Processing for Android

Create Mobile, Sensor-Aware, and VR Applications Using Processing

Andrés Colubri

Apress®

Processing for Android: Create Mobile, Sensor-Aware, and VR Applications Using Processing

Andrés Colubri
Cambridge, Massachusetts, USA

ISBN-13 (pbk): 978-1-4842-2718-3   ISBN-13 (electronic): 978-1-4842-2719-0
https://doi.org/10.1007/978-1-4842-2719-0

Library of Congress Control Number: 2017958640

Cover image designed by Freepik

Managing Director: Welmoed Spahr
Editorial Director: Todd Green
Acquisitions Editor: Natalie Pao
Development Editor: James Markham
Technical Reviewer: Anthony Tripoldi
Coordinating Editor: Jessica Vakili
Copy Editor: April Rondeau
Compositor: SPi Global
Indexer: SPi Global
Artist: SPi Global

Distributed to the book trade worldwide by Springer Science+Business Media New York, 233 Spring Street, 6th Floor, New York, NY 10013. Phone 1-800-SPRINGER, fax (201) 348-4505, email orders-ny@springer-sbm.com, or visit www.springeronline.com. Apress Media, LLC is a California LLC and the sole member (owner) is Springer Science + Business Media Finance Inc (SSBM Finance Inc). SSBM Finance Inc is a **Delaware** corporation.

For information on translations, please email rights@apress.com, or visit http://www.apress.com/rights-permissions.

Apress titles may be purchased in bulk for academic, corporate, or promotional use. eBook versions and licenses are also available for most titles. For more information, reference our Print and eBook Bulk Sales web page at http://www.apress.com/bulk-sales.

Any source code or other supplementary material referenced by the author in this book is available to readers on GitHub via the book's product page, located at www.apress.com/978-1-4842-2718-3. For more detailed information, please visit http://www.apress.com/source-code.

Printed on acid-free paper

To Jihyun, for her encouragement to take on new challenges.
To my family, for their support while being far away.

Contents at a Glance

About the Author xvii

About the Technical Reviewers xix

Acknowledgments xxi

Preface xxiii

■Part I: First Steps with Processing for Android 1

■Chapter 1: Getting Started with Android Mode 3

■Chapter 2: The Processing Language 17

■Chapter 3: From Sketch to Play Store 41

■Part II: Drawing and Interaction 57

■Chapter 4: Drawing Graphics and Text 59

■Chapter 5: Touchscreen Interaction 89

■Chapter 6: Live Wallpapers 111

■Part III: Sensors 141

■Chapter 7: Reading Sensor Data 143

■Chapter 8: Driving Graphics and Sound with Sensor Data 157

■Chapter 9: Geolocation 181

Part IV: Wearables and Watch Faces 211

Chapter 10: Wearable Devices 213

Chapter 11: Visualizing Time 227

Chapter 12: Visualizing Physical Activity 243

Part V: 3D and VR 273

Chapter 13: 3D in Processing 275

Chapter 14: VR Basics 303

Chapter 15: Drawing in VR 331

Appendix A: Gradle and Android Studio Integration 357

Appendix B: Processing Libraries 371

Index 377

Contents

About the Author xvii

About the Technical Reviewers xix

Acknowledgments xxi

Preface xxiii

■Part I: First Steps with Processing for Android 1

■Chapter 1: Getting Started with Android Mode 3

What Is the Processing Project? 3

    The Processing Language 3

    The Processing Development Environment 4

Extending Processing 7

    The Contribution Manager 7

Processing for Android 8

    Installing the Android mode 9

    Interface of Android Mode 10

    Running a Sketch on a Device 12

    Running a Sketch in the Emulator 14

Summary 16

■Chapter 2: The Processing Language 17

A Programming Sketchbook for Artists and Designers 17

The Setup/Draw Structure of a Processing Sketch 17

Drawing with Code 20

    Screen Coordinates 21

    Form 23

    Color 27

    Geometric Transformations 30

Responding to User Input 32

Creating a Vine-Drawing App 34

Summary 40

■Chapter 3: From Sketch to Play Store 41

Sketching and Debugging 41

    Getting Information from the Console 41

    Getting More Information with logcat 43

    Using the Integrated Debugger 44

    Reporting Processing Bugs 45

Preparing a Sketch for Release 45

    Adjusting for Device's DPI 45

    Using the Emulator 48

    Setting Icons and Package Name 51

    Setting Package Name and Version 51

    Exporting as a Signed Package 52

Summary 55

■Part II: Drawing and Interaction 57

■Chapter 4: Drawing Graphics and Text 59

Renderers in Processing 59

Drawing Shapes 60

    More Shape Types 60

    Curve Shapes 62

Shape Attributes 70

Shape Styles 72

Shape Contours 73

The PShape Class 74

Creating PShapes 75

Loading Shapes from SVG 78

Drawing Images 80

Texturing Shapes 81

Drawing Text 82

Loading and Creating Fonts 83

Text Attributes 85

Scaling Text 86

Summary 87

Chapter 5: Touchscreen Interaction 89

Touch Events in Android 89

Basic Touch Events 89

Multi-touch Events 96

Touch-based Interaction 100

Shape Selection 101

Scrolling 102

Swipe and Pinch 105

Using the Keyboard 108

Summary 109

Chapter 6: Live Wallpapers 111

Live Wallpapers 111

Writing and Installing Live Wallpapers 111

Using Multiple Home Screens 113

Handling Permissions 116

Particle Systems 120

    Autonomous Agents... 121

    Image Flow Field 126

An Image-flow Wallpaper 128

    Loading, Resizing, and Cropping Images.. 128

    Putting Everything Together.. 130

    Using Threads... 134

    Controlling the Hue.. 136

    Wrapping the Project Up.. 138

Summary.. 139

■Part III: Sensors.. 141

■Chapter 7: Reading Sensor Data............................... 143

Sensors in Android Devices... 143

    Accelerometer 143

    Gyroscope... 144

    Magnetometer 144

    Location.. 144

Accessing Sensors from Processing 145

    Creating a Sensor Manager.. 145

    Adding a Sensor Listener... 146

    Reading Data from the Sensor 147

    Reading from Other Sensors 149

The Ketai Library 150

    Installing Ketai.. 150

    Using Ketai 151

    Event Handlers in Ketai 153

Summary.. 156

Chapter 8: Driving Graphics and Sound with Sensor Data 157

Using Ketai to Read Sensor Data.. 157

Measuring Acceleration.. 157

Shake Detection 158

Step Counter.. 159

Audio-Visual Mapping of Step Data... 160

Playing Audio 165

Using the Magnetic Sensor 169

Creating a Compass App... 170

The Gyroscope.. 174

Controlling Navigation with the Gyroscope.. 177

Summary... 180

Chapter 9: Geolocation 181

Location Data in Android 181

Using Location API in Processing 182

Location Permissions 183

Event Threads and Concurrency 186

Location with Ketai.. 190

Using Additional Location Data.. 192

A Street View Collage 193

Using Google Street View Image API... 195

Voronoi Tessellations 197

Using an Offscreen Drawing Surface... 202

Putting Everything Together... 204

Summary... 210

■Part IV: Wearables and Watch Faces 211

■Chapter 10: Wearable Devices 213

From Activity Trackers to Smartwatches 213

Smartwatches 214

Running Watch Face Sketches 215

Using a Watch 215

Using the Emulator 218

Displaying Time 220

Counting Steps 221

Designing for Smartwatches 222

Screen Shape and Insets 223

Watch Face Preview Icons 225

Summary 226

■Chapter 11: Visualizing Time 227

From Sundials to Smartwatches 227

Using Time to Control Motion 228

Square Versus Round Watch Faces 231

Working with a Watch Face Concept 235

Elapsed/Remaining Time 235

Adding Interaction 237

Loading/Displaying Images 239

Summary 241

■Chapter 12: Visualizing Physical Activity 243

Body Sensors 243

Step Counter 243

Heart Rate 244

Visualizing Physical Activity in Real-time 245

Simple Step Counter 245

Accessing the Heart-rate Sensor 246

Visualizing Step-count Data 249

A Beating Heart 250

Sensor Debugging 253

Growing a Tree as You Exercise 257

Generating a Tree with a Particle System 258

Incorporating Step-count Data 260

Tweaking the Watch Face 263

Blooming the Tree 264

Summary 272

■Part V: 3D and VR 273

■Chapter 13: 3D in Processing 275

The P3D Renderer 275

A 3D Hello World 275

The Camera 277

Immediate Versus Retained Rendering 279

3D Transformations 281

Combining Transformations 282

3D Shapes 284

Custom Shapes 286

PShape Objects 288

Loading OBJ Shapes 291

Lighting and Texturing 293

Light Sources and Material Properties 294

Texture Mapping 298

Summary 302

xiii

■Chapter 14: VR Basics 303

Google VR 303

    Cardboard and Daydream.. 303

    Hardware Requirements.. 304

VR in Processing 304

    Stereo Rendering.. 306

    Monoscopic Rendering 308

VR Interaction 309

    Eye and World Coordinates... 310

    The Line of Sight.. 312

    Selecting a Shape with Screen Coordinates.................................... 315

    Bounding Box Selection... 318

Movement in VR 322

    Automatic Movement... 324

    Free-range Movement 326

Summary... 329

■Chapter 15: Drawing in VR 331

Creating a Successful VR Experience...................................... 331

    Drawing in VR 332

    Initial Sketches 333

A Simple VR UI... 334

Drawing in 3D.. 339

Flying Around 347

Final Tweaks and Packaging 352

    Intro Text... 353

    Icons and Package Export 354

Summary... 356

■Appendix A: Gradle and Android Studio Integration 357

Google's Tools for Android Development 357

Exporting a Sketch as a Gradle Project 359

Importing into Android Studio 361

Adding a Processing Sketch to a Layout 366

■Appendix B: Processing Libraries 371

Extending Processing with Libraries 371

Data 373

GUI 373

Hardware/Sensors 374

Geometry/Utilities 374

Sound and Video 374

Writing New Libraries 375

Index 377

About the Author

Andrés Colubri is a programmer, scientist, and artist, and long-time contributor to the Processing project. He originally obtained a doctoral degree in mathematics at the Universidad Nacional del Sur in Bahía Blanca, Argentina, and was a Burroughs Wellcome postdoctoral fellow at the University of Chicago, where he studied the protein folding problem. Later on, he completed an MFA from the Design Media Arts department at the University of California, Los Angeles. Andrés uses Processing to carry out research at the intersection between interaction, visualization, and computing. He currently works at the Broad Institute of Harvard and MIT, developing new methods and tools for analysis of biomedical data. http://andrescolubri.net/

About the Technical Reviewers

Jose Luis Garcia del Castillo is an architect, computational designer, and educator. He advocates for a future where programming and code are tools as natural to designers as paper and pencil. In his work, he explores creative opportunities at the intersection of design, technology, fabrication, data and art. His current research focuses on the development of digital frameworks that help democratize access to robotic technologies for designers and artists.

Jose Luis is a registered architect, and holds a Master in Architectural Technological Innovation from Universidad de Sevilla and a Master of Design Studies in Technology from the Harvard University Graduate School of Design. He has worked as a structural consultant for several international firms, such as OMA, Mecanoo, and Cesar Pelli, as well as data visualization architect at Fathom Information Design. He is also the co-founder of ParametricCamp, an international organization whose mission is to spread the knowledge of computational design among designers and architects.

Jose Luis currently pursues his Doctor of Design degree at the Material Processing and Systems group at the Harvard Graduate School of Design, works as Research Engineer in the Generative Design Team at Autodesk Inc., and teaches computational creativity in the Arts+Design Department at Northeastern University.

Anthony Tripaldi started programming in 2004, with a background in design and animation. By 2007 he went all in on Flash as the future of the web. Once realizing his devastating mistake, he pivoted, making Android apps and interactive installations with Processing for clients of all types. Once the ad industry had taken its toll, he found his way into Google Creative Lab, where he helped lead the creation of Android Experiments, a platform for artists and engineers alike to celebrate creativity on Android.

Gottfried Haider, born 1985 in Vienna, works as an artist, educator and software tool-maker. He received a degree in Digital Arts at University of Applied Arts Vienna in 2009. After receiving a Fulbright Scholarship in 2010, he pursued a MFA in Design Media Arts at University of California Los Angeles, which he finished in 2013. His artwork has been displayed in various venues and publications internationally.

Acknowledgments

During the past few months, I have learned that writing a book demands a significant personal effort, but, at the same time, it is the unequivocal confluence of the work, ideas, dreams, and passions of countless individuals. Since it would be impossible to track all the threads coming into the junction represented by this book, I will acknowledge the invaluable contributions of those who are most directly related to this project, knowing I will leave out many others.

I would like to start by extending my most earnest gratitude to Ben Fry, Casey Reas, and Daniel Shiffman, without whom this book would not have been possible. Their tireless work with Processing has enabled people from all over the world to use code in art and design, and made it possible for those coming from the sciences and engineering (like myself) to discover the possibilities of visual literacy within technology. Very special recognition goes to Jonathan Feinberg, who together with Ben, wrote the initial version of the Android mode the book is based upon, as well as to Pardis Sabeti, for supporting and encouraging my Processing work with her tireless enthusiasm. I also want to thank all the members of the Processing Foundation for putting forward a framework that promotes learning, diversity, and inclusion in the creative coding community and that empowers work such as mine.

Daniel Sauter and Jesus Duran made very important contributions to the Processing for Android project early on with their Ketai library, and also by organizing the Mobile Processing Conference at the School of Art and Design at the University of Illinois at Chicago, to which I was invited as speaker and workshop instructor in all editions from 2011 to 2013. These events were key to sustaining the initial momentum of the project into the present, and so my deepest recognition goes to them.

I would like to make a very special mention of all the Google Summer of Code students who worked on various Processing for Android projects during the past years: Sara Di Bartolomeo and Rupak Daas (GSoC 2017), Mohammad Umair (GSoC 2015), and Imil Ziyaztdinov (2014). Their contributions were absolutely crucial to the continued improvement and growth of Processing for Android. I am also very grateful for the existence of the GSoC program, which allowed these extraordinary coding and mentorship experiences with students of diverse backgrounds and origins.

Many thanks to Daniel Murphy, Shayan Amir-hosseini, Richard The, and Jen Kurtzman from Google Creative Lab in New York, who supported the renewed efforts behind the Processing for Android project during 2016, which led to this book.

As I mentioned at the beginning, a book like this is the result of the work of many people, but among them the technical reviewers played a critical role in ensuring that the book is correct, well structured, and easy to understand by its final audience. My reviewers, to whom I am deeply indebted, are Anthony Tripaldi, Kate Hollenbach, Jose Luis García del Castillo y López, and Gottfried Haider.

Likewise, I am very grateful to the Apress editors, Natalie Pao, Jessica Vakili, and James Markham, who, with their hard work and professionalism (and their patience with a novice writer), accompanied me along the way from draft idea to published book.

I would like to acknowledge Neil Zhao and Dean Kessey (on behalf of her late mother, Dr. Masumi Hayashi) for graciously allowing me to use reproductions of their work in the book.

Last, but not least, I thank the entire Processing community for their endless creativity, enthusiasm, and appreciation, which has been one of my most important motivations over the years.

Preface

By Ben Fry

The Android version of Processing got its start when I received an email from Andy Rubin back in February 2009. He was interested in having Processing be more tightly integrated with Android. The discussion led to initial funding, which helped us work on building an Android version of the project during the year or two that followed. For one of the test applications, I used some code developed by Casey Reas (the co-founder of the Processing project), and we were elated to see the first version of it up and running on the G1, the very first widely available Android device.

I was especially excited, and still am, about the Android platform as an incredible canvas to work from. You have mobile devices with a range of ways to communicate with the outside world (mobile network, wi-fi, Bluetooth, etc.), higher-performance CPUs than even the desktop machines we first used to develop Processing in 2001 (not to mention GPU performance better than the SGI workstations we were using around the same time), and a broad range of sensors—accelerometer, magnetometer, GPS, and gyroscope—that opened an amazing number of possibilities for applications and ideas. It's the platform I wish we'd had when we first started the project, with its focus on all the interesting use cases that come from openness and having the right set of tools and APIs to go along with it.

I'm especially excited, for instance, about possibilities like completely reinventing the mobile phone interface, because all those pieces are available to be customized, and you're just a few activities or fragments away from an entirely different end-user experience. Since the Handspring (later Palm) Treo, mobile phone interfaces really haven't changed much—a grid of applications as a home screen, and a phone "app" that essentially emulates the interface of a touch-tone phone. The Treo's interface dates to 2008 and built on the Palm Pilot interface from 1997, which itself referenced other organizer tools and too many icon-driven interfaces to mention from decades prior. The touch-tone phone, meanwhile, dates to at least 1968. Suffice to say, we're still working with a set of forms, interactions, and metaphors that have been heavily repurposed over the years, and I'm drawn to the idea of people experimenting with alternative interfaces and having the ability to rethink how those elements might work. Innovation comes from getting people the right tools to play with ideas, and while a new phone interface may not necessarily be around the corner, there's so much to be learned during the process itself.

This idea of experimentation and exploration is at the core of the Processing project. Projects are called "sketches" to keep people in the mindset of writing a small amount of code to get started, not overthinking it too much until they understand their problem better. This is not unlike scribbling something in a sketchbook and flipping to a new page—perhaps even tearing out the previous page and throwing it out. This approach is a little backward, as typical software engineering practice encourages figuring out structure first and filling in the details over time. However, we found that our iterative approach was helpful not just for our professional work, but also for teaching beginners how to get started. We built Processing in a way that allowed people to write a few lines of code that would make something happen—no knowledge of classes, threads, animation loops, or double-buffering necessary. Over time, as the user's experience grew and their ideas became more ambitious, they could learn the details of these more complex concepts. Interestingly, this mirrored things that we, as more seasoned developers, also wanted: why write a lot of the same boilerplate to do the same things? Why get RSI retyping the same handler and utility functions? Could we give people a toolbox that was useful enough on its own that starting a project didn't mean collecting the initial set of libraries that were required just to get things done?

A related idea was simply how one gets started. Most integrated development environments (IDEs) require a lot of background—even training—to use. Even though I had 20 years of coding experience, a friend had to sit me down to explain how to use Eclipse to set up a project. With Processing, it's a matter of downloading the software, writing a single line of code, and hitting the Run button. This gets even more important with a platform like Android, and we set out to make the Android version of Processing just as simple. We wanted users to be able to download the software, write a little code (or open an example), plug in their phone (or tablet, or who-knows-what), and hit the Run button to see something show up on the device. Once that works, it should be all set, and hopefully you're having enough fun that you lose the rest of the afternoon hacking away at your idea.

This book covers a wide range of ideas on how the Android platform can be used and how Processing can be a helpful bridge to creating everything from quick experiments to professionally developed applications. It's exciting to have Andrés writing it, as we want to see even more people building and playing with the platform, and also because you couldn't have a better expert in how Processing itself works. Andrés first started working as a core committer to the Processing project when we folded his popular OpenGL and Video libraries into the main project, which over the years led to his overseeing the 3D and Video portions of Processing. His experience with 3D got him deeply involved in the internals of how OpenGL works on Android, and his work there was the basis for his rebuilding the desktop version to move from the old-style fixed-function pipeline used in GL to the brave new world of shaders and highly multicore GPUs. It was through this experience, combined with his being an avid Android user, that Andrés became a core maintainer for the Android portion of the Processing project. He has helped shepherd it ever since, including everything from ongoing development to mentoring Google Summer of Code projects to, finally, writing this book. Suffice to say, you're in good hands.

I hope you'll enjoy this book, and we can't wait to see what you build with Processing!

PART I

First Steps with Processing for Android

CHAPTER 1

Getting Started with Android Mode

In this chapter, we will introduce the Processing software and Android mode, the community project behind them, and how we can begin using the mode to create apps for Android devices.

What Is the Processing Project?

The Processing project is a community initiative focused on sharing knowledge, fostering education, and promoting diversity in code-based art and design. The Processing software is a central part of this initiative, now guided by the Processing Foundation (https://processingfoundation.org/). The Processing software was created in 2001 by Casey Reas and Ben Fry at the MIT Media Lab as a teaching and production tool in computational arts and design, and has been evolving continuously since then. It is available for download at https://processing.org/, and its source code is released under free software licenses (GPL and LGPL). From now on, I will simply refer to Processing when talking about the Processing software.

Processing consists of two complementary pieces: the language and the development environment. Together, they form a "software sketchbook" designed to allow the expression of visual ideas quickly with code, while also providing enough room to let those ideas develop into full-blown projects. Processing has been used to create many beautiful and inspiring works in generative art, data visualization, and interactive installations, some of which are included in a curated list on the Processing site (https://processing.org/exhibition/).

The Processing Language

The Processing language comprises a set of functions for handling screen drawing, data input/output, and user interaction. A small team of volunteers behind the Processing project (https://processing.org/people/) has carefully constructed this set of functions, technically called an Application Program Interface or API, to simplify the development of graphical and interactive applications by means of a simple and consistent naming convention, unambiguous behavior, and a well-defined scope.

© Andrés Colubri 2017
A. Colubri, *Processing for Android*, https://doi.org/10.1007/978-1-4842-2719-0_1

3

While originally implemented in Java, the Processing API is currently available in many programming languages, including Python, JavaScript, and R. However, it is the Java implementation of this API, together with some simplifications to the Java language, what defines the Processing language. Despite this distinction, throughout the book I will use the terms Processing language and API interchangeably, since in the context of Android, we will essentially be using the Java implementation of the Processing API.

In active development since 2001, the Processing language now encompasses around 300 items between not only functions, but also classes and constants (https://processing. org/reference/). One defining feature of this language is that it offers the possibility to create a program capable of displaying interactive graphics using very little code. As I mentioned, it also includes a number of simplifications with respect to the Java language, with the purpose of making it easier to teach to people who are not familiar with computer code. The following program exemplifies these features of the Processing language:

```
color bg = 150;

void setup() {
  size(200, 200);
}

void draw() {
  background(bg);
  ellipse(mouseX, mouseY, 100, 100);
}
```

The output of this program is a window of 200 by 200 pixels that contains a white circle that follows the movement of the mouse; the window has a gray background. The functions setup() and draw() are present in almost any Processing program and drive its "drawing loop." All the initialization of the program should take place in setup(), which is executed just once when the program starts up. The draw() function, which contains all the drawing instructions, is then called continuously several times per second (by default, 60 times) so that the graphical output of the program can be animated through time.

However, if you are familiar with Java, you have probably noticed that this code is not a valid Java program. For example, there is no explicit definition of a main class encapsulating all the code, nor additional instructions required in Java to initialize the "windowing toolkit" that handles the display and the user input. This program, as it is, needs to be run inside the Processing development environment, which applies a "preprocessing" step to the Processing code in order to convert it into a valid Java program. However, this transformation occurs behind the scenes, and the Processing user does not need to worry about it at all.

The Processing Development Environment

The Processing development environment (PDE) is the application that provides us with a simplified code editor to write, debug, and run Processing programs, called *sketches* (Figure 1-1). The PDE also incorporates an uncluttered user interface to handle all the sketches created with it and to add libraries and other external components that extend the core functionality of the PDE, such as p5.js, Python, or Android modes.

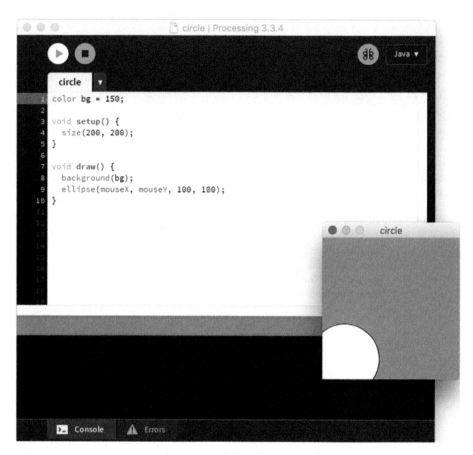

Figure 1-1. *The Processing development environment showing a running sketch in Java mode*

The simplicity and ease of use of the PDE and the Processing language are the key elements of this "code sketchbook." A stumbling block for many people wanting to start working with code is the complexity of a modern development environment, like Eclipse or IntelliJ, in terms of a lengthy installation and an overwhelming user interface. In contrast, the PDE addresses these issues by providing an easy install process and a minimal interface, while the simple structure of a Processing sketch enables users to obtain visual feedback rapidly. Processing's aim is to support an iterative development process analogous to sketching with pen and paper, where one can start with a simple idea and refine it through successive sketches.

■ **Note** The Processing API can be used outside of the PDE; for example, in a more advanced integrated development environment, or IDE, such as Eclipse, NetBeans, or IntelliJ. All of Processing's drawing, data, and interaction APIs are available when writing a program with any of these IDEs; however, the simplifications that the Processing language has with respect to Java will be lost.

We can download the latest version of Processing from the main website (https:// processing.org/download). As pointed out in the previous paragraph, installation is fairly straightforward, only requiring the unpacking of the .zip (on Windows and Mac) or .tgz (on Linux) package that contains the PDE and all other core files. We should be able to then run the PDE without any additional steps from any location inside the Home or Applications folders.

The PDE organizes user sketches in a sketchbook folder. Each sketch is stored in a subfolder inside the sketchbook, which in turn contains one or more source-code files with the .pde extension. By default, Processing creates the sketchbook folder inside the Documents folder located in the user's account (for instance, /Users/andres/Documents/ Processing on Mac), but this location can be changed by selecting the desired sketchbook folder in the Preferences window, available under the Processing menu on Mac and File menu on Windows and Linux (Figure 1-2). Notice the sketchbook location at the top.

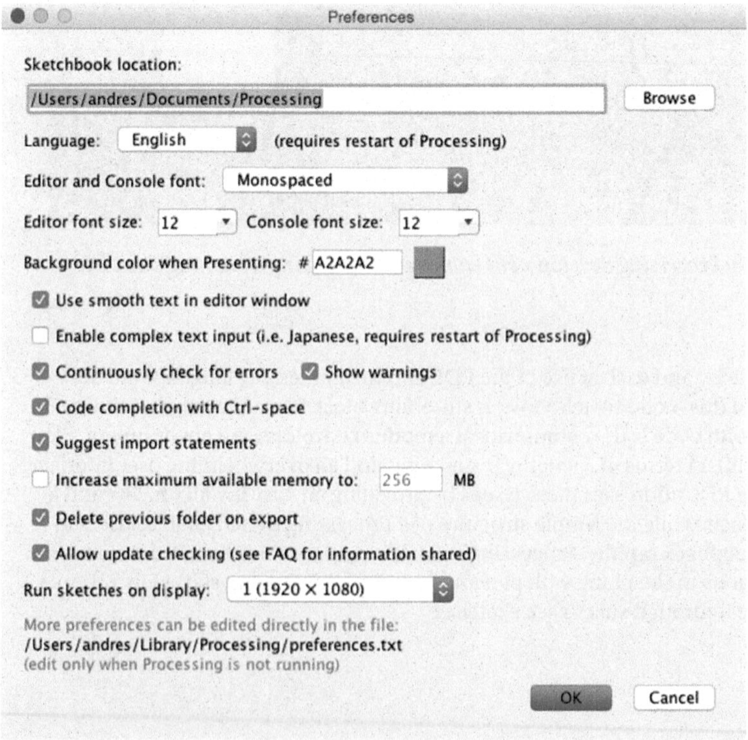

Figure 1-2. *The Preferences window on Mac*

Extending Processing

As I mentioned at the beginning, the Processing project is not only the PDE or the language, but also, and very importantly, the community built around the use of the software and the goals of sharing, teaching, and inclusiveness. Thanks to Processing's open nature and modular architecture, many people have contributed improvements and extensions to the "core" software. These contributions fall within one of the following four categories:

> **Libraries:** Modules (comprising one or more Java code files built into a jar package, and additional documentation and example files) that make it possible to access new functionality in the sketches. E.g., OpenCV library for computer vision (which is PC/Mac only), or Ketai for Android sensors (covered in Chapters 7 and 8).

> **Programming Modes:** Alternative code editors and related PDE customizations that allow the use of an entire different language within the PDE. E.g., Android mode. We will see in the next sections of this chapter how to install Android mode.

> **Tools:** Applications that can only run from Processing and provide specific functionality to aid in writing code, debugging, and testing the sketch. E.g., the color picker (discussed in Chapter 2).

> **Examples:** Packages of contributed code sketches that can be used as learning material or reference. E.g., the sketches from the book *Learning Processing* by Daniel Shiffman (`http://learningprocessing.com/`).

The extension of Processing through contributed libraries, modes, tools, and examples has enabled its growth into application domains that were not part of the original software, such as mobile apps, computer vision, and physical computing, while keeping the core functionality simple and accessible for new programmers.

The Contribution Manager

By default, Processing includes one default mode, Java, where we can write and run sketches on Windows, Mac, and Linux computers using the Java implementation of the Processing language. Processing also bundles several "core" libraries, some of which are OpenGL (for drawing hardware-accelerated 2D and 3D scenes), pdf (to export graphics as pdf files), and data (which allows the handling of data files in formats such as CSV and JSON).

To install additional contributions, we can use the Contribution Manager (CM), which makes the process seamless. A screenshot of the CM is shown in Figure 1-3. The CM has five tabs, the first four for each type of contribution—libraries, modes, tools, and examples—and the fifth for updates. All the contributions that are registered by their authors in a central repository are accessible through the CM and can also be updated through the CM when new versions become available.

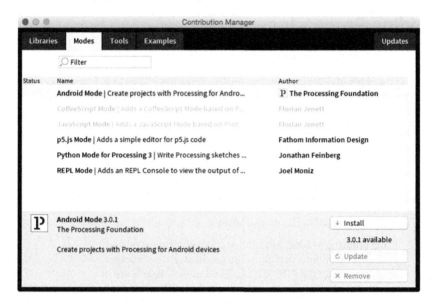

Figure 1-3. *The Contribution Manager in Processing, showing the Modes tab*

■ **Note** Contributions that were not registered by their authors and hence are not available through the CM, can still be installed manually. We would need to download the package containing the library, mode, tool, or examples, typically in zip format, and extract it into the sketchbook folder. There are separate subfolders for libraries, modes, tools, and examples. See `https://processing.org/reference/libraries/` for more info.

Processing for Android

Processing for Android, not unlike the Processing software itself, is several things. Primarily, it is a community effort that started in 2009 with the purpose of supporting the development of Android apps using Processing, as well as translating some of the concepts of the project to the context of mobile apps: iterative sketching, simplicity, and accessibility.

From a software point of view, Processing for Android is composed of the processing-android library and the custom PDE programming mode itself. The library is the package that contains all the functions of the Processing API, but reimplemented for the Android platform. Android mode provides a customized version of the PDE that allows us to write Processing code and run it on an Android device or in the emulator. Android mode includes the processing-android library, which we need for our Processing code to run without errors. However, these distinctions are not critical at this point, since Processing will let us install and use Android mode without our having to worry about the processing-android library. This library would become more important for those among you who may be planning to use Processing for Android in more advanced applications.

≡ **Note** The processing-android library can be imported from an IDE like Android Studio, allowing the use of all the Processing functionality in a regular Android app. This advanced use is covered in Appendix A.

Installing the Android mode

Once we have installed Processing on our computer, we should be able to open the PDE by running the Processing application, and then we can install the most recent release of Android mode through the CM. The mode also requires the Android Software Development Kit (SDK) in order to work. The Android SDK is the set of libraries, tools, documentation, and other supporting files provided by Google to develop and debug Android apps. So, to install Android mode and, if needed, the SDK, follow these steps:

1. Open the CM by clicking the "Add Mode..." option that appears in the drop-down menu in the upper-right corner of the PDE (Figure 1-4).

Figure 1-4. *Opening the Contribution Manager to add a new mode*

2. Select the entry for Android mode in the Modes tab, then click the Install button.

3. After installation is complete, close the CM and switch to Android mode using the same drop-down menu from Figure 1-4.

   If a valid SDK is detected on the computer, Processing will ask if we want to use it or download a new one (Figure 1-5). Because the SDK is very large (up to several GBs), it can be a good idea to use the one that is already installed to save disk space. However, if that SDK is also used by another development tool, such as Android Studio, it may get updated outside Processing, which may lead to incompatibilities with the mode.

   If no valid Android SDK is detected, Processing will ask to either manually locate an SDK or automatically download one (Figure 1-5).

9

Figure 1-5. *Choosing between using an existing SDK or downloading a new one automatically (top), and between locating an SDK manually or downloading one automatically (bottom)*

■ **Note** Version 4.0 of Android mode requires Android version 8.0 (Oreo), corresponding to API level 26 (`https://source.android.com/source/build-numbers`). The mode's automatic SDK download will retrieve this version from the Google servers.

Pre-releases of Android mode, as well as older, unsupported versions, are no longer available through the CM, but rather are deposited on the GitHub releases page (`https://github.com/processing/processing-android/releases`) and can be installed manually by downloading the corresponding file and extracting it into the Modes folder in Processing's sketchbook.

Interface of Android Mode

The editor in Android mode is very similar to that of Java mode. The toolbar contains the Play and Stop buttons to launch a sketch and to stop its execution (on the device or in the emulator). Code autocompletion in the editor is available as well. However, version 4.0 of Android mode does not offer an integrated debugger. The main menu contains a number of Android-specific options as well (Figure 1-6). The File menu has options to export the current sketch as a package ready for upload to the Google Play Store or as a project that can be opened with Android Studio. The Sketch menu contains separate options to run the sketch on a device or in the emulator, as well as a separate Android menu containing several options, among them the type of output to target with the sketch—regular app, wallpaper, watch face, or VR app—and a list of Android devices currently connected to the computer. All of these options will be covered in subsequent chapters.

Figure 1-6. *Android-specific options in the interface of Android mode*

Running a Sketch on a Device

Once we have written some sketch code with the PDE, we can run it on an Android phone, tablet, or watch. We need to first make sure that "USB Debugging" is turned on for our device. The process to do so varies by device and by which version of the Android OS is installed on it. In most cases, this setting is located in the Developer Options, under System Setting. On Android 4.2 and higher, the Developer Options are hidden by default, but we can enable them by following these instructions:

1. Open the Settings app.

2. Scroll to the bottom and select "About Phone."

3. Scroll to the bottom and tap "Build Number" seven times.

4. Return to the previous screen to find Developer Options near the bottom.

After turning USB Debugging on (which we need to do only once), we have to connect the device to the computer through the USB port. Processing will then try to recognize it and add it to the list of available devices in the Android menu.

▨ **Note** Version 4.0 of Android mode only supports devices that are running Android 4.2 (Jelly Bean, API level 17) or newer.

Let's use the code in Listing 1-1 as our first Processing for Android sketch! It is not important to understand each line of code in it, as we will go over the Processing API in detail in the following chapters. This code simply draws a black square on the half of the screen that receives a touch press.

Listing 1-1. Our First Processing for Android Sketch

```
void setup() {
  fill(0);
}

void draw() {
  background(204);
  if (mousePressed) {
    if (mouseX < width/2) rect(0, 0, width/2, height);
    else rect(width/2, 0, width/2, height);
  }
}
```

It is possible to have multiple devices connected simultaneously to the computer, but only one can be selected in the Devices menu as the "active" device, which is where our sketch will be installed and run. Figure 1-7 shows our first sketch already loaded in the PDE, along with the selected device to run it on.

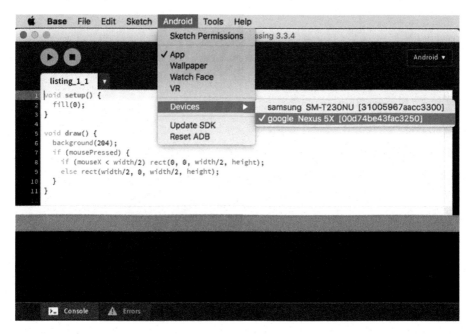

Figure 1-7. *Selecting the device to run the sketch on*

After we have picked the active device, we can hit the Run button or select "Run on Device" under the Sketch menu. We should see some messages scrolling down the PDE's console while Processing compiles the sketch, packages it as a debug app, and installs it on the device. One important detail is that the computer needs to be connected to the Internet the first time a sketch is run. Processing uses a tool called Gradle to build the app from the sketch's source code. Android mode comes with a "Gradle wrapper," so we don't need to install Gradle manually, but the wrapper will automatically download the rest of the Gradle tool the first time it is invoked. We can be offline when running sketches after the first time. If everything goes well, the sketch should launch and show up on the screen of the device, as depicted in Figure 1-8.

Figure 1-8. *Running a sketch on a connected phone*

■ **Note**   If we are running Windows, we need to install a special USB driver to connect to the device (`https://developer.android.com/studio/run/oem-usb.html`). If we downloaded the Android SDK automatically in Processing, then the latest Google USB drivers for Nexus devices will be inside the `sketchbook` folder, under the `android\sdk` subfolder; e.g., `C:\Users\andres\Documents\Processing\android\sdk\extras\google\usb_driver`.

If we are running Linux, we may need to install some additional packages (`https://developer.android.com/studio/run/device.html`). Also, make sure that the USB connection is not configured as "Charge Only."

Running a Sketch in the Emulator

If we do not have a device on which to run our sketch, we can use the emulator. The emulator is a program that creates a software replica of a physical device. This replica is called an Android Virtual Device (AVD), and even though it is generally slower than a real device, it can be useful for testing a sketch on hardware we don't currently have.

The first time we run a sketch in the emulator, Processing will download the system image containing all the information needed to create the AVD on our computer (Figure 1-9). However, it will initially ask if we want to use the "ARM" or the "x86" images. The reason for this is that Android devices use ARM CPUs, while desktop computers have x86 processors. When working with an AVD with an ARM image, the emulator will convert ARM instructions into x86 instructions one by one, which is slow. But if we use the x86 image, the CPU in our computer will be able to simulate the AVD's CPU much more directly and quickly. One drawback of using x86 images is that we must install additional software on Mac or Windows called HAXM. Since Processing downloaded HAXM together with the SDK, it will install it for us in case we decide to use x86 images.

Figure 1-9. *System image download dialog in Android mode*

We also have to keep in mind that HAXM is only compatible with Intel processors, so the emulator won't work with x86 images if our computer has an AMD CPU. Linux has its own AVD acceleration system and does not require HAXM, so we can use x86 images on a Linux computer with an AMD CPU. We would need to perform some extra configuration steps though, which are described here: `https://developer.android.com/studio/run/emulator-acceleration.html#vm-linux`.

After finishing the download, which can take several minutes, depending on the Internet connection (the system images for the emulator are around 900 MB in size), Processing will boot up the emulator and then launch the sketch in it. Once our Listing 1-1 is running in the emulator, it should look like Figure 1-10.

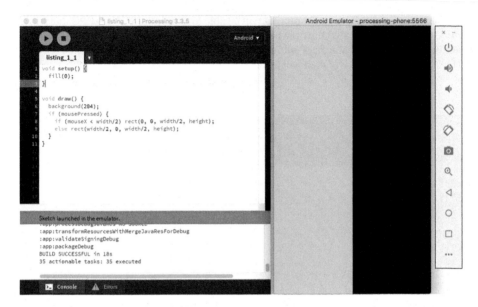

Figure 1-10. *Running our sketch in the emulator*

Summary

In this first chapter, we have learned what the Processing project and software are, and how we can use Processing to create apps via the Android programming mode. As we saw, some of the main features of the Processing software are its minimal interface and the simple structure of a code project, which is called a sketch. These features allow us to start writing and testing our own sketches, either on a device or in the emulator, very quickly.

CHAPTER 2

■ ■ ■

The Processing Language

If you are not familiar with the Processing language, read this chapter for an introduction to the creation of 2D shapes, use of geometry transformations and color, and how to handle touchscreen input. The chapter ends with a step-by-step example of a drawing sketch, which we will use in Chapter 3 to learn how to export and upload an app created with Processing to the Google Play Store.

A Programming Sketchbook for Artists and Designers

As we learned in the previous chapter, the Processing language, in conjunction with the PDE, makes it easier for users who are new to programming to start creating interactive graphics. The language has been designed to be minimal and simple for learning and yet expressive enough to create code-based projects in diverse fields: generative art, data visualization, sound art, film, performance, and so on. It includes around 200 functions across different categories—drawing, interaction, typography, and so forth—as well as several classes that help with the handling of form, color, and data.

We can also see Processing as a "coding sketchbook," analogous to a paper sketchbook that we use to quickly draft and refine ideas. An important part of this analogy is that, as with the paper sketchbook, Processing gives us the ability to obtain visual feedback from the code as quickly as possible. The next section describes the basic structure in Processing that allows us to easily generate animated output on the screen.

The Setup/Draw Structure of a Processing Sketch

In most cases, we need our Processing sketches to run continuously in order to animate graphics on the screen and keep track of user input. We can implement such interactive sketches using a basic code structure where we first carry out all initialization operations inside a setup() function and then run a draw() function every time Processing needs to render a new frame.

© Andrés Colubri 2017

A. Colubri, *Processing for Android*, https://doi.org/10.1007/978-1-4842-2719-0_2

■ **Note**   All the code examples in this chapter can be run in either Java or Android modes since they don't rely on any features of the Processing language specific to either one. Also, because a requirement for this book is some level of knowledge of a programming language, we will not go over the basic concepts of programming (e.g., conditions, loops, comments).

With this structure, we can create an animation that is updated a fixed number of times per second, 60 by default. In each call of the draw() function, we need to not only draw the visual elements that form our composition, but also perform all the calculations needed to update the composition. For example, in Listing 2-1, we draw a vertical line moving horizontally across the screen from left to right using the function line(x, 0, x, height). The horizontal position of the line is contained in the variable x, which we update in every frame with x = (x + 1) % width. In this line of code, we increment x by 1 and then calculate the result modulo the screen width. Since "a modulo b" is defined as the remainder of the integer division of a by b (for example 9 % 4 is 1), the result can only be a number between 0 and b - 1. Hence, x in our sketch cannot be smaller than 0 nor greater than the width - 1, which is exactly what we need: x increments 1 unit at a time and wraps back to 0 after reaching the right edge. The output of this sketch is shown in Figure 2-1.

Listing 2-1. A Sketch That Draws a Vertical Line Moving Horizontally Across the Screen

```
int x = 0;

void setup() {
  size(600, 200);
  strokeWeight(2);
  stroke(255);
}

void draw() {
  background(50);
  line(x, 0, x, height);
  x = (x + 1) % width;
}
```

Figure 2-1. *Output of the animated line sketch*

Processing calls the draw() function at a default frame rate of 60 frames per second; however, we can change this default using the function frameRate(int fps). For instance, if we add frameRate(1) in setup(), the sketch will draw 1 frame per second.

Sometimes, we may need to stop Processing from running its animation after a number of frames. We can use the noLoop() and loop() functions to stop and resume the animation, respectively. Processing has a Boolean (logical) variable named looping that is true or false depending on whether or not the sketch is running the animation loop. We can add simple keystroke-detection functionality to our previous code to stop/resume the sketch, which is implemented in Listing 2-2.

Listing 2-2. Pausing/Resuming the Animation Loop

```
int x = 0;

void setup() {
  size(600, 200);
  strokeWeight(2);
  stroke(255);
}

void draw() {
  background(50);
  line(x, 0, x, height);
  x = (x + 1) % width;
}

void keyPressed() {
  if (looping) {
    noLoop();
  } else {
    loop();
  }
}
```

In addition to these interactive sketches, we can also create static sketches without setup/draw, which are typically useful if we only want to generate a fixed composition that does not need to be updated. Processing runs the code in these sketches only one time. Listing 2-3 contains a simple static sketch that draws the white circle seen in Figure 2-2.

Listing 2-3. Static Sketch Without setup() and draw() Functions

```
size(400, 400);
ellipse(200, 200, 150, 150);
```

Figure 2-2. *Output of the static sketch*

Drawing with Code

The examples from the previous section point to some important concepts in code-based drawing. First, we need to specify the coordinates of the elements we want to draw on the screen; second, there are functions, such as line(), that allow us to draw various graphical primitives or shapes by setting the appropriate numerical values that define the shapes; and third, we can set the visual "style" of these shapes (e.g., stroke color and weight).

In Processing, we can draw shapes of different kinds (points, lines, polygons) and with certain attributes (stroke weight and color, fill color, and so on). These attributes can be thought of as "style parameters" that, once set, affect everything drawn after. For example, each circle in Listing 2-4 has a different fill color, but if we comment out the second fill() call, the first and second circles will be red, since the fill color set at the beginning affects the first two ellipse calls. Figure 2-3 shows the output of this sketch in these situations.

Listing 2-4. Setting Style Attributes

```
size(460, 200);
strokeWeight(5);
fill(255, 0, 0);
stroke(0, 255, 0);
ellipse(100, 100, 200, 200);
fill(255, 0, 200); // Comment this line out to make second circle red
stroke(0);
ellipse(250, 100, 100, 100);
fill(0, 200, 200);
ellipse(380, 100, 160, 160);
```

Figure 2-3. *Effect of the calling order of style functions*

Screen Coordinates

Processing draws its graphical output into a rectangular grid of pixels, numbered from 0 to width – 1 along the horizontal direction (the x-axis) and 0 to height – 1 along the vertical direction (the y-axis), as illustrated in Figure 2-4. This grid will be contained in a separate output window when running the code in Java mode, or centered in the device's screen when using Android mode.

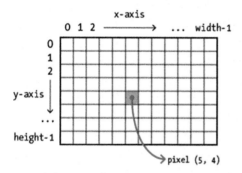

Figure 2-4. *Diagram of the screen's pixels*

When drawing with Processing, we need to keep in mind that x coordinates run from left to right, while y coordinates run from top to bottom. So, the pixel (0, 0) represents the upper-left corner of the screen, and the pixel (width-1, height-1) represents the lower-right corner. The arguments of most of the 2D drawing functions in Processing refer to the pixel coordinates of the screen. For example, the following sample code would produce the output seen in Figure 2-5 (where each square represents a single pixel, for clarity).

```
stroke(200, 0, 0);
fill(100, 200, 100);
rect(2, 1, width - 1, height - 2);
```

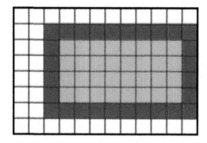

Figure 2-5. *Pixels covered by a stroked rectangle in Processing*

We should size the shapes we draw with Processing according to the constraints of our screen size. In general, it is recommended to use the width and height internal variables when referring to the size of the screen instead of the actual values; in this way, we can readjust the size without having to modify the drawing code, as is done in Listing 2-5.

Listing 2-5. Using screen coordinates.

```
Size(800, 800);
stroke(0);
fill(180);
background(97);
line(width/2, 0, width/2, height);
line(0, height/2, width, height/2);
rect(0, 0, 200, 200);
rect(width - 200, 0, 199, 200);
rect(width - 200, height - 200, 199, 199);
rect(0, height - 200, 199, 199);
rect(200, 200, width - 400, height - 400);
```

In this code, some rectangles have an unusual width/height of 199. This is so the stroke lines on the outer border of the screen are visible since, as we just saw, the x coordinates of the last row/column of pixels are height-1/width-1. The sketch's output, with all the outer strokes falling on the edge pixels, is shown in Figure 2-6, as it would appear on a Nexus 5X phone. You will also notice that this output only occupies a screen-centered 800 × 800 square, since that's the size we specified in the code. We will see later in this chapter how to use the entire screen, and in Chapter 4 we will see how to scale our graphics per the device's resolution.

Figure 2-6. *Output of code Listing 2-5, on a Nexus 5X phone*

Form

All visual forms we can generate with Processing are drawn as two- or three-dimensional shapes. Typically, we construct these shapes by explicitly specifying all the vertices that define their boundaries inside the beginShape() and endShape() functions, as shown in Listing 2-6 (the output of which is presented in Figure 2-7).

Listing 2-6. Using beginShape() and endShape()

```
size(600, 300);

beginShape(QUADS);
vertex(5, 250);
vertex(590, 250);
vertex(590, 290);
vertex(5, 290);
endShape();

beginShape();
vertex(30, 25);
vertex(90, 90);
vertex(210, 10);
vertex(160, 120);
vertex(210, 270);
vertex(110, 180);
vertex(10, 270);
vertex(60, 150);
endShape(CLOSE);

beginShape(TRIANGLES);
vertex(50, 30);
vertex(90, 75);
vertex(110, 30);
endShape();

ellipse(470, 80, 70, 70);
```

23

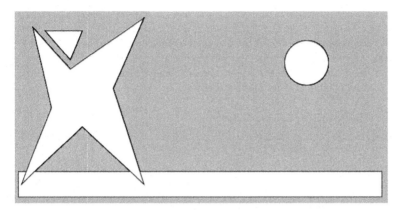

Figure 2-7. *Composition created with several shapes*

Even though we did not use beginShape/endShape in our first examples, where we created primitive shapes with the built-in functions ellipse() and rect(), these are nothing more than shorthand calls for their corresponding beginShape/endShape calls. We can, in fact, create other types of primitive shapes using beginShape(int kind), where the kind argument indicates the desired primitive. For example, in Listing 2-7 we construct a regular polygon with a group of triangles than fan out from a central vertex.

Listing 2-7. Creating a Triangle Fan

```
size(300, 300);
int numTriangles = 10;
beginShape(TRIANGLE_FAN);
vertex(width/2, height/2);
for (int i = 0; i <= numTriangles; i++) {
  float a = map(i, 0, numTriangles, 0, TWO_PI);
  float x = width/2 + 100 * cos(a);
  float y = height/2 + 100 * sin(a);
  vertex(x, y);
}
endShape();
```

In this example, we use a for loop to iterate over the number of divisions of the triangle fan. Processing, as an extension of the Java language, inherits all the control structures from Java, which we need for algorithmic drawing. Also, notice the use of the function map(), which is part of the Processing API. This function is very useful and allows us to convert a numeric value within a range to the corresponding value in a different range. In this case, the index i varies between 0 and numTriangles, and we want to transform it into an angle between 0 and 2π.

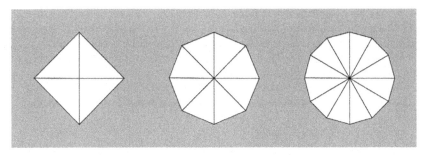

Figure 2-8. *Outputs of the triangle fan example for different numbers of vertices*

Other kinds of primitive shapes are TRIANGLE_STRIP, QUAD_STRIP, LINES, and POINTS, which are all fully documented in Processing's reference material. For instance, QUAD_STRIP becomes handy when one needs to create a rectangular grid or a hollowed-out circle, like we do in Listing 2-8.

Listing 2-8. Creating a Quad Strip

```
size(300, 300);
beginShape(QUAD_STRIP);
int numQuads = 10;
for (int i = 0; i <= numQuads; i++) {
  float a = map(i, 0, numQuads, 0, TWO_PI);
  float x0 = width/2 + 100 * cos(a);
  float y0 = height/2 + 100 * sin(a);
  float x1 = width/2 + 130 * cos(a);
  float y1 = height/2 + 130 * sin(a);
  vertex(x0, y0);
  vertex(x1, y1);
}
endShape();
```

By adjusting the value of the numQuads variable, we can obtain geometries of increasing detail, as seen in Figure 2-9.

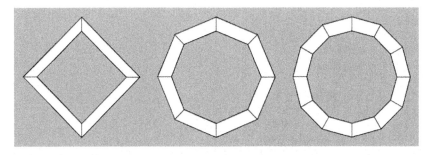

Figure 2-9. *Quad strip example with different values for numQuads*

However, we often need to create more complex shapes, such as curves. Even though we could calculate the vertices along the curves manually, Processing provides a number of functions that do precisely that for us, specifically for Catmull-Rom splines and quadratic and cubic Bezier curves. The `bezierVertex()` function, for instance, allows us to define a point on a cubic Bezier curve. It requires the anchor point the curve must pass through as well as the control points defining the starting and ending directions. When starting a Bezier curve, the first anchor is set with a regular `vertex()` call, as shown in Figure 2-10.

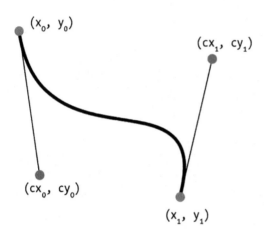

```
vertex(x0, y0);
bezierVertex(cx0, cy0, cx1, cy1, x1, y1);
```

Figure 2-10. *Parameters of the bezierVertex() function*

We can combine several Bezier curves into a single shape in order to generate more complex figures, as shown in Listing 2-9.

Listing 2-9. Creating Multi-lobed Shape with Bezier Curves

```
size(300, 300);
int numLobes = 4;
float radAnchor = 50;
float radControl = 150;
float centerX = width/2;
float centerY = height/2;
beginShape();
for (int i = 0; i < numLobes; i++) {
  float a = map(i, 0, numLobes, 0, TWO_PI);
  float a1 = map(i + 1, 0, numLobes, 0, TWO_PI);
  float cx0 = centerX + radControl * cos(a);
  float cy0 = centerY + radControl * sin(a);
```

```
  float cx1 = centerX + radControl * cos(a1);
  float cy1 = centerY + radControl * sin(a1);
  float x0 = centerX + radAnchor * cos(a);
  float y0 = centerY + radAnchor * sin(a);
  float x1 = centerX + radAnchor * cos(a1);
  float y1 = centerY + radAnchor * sin(a1);
  vertex(x0, y0);
  bezierVertex(cx0, cy0, cx1, cy1, x1, y1);
}
endShape();
```

By playing with the parameters in this sketch (number of lobes, radius of the anchor points, radius of the control points), we can obtain an entire family of shapes, some of which we can see in Figure 2-11.

Figure 2-11. *Family of multi-lobed shapes created with Bezier curves*

Color

Color is another important component of visual design, and Processing provides numerous functions to set the color of shape interiors (the fill color) and edges (the stroke color), in addition to the background color of the entire output screen.

By default, we can set colors using RGB (red, green, and blue) values between 0 and 255, as illustrated in the code of Listing 2-10 and its output in Figure 2-12.

Listing 2-10. Setting Fill and Stroke Colors Using RGB Values

```
size(600, 300);
strokeWeight(5);
fill(214, 87, 58);
stroke(53, 124, 115);
rect(10, 10, 180, 280);
stroke(115, 48, 128);
fill(252, 215, 51);
rect(210, 10, 180, 280);
stroke(224, 155, 73);
fill(17, 76, 131);
rect(410, 10, 180, 280);
```

Figure 2-12. *Output of setting stroke and fill RGB colors*

Even though we can create almost any imaginable color using RGB values, it can be hard to find the right combination of numbers for the color we need. Processing includes a handy Color Selector tool to help us to pick a color interactively, which we can then copy into our sketches as RGB values. The Color Selector is available, along with any other installed tools, under the Tools menu in the PDE (Figure 2-13).

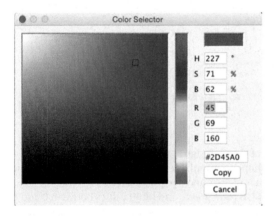

Figure 2-13. *Color Selector tool*

We can also specify colors in the HSB (Hue, Saturation, and Brightness) space. HSB mode can be set with the colorMode() function, which also allows us to set the ranges for each component. In code Listing 2-11, we draw a color wheel by mapping the position around a circle to the color hue.

Listing 2-11. Drawing a Color Wheel Using HSB Values

```
size(300, 300);
colorMode(HSB, TWO_PI, 1, 1);
float centerX = width/2;
float centerY = height/2;
float maxRad = width/2;
strokeWeight(2);
stroke(0, 0, 1);
for (int i = 0; i < 6; i++) {
  float r0 = map(i, 0, 6, 0, 1);
  float r1 = map(i + 1, 0, 6, 0, 1);
  beginShape(QUADS);
  for (int j = 0; j <= 10; j++) {
    float a0 = map(j, 0, 10, 0, TWO_PI);
    float a1 = map(j + 1, 0, 10, 0, TWO_PI);
    float x0 = centerX + maxRad * r0 * cos(a0);
    float y0 = centerY + maxRad * r0 * sin(a0);
    float x1 = centerX + maxRad * r1 * cos(a0);
    float y1 = centerY + maxRad * r1 * sin(a0);
    float x2 = centerX + maxRad * r1 * cos(a1);
    float y2 = centerY + maxRad * r1 * sin(a1);
    float x3 = centerX + maxRad * r0 * cos(a1);
    float y3 = centerY + maxRad * r0 * sin(a1);
    fill(a0, r0, 1);
    vertex(x0, y0);
    vertex(x1, y1);
    vertex(x2, y2);
    vertex(x3, y3);
  }
  endShape();
}
```

Let's note a few important things in this example. First, we set the range for the hue to 2π in order to make the transformation between indices and color more direct. Second, we use QUADS instead of QUAD_STRIP. We would not be able to set separate colors for each quad in a strip, because they all share a common edge with the previous and next quad. Instead, in a QUADS shape, each quad is defined independently of the others and so can have different style attributes. Our final color wheel is shown in Figure 2-14.

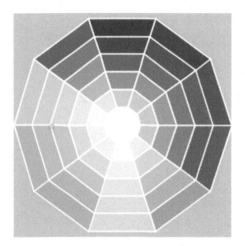

Figure 2-14. *Output of HSB color wheel example*

■ **Note**   We can also specify colors in hexadecimal (hex) format, which is very common in web development; i.e., fill(#FF0000) or stroke(#FFFFFF).

Geometric Transformations

So far, we have seen how to construct shapes and pick their colors. In addition, we need to be able to move them around and change their size by applying translations, rotations, and scaling transformations (Figure 2-15).

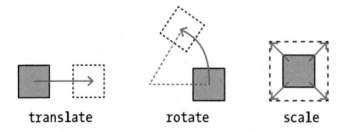

Figure 2-15. *The three types of geometric transformations*

While the ideas of translation, rotation, and scaling are intuitive, it is difficult to anticipate the effect of several consecutive transformations. It can help us when thinking about transformations to imagine that a transformation only affects the coordinates after it has been applied. For instance, if we apply a translation of 20 units along the x-axis and 30 units along the y-axis, then a subsequent rotation will occur around the point (20, 30). Conversely, if the rotation is applied first, the axes will then be rotated, and a translation will occur along the rotated axes. Therefore, if we draw a shape at the end of this chain of transformations, its final position may be different depending on the order in which they were done (Figure 2-16).

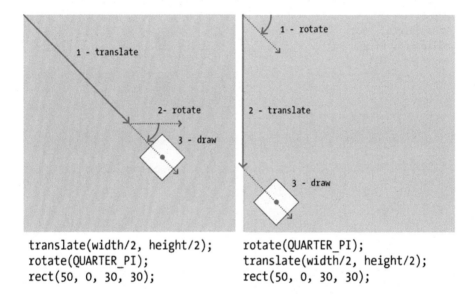

```
translate(width/2, height/2);      rotate(QUARTER_PI);
rotate(QUARTER_PI);                translate(width/2, height/2);
rect(50, 0, 30, 30);               rect(50, 0, 30, 30);
```

Figure 2-16. *Geometric transformations cannot be exchanged*

We can save the current transformation "state" with the pushMatrix() function and restore it with the corresponding popMatrix() function. We must always use these two functions in pairs. They allow us to create complex relative movements by setting transformations only to specific subsets of the shapes. For example, Listing 2-12 generates an animation of an ellipse and a square rotating around a larger square placed at the center of the screen, with the smaller square also rotating around its own center. Figure 2-17 shows a snapshot of this animation.

Listing 2-12. Using pushMatrix() and popMatrix()

```
float angle;

void setup() {
  size(400, 400);
  rectMode(CENTER);
  noStroke();
}
```

```
void draw() {
  background(170);
  translate(width/2, height/2);
  rotate(angle);
  rect(0, 0, 100, 100);
  pushMatrix();
  translate(150, 0);
  rotate(2 * angle);
  scale(0.5);
  rect(0, 0, 100, 100);
  popMatrix();
  translate(0, 180);
  ellipse(0, 0, 30, 30);
  angle += 0.01;
}
```

Figure 2-17. *Using pushMatrix() and popMatrix() to keep transformations separate*

Responding to User Input

Keyboard input and touchscreen input allow us to enter information into the sketch to control its behavior. Since the user can touch the screen or press a key at any moment, not necessarily when Processing is drawing a frame, we need a way to retrieve this information no matter what stage of drawing we are in within our sketch.

Processing provides several built-in variables and functions to handle user input. The variables mouseX and mouseY give us the current position of the mouse when working in Java mode. These variables are still available in Android mode, although mobile devices do not usually have a mouse. In this case, they just represent the position of the first touch point on the screen (Processing also supports multi-touch interaction, which is covered in Chapter 5). Both mouseX and mouseY are complemented by mousePressed, which indicates whether the mouse/touchscreen is being pressed. Using these variables, we can create a simple drawing sketch with very little code, like the one in Listing 2-13. Its output on a phone would look like Figure 2-18. Since the width and height set via the size() function are smaller than the screen resolution, we see the output area surrounded by a light background we cannot draw on. However, we can use the entire screen if, instead of initializing the sketch with size(width, height), we use the fullScreen() function. This also has the advantage of hiding the status bar at the top of the screen and the navigation bar at the bottom.

Listing 2-13. A Free-hand Drawing Sketch Using Circles

```
void setup() {
  size(1000, 500);
  noStroke();
  fill(255, 100);
}

void draw() {
  if (mousePressed) {
    ellipse(mouseX, mouseY, 50, 50);
  }
}
```

Figure 2-18. *Drawing with ellipses*

While mouseX/Y stores the current position of the mouse/touch, Processing also provides the variables pmouseX and pmouseY, which store the previous position. By connecting the pmouseX/Y coordinates with the ones in mouseX/Y, we can draw continuous lines that follow the movement of the pointer. Listing 2-14 illustrates this technique, and it also uses fullScreen() so we can draw on the entire screen surface, as seen in Figure 2-19.

Listing 2-14. Another Free-hand Drawing Sketch

```
void setup() {
  fullScreen();
}

void draw() {
  if (mousePressed) {
    line(pmouseX, pmouseY, mouseX, mouseY);
  }
}
```

Figure 2-19. *Output of our simple drawing sketch, in full-screen mode*

Creating a Vine-Drawing App

Our goal in this final section is to code a drawing app that incorporates algorithmic shapes into the hand-drawn lines. One possibility is to augment the scaffold provided by the lines with shapes that resemble growing vegetation, vines, leaves, and flowers. The Bezier curves we learned about earlier could be used to generate organic-looking shapes. Some sketching with pen and paper (Figure 2-20) may also help us try out some visual ideas.

Figure 2-20. *Sketches for the vine-drawing app*

We can build on our previous sketches. One thing we were missing before is some degree of "randomness" in both form and color. The random(float a, float b) function in Processing allows us to select random numbers between a and b, which we can then use in the leaf/flower shapes constructed via the bezierVertex() function. In Listing 2-15, we apply the random function to introduce variation in the color and number of lobes of our shapes, and Figure 2-21 shows the output of this sketch for three separate runs.

Listing 2-15. Generating Randomized Flowers/Leaves with Bezier Curves

```
void setup() {
  size(600, 200);
  frameRate(1);
}

void draw() {
  background(180);
  drawFlower(100, 100);
  drawFlower(300, 100);
  drawFlower(500, 100);
}

void drawFlower(float posx, float posy) {
  pushMatrix();
  translate(posx, posy);
  fill(random(255), random(255), random(255), 200);
  beginShape();
  int n = int(random(4, 10));
  for (int i = 0; i < n; i++) {
    float a = map(i, 0, n, 0, TWO_PI);
    float a1 = map(i + 1, 0, n, 0, TWO_PI);
    float r = random(10, 100);
```

```
    float x = r * cos(a);
    float y = r * sin(a);
    float x1 = r * cos(a1);
    float y1 = r * sin(a1);
    vertex(0, 0);
    bezierVertex(x, y, x1, y1, 0, 0);
  }
  endShape();
  popMatrix();
}
```

Figure 2-21. *Output of the flower/leaf sketch*

In addition to the flowers/leaves, we can add some additional elements; for instance, a growing spiral branch that finishes in a fruit. Spirals have a parametric formula (https://www.khanacademy.org/tag/parametric-equations) of the form x(t) = r(t) cos(a(t)), y(t) = r(t) sin(a(t)), where the parameter t goes from 0 to 1 and controls the growth of the curve. After tweaking the radial function, I reached a satisfactory growth behavior with r(t) = 1/t, so we can start with the code in Listing 2-16 to draw a single spiral (Figure 2-22).

Listing 2-16. Drawing a Spiral Using Parametric Equations

```
size(300, 300);
noFill();
translate(width/2, height/2);
beginShape();
float maxt = 10;
float maxr = 150;
for (float t = 1; t < maxt; t += 0.1) {
  float r = maxr/t;
  float x = r  * cos(t);
  float y = r  * sin(t);
  vertex(x, y);
}
endShape();
```

Figure 2-22. *Output of our spiral parametric equation sketch*

The number of turns is controlled by the maximum value of the parameter t, while the maximum radius determines how much the spiral extends outward. These two parameters will give us some visual variation with the aid of the random() function, as we did before. One issue is that we will need the stem of the spiral to be aligned with the direction of the line drawing. We can orient the spiral along a desired angle by rotating by the angle plus 180 degrees (π). This is what we do in Listing 2-17, with three different spirals generated by it shown in Figure 2-23.

Listing 2-17. Adding Random Variability to Our Spiral-Generation Algorithm

```
void setup() {
  size(600, 200);
  frameRate(1);
}

void draw() {
  background(180);
  drawSpiral(100, 100, 0);
  drawSpiral(300, 100, QUARTER_PI);
  drawSpiral(500, 100, PI);
}

void drawSpiral(float posx, float posy, float angle) {
  pushMatrix();
  translate(posx, posy);
  rotate(angle + PI);
  noFill();
  beginShape();
  float maxt = random(5, 20);
  float maxr = random(50, 80);
  float x0 = maxr * cos(1);
  float y0 = maxr * sin(1);
  for (float t = 1; t < maxt; t += 0.1) {
    float r = maxr/t;
    float x = r  * cos(t) - x0;
    float y = r  * sin(t) - y0;
    vertex(x, y);
  }
  endShape();
  popMatrix();
}
```

Figure 2-23. *Output of the randomized spirals sketch*

We can now put all these elements together in a simple drawing app that adds leaves, vines, and fruit to the hand-drawn line (Listing 2-18). Leaves and vines are randomly added when the mouse/touchscreen is pressed. We can control the amount of detail by setting the probability of drawing a new leave or vine in each frame. By using a value of 0.05, in average we will be adding a new element every 20 frames that have a press event. The angle of the connection of the spiral vines to the last line segment is calculated by constructing a PVector object from the difference between the current and previous mouse/touch positions. PVector is a built-in class that handles 2D and 3D vectors. This class contains several utility functions, one of which gives us the heading angle of the vector; that is, the angle of the vector along the x-axis. Figure 2-24 shows a drawing made with this app.

Listing 2-18. Full Vine-Drawing Sketch

```
void setup() {
  fullScreen();
  noFill();
  colorMode(HSB, 360, 99, 99);
  strokeWeight(2);
  stroke(210);
  background(0, 0, 99);
}

void draw() {
  if (mousePressed) {
    line(pmouseX, pmouseY, mouseX, mouseY);
    if (random(1) < 0.05) {
      PVector dir = new PVector(mouseX - pmouseX, mouseY - pmouseY);
      float a = dir.heading();
      drawSpiral(mouseX, mouseY, a);
    }
    if (random(1) < 0.05) {
      drawFlower(mouseX, mouseY);
    }
  }
}
```

```
void keyPressed() {
  background(0, 0, 99);
}

void drawFlower(float xc, float yc) {
  pushMatrix();
  pushStyle();
  noStroke();
  translate(xc, yc);
  fill(random(60, 79), random(50, 60), 85, 190);
  beginShape();
  int numLobes = int(random(4, 10));
  for (int i = 0; i <= numLobes; i++) {
    float a = map(i, 0, numLobes, 0, TWO_PI);
    float a1 = map(i + 1, 0, numLobes, 0, TWO_PI);
    float r = random(10, 50);
    float x = r * cos(a);
    float y = r * sin(a);
    float x1 = r * cos(a1);
    float y1 = r * sin(a1);
    vertex(0, 0);
    vertex(0, 0);
    bezierVertex(x, y, x1, y1, 0, 0);
  }
  endShape();
  popStyle();
  popMatrix();
}

void drawSpiral(float xc, float yc, float a) {
  pushMatrix();
  pushStyle();
  translate(xc, yc);
  rotate(PI + a);
  noFill();
  beginShape();
  float maxt = random(5, 10);
  float maxr = random(20, 70);
  float sign = (random(1) < 0.5) ? -1 : +1;
  float x0 = maxr * cos(sign);
  float y0 = maxr * sin(sign);
  for (float t = 1; t < maxt; t += 0.5) {
    float r = maxr/t;
    float x = r  * cos(sign * t) - x0;
    float y = r  * sin(sign * t) - y0;
    vertex(x, y);
  }
  endShape();
```

```
  noStroke();
  fill(random(310, 360), 80, 80);
  float x1 = (maxr/maxt) * cos(sign * maxt) - x0;
  float y1 = (maxr/maxt) * sin(sign * maxt) - y0;
  float r = random(5, 10);
  ellipse(x1, y1, r, r);
  popStyle();
  popMatrix();
}
```

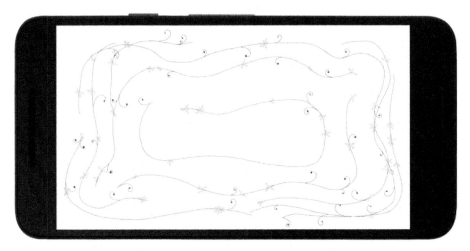

Figure 2-24. *Output of the vine-drawing sketch*

Summary

We now have a general overview of the Processing language and would be able to use some of its functions and variables to draw shapes, set colors, apply transformations, and handle user interaction through the mouse or touchscreen. Even though we covered only a small fraction of all the functionality available in Processing, what we saw here should give us enough material with which to explore algorithmic drawing, make our own interactive sketches, and run them as Android apps.

CHAPTER 3

From Sketch to Play Store

In this chapter, we will go over the steps involved in the creation of a complete Processing for Android project, from sketching and debugging to exporting the project as a signed app ready for upload to the Google Play Store. We will use the drawing sketch from the previous chapter as our example.

Sketching and Debugging

In the previous chapters, we emphasized the importance of "code sketching," where immediate visual output and quick iteration are central elements to the development of Processing projects. Another crucial component is the identification and resolution of errors or "bugs" in the code, a process called *debugging*.

Debugging can take as much time as writing the code itself. What makes debugging challenging is that some bugs are the result of faulty logic or incorrect calculations, and because there are no typos or any other syntactical errors in the code, Processing is able to run the sketch. Unfortunately, there is no foolproof technique for eliminating all bugs in a program, but Processing provides some utilities to help us.

Getting Information from the Console

The simplest way to debug a program is by printing the values of variables and messages at various points of the program's execution flow. Processing's API includes the text-printing functions print() and println(), which output to the console area in the PDE. The only difference between these two functions is that println() adds a new line break at the end, while print() does not. Listing 3-1 shows a sketch that uses println() to indicate the occurrence of an event (a mouse press, in this case) and the value of a built-in variable.

Listing 3-1. Using println() in a Sketch to Show Information on the Console

```
void setup() {
  fullScreen();
}
```

© Andrés Colubri 2017
A. Colubri, *Processing for Android*, https://doi.org/10.1007/978-1-4842-2719-0_3

```
void draw() {
  println("frame #", frameCount);
}

void mousePressed() {
  println("Press event");
}
```

Processing's console shows anything that is printed with these functions, and also any warning or error messages indicating a problem in the execution of the sketch (Figure 3-1).

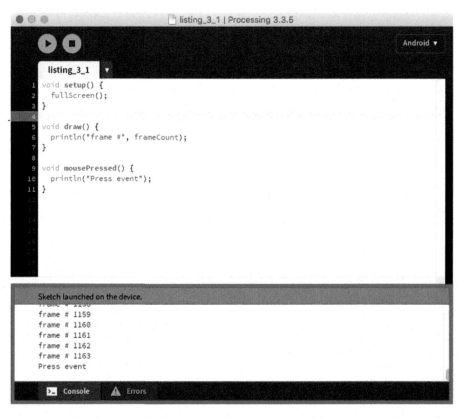

Figure 3-1. *PDE's console outlined with red*

The main problem with printing messages to the console for debugging is that it requires adding these additional function calls for each variable we want to keep track of. Once we are done with debugging, we need remove or comment out all these calls, which can become cumbersome for large sketches.

■ **Note**   Comments in Processing work exactly the same way as in Java: we can comment out a single line of code using two consecutive forward slashes, //, and an entire block of text with /* at the beginning of the block and */ at the end. We can also use the "Comment/ Uncomment" option under the Edit menu in the PDE.

Getting More Information with logcat

We can obtain a lot of useful information from the Processing console, but sometimes this won't be enough to find out what is wrong with our sketch. The Android SDK includes several command-line tools that can help us with debugging. The most important SDK tool is adb (Android Debug Bridge), which makes communication possible between the computer we are using for development and the device or emulator. In fact, Processing uses adb under the hood to query what devices are available and to push the sketch to the device or emulator when running it from the PDE.

We can also use adb manually—for example, to get more-detailed debug messages. To do so, we need to open a terminal console, and once in it we have to change to the directory where the Android SDK is installed. If the SDK was automatically installed by Processing, it should be located inside the sketchbook folder in the android sub-folder. Within that folder, the SDK tools are found in sdk/platform-tools. Once there, we can run the adb tool with the logcat option, which prints out the log with all the messages. For instance, Figure 3-2 shows the sequence of commands we would need on Mac to run logcat.

Figure 3-2. Terminal session on Mac displaying the commands to run logcat

By default, logcat prints all messages generated by the Android device or emulator—not only those from the sketch we are debugging, but also those from all other processes currently running—so we might get too many messages. The print messages from Processing can be displayed if using logcat with the –I option. Logcat has additional options to only show error messages (-E) or warnings (-W). The full list of options is available on the Google's developer site (https://developer.android.com/ studio/command-line/logcat.html).

Using the Integrated Debugger

Java mode in Processing 3.0 introduced an integrated debugger that makes it easier for us to keep track of the internal state of a running sketch. Even though the debugger is not available in Android mode, we can still use it to debug Android sketches. If a Processing sketch does not rely on Android-specific functionality, it should be compatible with both Android and Java modes, since the code API is (almost) identical for the two modes. In that case, we can momentarily switch to Java mode to take advantage of its debugger and then come back to Android mode to continue working on the device or emulator.

We turn the debugger on by pressing the button with the butterfly icon on the left of the menu bar, next to the mode selector, or by selecting "Enable Debugger" in the Debug menu. Once it is enabled, we can access several additional options in the PDE to use when the sketch is running. For example, we can add *checkpoints* to any line in the code of our sketch. A checkpoint signals where the execution of the sketch should stop to allow us to inspect the value of all variables in the sketch, both user-defined and built-in ones.

We can create a new checkpoint by double-clicking on the line number in the left margin of the code editor. A diamond sign will indicate that the line has been flagged with a checkpoint. When we run a sketch containing one or more checkpoints, Processing will stop execution when it reaches each checkpoint, at which moment we can inspect the value of the variables using the variable-inspector window (Figure 3-3). We resume execution by pressing the Continue button on the toolbar. We can also step line by line by pressing the Step button to see how each variable changes its value after each line.

Figure 3-3. *Debugging session with the integrated debugger in Java mode*

All this functionality in the integrated debugger could help us identify bugs in the code without adding print instructions, although fixing a tricky bug is always challenging and can take a long time even with the debugger. In the end, it comes down to understanding the logic of the code in the sketch and its possible consequences and edge cases based on information we get from the debugger or print instructions. In this way, we can narrow down the portion of the code containing the bug.

Reporting Processing Bugs

Sometimes an unexpected or erroneous behavior in a Processing sketch may be the result of not a bug in the sketch itself, but rather one in Processing's core. If you have a strong suspicion that you have found a Processing bug, you can report it on the GitHub page of the project. If it is a bug affecting Android mode, open a new issue in the processing-android repository at `https://github.com/processing/processing-android/issues` and include as much information as possible to reproduce the bug and help the developers examine the issue and eventually fix it.

Preparing a Sketch for Release

After debugging a sketch in the PDE, we may want to package it for public release through Google Play Store. When working from the PDE, Processing creates a debug app package that can only be installed on our own device for testing purposes. Creating an app suitable for general distribution requires some additional steps and considerations to ensure it can be uploaded to the Play Store.

Adjusting for Device's DPI

To ready our sketch for public release, we must first make sure that it can be run on (most) of the Android devices in use. When writing and debugging sketches, it is often the case that we work with one or only a few different devices, so it may be hard to anticipate issues on hardware we do not have access to. A common situation is that the graphics look either too big or too small when running Processing sketches on different devices. Both resolution (number of pixels) and physical screen size can vary quite substantially across phones, tablets, and watches, so graphic elements designed with one resolution in mind and viewed on a screen of a particular size will likely look wrong on another device. Since Android is designed to support various combinations of screen sizes and resolutions, we need a way in Processing to adapt the visual design of our sketch so it looks as intended across different devices.

The ratio of the resolution to the screen size gives us what is called the DPI (dots per inch, which in the context of computer screens is equivalent to pixels per inch, or PPI). The DPI is the basic magnitude to compare across devices. It is important to keep in mind that a higher DPI does not necessarily mean a higher resolution, since two different devices with the same resolution may have different screen sizes. For example, the Galaxy Nexus (4.65" diagonal) has a 720 × 1280 pixels resolution, while the Nexus 7 (7" diagonal) has an 800 × 1280 pixels resolution. The DPIs of these devices are respectively 316 and 216, even though the resolution of the Galaxy Nexus is actually slightly lower than that of the Nexus 7.

Android classifies devices in "density buckets" according to the following six generalized densities (a specific device will fall into one of these categories depending on which one is closest to its actual DPI):

- ldpi (low) ~120 dpi

- mdpi (medium) ~160 dpi

- hdpi (high) ~240 dpi

- xhdpi (extra-high) ~320 dpi

- xxhdpi (extra-extra-high) ~480 dpi

- xxxhdpi (extra-extra-extra-high) ~640 dpi

The generalized density levels are important in Processing when generating the app icons, as we will see later in this chapter, but not so much when writing our code. To make sure that the visual elements in our sketch scale properly across different devices, there is another parameter from Android that Processing makes available through its API. This is the *display density*, a number that represents how much bigger (or smaller) the pixel in our device is when compared with a reference 160 dpi screen (for example, a 320 × 480, 3.5" screen). Thus, on a 160 dpi screen, this density value will be 1; on a 120 dpi screen, it would be .75, etc.

■ **Note**   Google's API Guide on Multiple Screen Support gives detailed information about density independence on Android: `https://developer.android.com/guide/practices/screens_support.html`.

The display density is available in Processing as the constant named `displayDensity`, which we can use from anywhere in our code. The simplest way of adjusting the output to the device's DPI is to multiply the size of all of the graphical elements in the sketch by `displayDensity,` which is the approach shown in Listing 3-2. As we can see in Figure 3-4, the size of the circles drawn by the sketch is the same across devices with different DPIs. Also, this example uses `fullScreen()` to initialize the size of the output of our sketch to the entire screen, regardless of its resolution.

Listing 3-2.   Using displayDensity to Adjust Our Sketch to Different Screen Sizes and Resolutions

```
void setup() {
  fullScreen();
  noStroke();
}

void draw() {
  background(0);
  float r = 50 * displayDensity;
  int maxi = int(width/r);
```

```
  int maxj = int(height/r);
  for (int i = 0; i <= maxi; i++) {
    float x = map(i, 0, maxi, 0, width);
    for (int j = 0; j <= maxj; j++) {
      float y = map(j, 0, maxj, 0, height);
      ellipse(x, y, r, r);
    }
  }
}
```

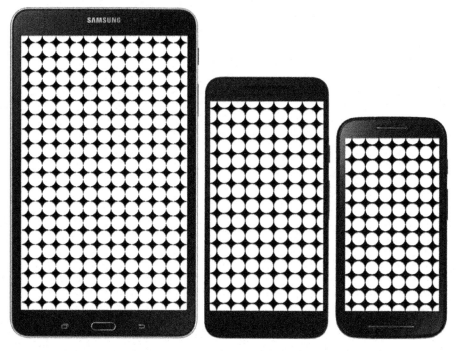

Figure 3-4. *From left to right: output of our sketch on a Samsung Galaxy Tab 4 (7", 1280 × 800 px, 216 dpi), Nexus 5X (5.2", 1920 × 800 px, 424 dpi), and a Moto E (4.3", 960 × 540 px, 256 dpi)*

We can return now to our vine-drawing sketch from the previous chapter and add displayDensity in the parts of the code where we need to scale the graphics. More specifically, any variable or value that represents the size of shapes or position of vertices on the screen should be multiplied by displayDensity. Listing 3-3 shows these changes applied to the original drawing sketch.

Listing 3-3. Adding displayDensity to the Vine-drawing Sketch from Chapter 2

```
void drawFlower(float xc, float yc) {
  pushMatrix();
  pushStyle();
  noStroke();
  translate(xc, yc);
  fill(random(60, 79), random(50, 60), 85, 190);
  beginShape();
  int numLobes = int(random(4, 10));
  for (int i = 0; i <= numLobes; i++) {
    float a = map(i, 0, numLobes, 0, TWO_PI);
    float a1 = map(i + 1, 0, numLobes, 0, TWO_PI);
    float r = random(10, 50) * displayDensity;
    ...
}

void drawSpiral(float xc, float yc, float a) {
  pushMatrix();
  pushStyle();
  translate(xc, yc);
  rotate(PI + a);
  noFill();
  beginShape();
  float maxr = random(20, 70) * displayDensity;
  ...
  fill(random(310, 360), 80, 80);
  float x1 = (maxr/maxt) * cos(sign * maxt) - x0;
  float y1 = (maxr/maxt) * sin(sign * maxt) - y0;
  float r = random(5, 10) * displayDensity;
  ellipse(x1, y1, r, r);
  popStyle();
  popMatrix();
}
```

Using the Emulator

We briefly discussed the emulator in the first chapter. Even when we have our own device, the emulator can be useful because it allows us to test hardware configurations we do not have access to. Processing creates a default Android Virtual Device (AVD) to run in the emulator, but one with a resolution of only 480 × 800 pixels to ensure a reasonable performance across different computers. We can create other AVDs with different properties by using the command-line tool avdmanager, which is included in the Android SDK. We have to keep in mind that the emulator will likely run slower than an actual device would, especially if you are using high-resolution AVDs or ones with other high-end capabilities.

Since avdmanager is a command-line tool, we first need to open a terminal console and change to the tools directory, where avdmanager and the emulator launcher are located inside the SDK folder. Figure 3-5 shows the sequence of steps to create a new AVD using the device definition for a Nexus 5X phone and then launch it with the emulator.

```
●  ●  ●                          tools — -bash — 100×10
~ $ cd ~/Documents/Processing/android/sdk/tools/
tools $ bin/avdmanager create avd -n n5x -k "system-images;android-26;google_apis;x86" -d "Nexus 5X"
 -p ~/Documents/Processing/android/avd/n5x
Auto-selecting single ABI x86
tools $ ./emulator -avd n5x -gpu auto -port 5566
```

Figure 3-5. *Creating and launching a new AVD from the command line using the avdmanager and emulator tools*

In the line running the avdmanager command, we provided four arguments:

- -n n5x: The name of the AVD, which could be any name we wish to use

- -k "system-images;android-26;google_apis;x86": The SDK package to use for the AVD; to find out which SDK packages are available in our SDK, we need to look at the system-images sub-folder inside the SDK folder.

- -d: "Nexus 5X": A device definition containing the hardware parameters of the device we want to emulate. We can list all the available device definitions by running the command './avdmanager list devices'.

- -p ~/Documents/Processing/android/avd/n5x: The folder where we will store this AVD; in this case, we are using android/ avd/n5x inside the sketchbook folder since this is the default location the Android mode uses for default AVDs.

The next line in Figure 3-5 actually launches the emulator, but before doing that we need to set up the AVD's "skin" by telling the emulator the actual dimensions it should render the phone screen at. Currently, the avdmanager does not have an option to set the device skin, but we can add it manually to the AVD's configuration file, which in this example is located inside ~/Documents/Processing/android/avd/n5x and named config.ini. We can open this file with any text editor and then add the line skin. name=widthxheight at the end, using the width and height of the device, although we can also use other values of our preference, as shown in Figure 3-6.

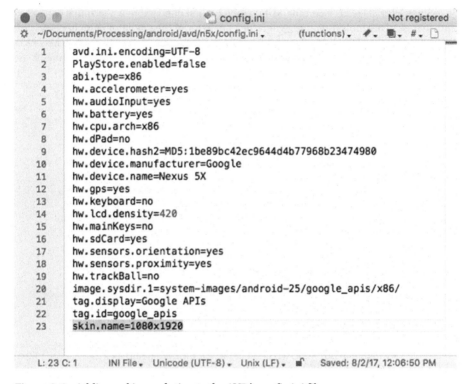

Figure 3-6. *Adding a skin resolution to the AVD's config.ini file*

Once we have added the skin resolution to the `config.ini` file of our AVD, we can run the emulator line shown earlier, which includes the following arguments:

- `-avd n5x`: The name of the AVD we want to launch

- `-gpu auto`: Enables the emulator to use hardware acceleration on the computer to render the AVD's screen faster, if it is available. Otherwise, it will use a slower software renderer.

- `-port 5566`: Sets the TCP port number to connect the console and adb with the emulator.

To use our new AVD in place of Processing's default one, we should launch it manually, as we did in this example, and then Processing will install our sketches in it instead of in the default AVD. However, we need to make sure to use the right port parameter, because Processing will only be able to communicate with phone emulators running on port 5566 and watch emulators on port 5576.

▦ **Note** Google's Android developer site includes pages on avdmanager (`https://developer.android.com/studio/command-line/avdmanager.html`) and running the emulator from the command line (`https://developer.android.com/studio/run/emulator-commandline.html`). There, we can find more information about these tools.

Setting Icons and Package Name

Android apps require icons of various sizes to be displayed at different pixel densities in the App Launcher menu. Processing uses a set of default generic icons when running a sketch from the PDE, but these icons should not be used for a public release.

In order to add our own icons to the project, we need to create the following files: icon-36, icon-48, icon-72, icon-96, icon-144, and icon-192 in .PNG format for the ldpi (36 × 36), mdpi (48 × 48), hdpi (72 × 27), xhdpi (96 × 96), xxhdpi (144 × 144), and xxxhdpi (192 × 192) resolutions. Once we have these files, we place them in the sketch's folder before exporting the signed package.

For the vine-drawing app from the previous chapter, we will use the set of icons shown in Figure 3-7.

Figure 3-7. *Set of icons for the vine-drawing app*

Google has published a set of guidelines and resources for icon creation that follows the company's material UI style, available at `https://www.google.com/design/spec/style/icons.html`

Setting Package Name and Version

Apps in the Google App Store are uniquely identified by a package name, which is a string of text that looks something like `com.example.helloworld`. This package name follows the Java package-naming convention, where the app name (`helloworld`) is last, preceded by the website of the company or person developing the app in reverse order (`com.example`).

Processing constructs this package name automatically by prepending processing.test to the sketch name. We can change the default package name by editing the manifest.xml file that Processing generates in the sketch folder after we run it for the first time from the PDE (either on a device or in the emulator). We can also set the version code and version name. For example, in the following manifest file generated by Processing, the package name is com.example.vines_draw, the version code 10, and version name 0.5.4:

```xml
<?xml version="1.0" encoding="UTF-8"?>
<manifest xmlns:android="http://schemas.android.com/apk/res/android"
          android:versionCode="10" android:versionName="0.5.4"
          package="com.example.vines_draw">
    <uses-sdk android:minSdkVersion="17" android:targetSdkVersion="25"/>
    <application android:icon="@drawable/icon"
                 android:label="Vines Draw">
        <activity android:name=".MainActivity"
                  android:theme=
                  "@style/Theme.AppCompat.Light.NoActionBar.FullScreen">
            <intent-filter>
                <action android:name="android.intent.action.MAIN"/>
                <category android:name="android.intent.category.LAUNCHER"/>
            </intent-filter>
        </activity>
    </application>
</manifest>
```

Note that our app's package name must be unique, since there cannot be two apps on the Google Play Store with the same package name. Also, we should set the application name by using the android:label attribute in the application tag. Android will use this label as the visible title of the app in the launcher and other parts of the UI.

Exporting as a Signed Package

Android Mode simplifies the publishing of our sketch by signing and aligning the app so we can upload it to the Google Play Developer Console very easily. The signing process involves creating a public-key certificate that contains the public key of a public/private key pair, so that when the app package is signed, it embeds a unique fingerprint that associates the package with its author. This ensures that any future updates of the app are authentic and come from the o riginal author (https://developer.android.com/studio/publish/appsigning.html). The alignment is required to optimize data storage inside the package, which reduces the amount of RAM consumed when running the application. While Processing will do the signing and alignment for us, we still need to create a Google Play Developer account to use the Play Console, which requires paying a one-time fee of $25, at the time of this writing (https://support.google.com/googleplay/androiddeveloper/answer/6112435). From Processing, all we need to do is select the "Export Signed Package" option under the File menu (Figure 3-8).

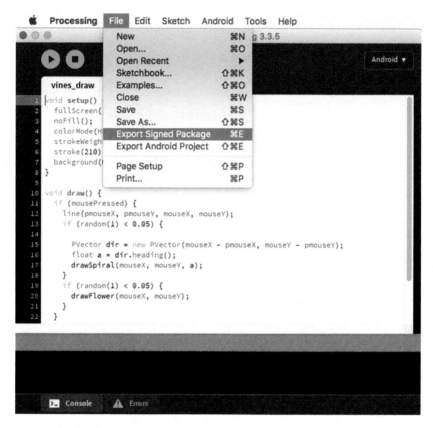

Figure 3-8. *"Export Signed Package" option in the PDE's File menu*

After selecting this option, Processing will ask to create a new keystore to save the release key to sign the app package. The keystore requires a password and additional information about the keystore issuer (name, organization, city, state, country), although those are optional. The Keystore Manager window that allows us to enter all this information is displayed in Figure 3-9.

53

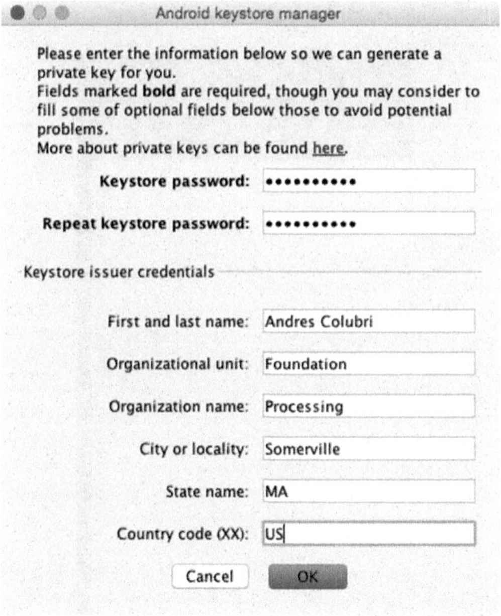

Figure 3-9. *Entering the information needed to create a keystore in Processing*

Remember this password, as you will have to use it every time you export a new signed package. Even though you could reset it and create a new key, you should keep in mind that you cannot change keys once an app is uploaded to the Play Store—any subsequent updates to the app need to be signed by the same key as the original, or else it will be denied, and you will have to create a new package with a new key.

The signed (and aligned) package will be saved in the build subfolder inside the sketch's folder, under the name [Sketch name in lowercase]_release_signed_aligned.apk. Once we have this package, we can follow the instructions from Google to complete the app-publishing process: https://support.google.com/googleplay/android-developer/answer/113469.

If we follow all these steps with our vine-drawing sketch, we should be able to generate a signed package that is ready to upload to the Play Store. We can also install it manually on our device using the adb tool (see Figure 3-10).

```
● ● ●                    📄 platform-tools — -bash — 100×10
~ $ cd ~/Documents/Processing/android/sdk/platform-tools/
platform-tools $ ./adb install ~/Documents/Processing/vines_draw/build/vines_draw_release_signed_ali
gned.apk
/Users/andres/Documents/Processing/vines_draw/bu... file pushed. 3.0 MB/s (2394241 bytes in 0.754s)
        pkg: /data/local/tmp/vines_draw_release_signed_aligned.apk
Success
platform-tools $ ▌
```

Figure 3-10. *Installing a signed package from the command line using adb*

If we install the final app package either manually or through the Play Store, we should see it in the app launcher with the icon we created for it (Figure 3-11).

Figure 3-11. *The vine-drawing app installed on our device*

Summary

This chapter covered a number of technical topics, including debugging our code using Processing's console, the integrated debugger, or the logcat option in adb; scaling the output of our sketches according to the device's DPI; and exporting our sketch as a signed package ready for upload to the Play Store. With these tools, we are ready to share our creations with Android users around the world!

PART II

Drawing and Interaction

CHAPTER 4

■ ■ ■

Drawing Graphics and Text

In this chapter, we will delve deeper into the Processing API for drawing shapes, images, and text, using several code examples to illustrate the different functions in the API. We will also learn how to use the P2D renderer and the PShape class for better 2D performance.

Renderers in Processing

In the previous chapters, we learned the basic structure of a Processing sketch, which consists of a setup() and a draw() function, with the former containing the sketch initialization and the latter the code that updates the screen in each frame. As part of the initialization, we need to indicate the size of the output area with the size() function, as shown in Listing 4-1. We also saw that the fullScreen() function allows us to use the entire area of the device's screen, irrespective of its resolution.

Both the size() and fullScreen() functions accept a "renderer" option. The renderer is the module in Processing that transforms the drawing commands in our sketch into a final image on the device's screen. The Processing renderer does this by communicating with the graphics hardware through an API provided by the Android system (https://source.android.com/devices/graphics/).

The default renderer (JAVA2D), enabled when no additional option is given to size() or fullScreen(), uses Android's Canvas API and offers high-quality 2D rendering. However, performance can be limited, especially when drawing many shapes and other graphic elements. The other two renderers, P2D and P3D, use the graphics processing unit (GPU) through the OpenGL API, which results in higher performance, but at the expense of increased battery consumption. We can select the renderer by calling size() or fullScreen() with the appropriate parameter; for example, size(w, h) or size(w, h, JAVA2D) will result in the sketch using the default renderer, while size(w, h, P2D) or fullScreen(P2D) will enable the P2D renderer, as we do in Listing 4-1. The output of this sketch is the same whether we use JAVA2D or P2D, but later in this chapter we will see some specific advantages of using P2D. We will cover the use of the P3D renderer to draw 3D graphics in Chapter 13.

© Andrés Colubri 2017

A. Colubri, *Processing for Android*, https://doi.org/10.1007/978-1-4842-2719-0_4

Listing 4-1. Using Full-screen Output with the P2D Renderer

```
void setup() {
  fullScreen(P2D);
  background(255);
  noFill();
  rectMode(CENTER);
}

void draw() {
  float w = 2*(width/2-mouseX);
  rect(width/2, height/2, w, w/width * height);
}
```

Figure 4-1. Output of the full-screen P2D sketch

Drawing Shapes

Chapter 2 gave us an overview of some important elements of the drawing API in Processing. We saw how primitive shapes are drawn using functions like ellipse() or rect(), while arbitrary shapes can be created vertex by vertex with the beginShape(), vertex(), and endShape() functions. In this section, we will go deeper into the shape-drawing API and will learn how to store shapes into objects for faster rendering using the PShape class and by loading vector graphics into a PShape object.

More Shape Types

Let's start by reviewing all the possible shape types that we have at our disposal. Essentially, depending on the type we specify in beginShape(), the vertices will be connected in different ways to construct the desired geometry, as shown in Figure 4-2.

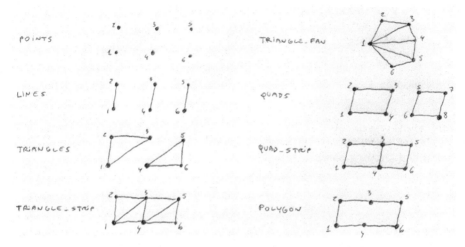

Figure 4-2. *All the shape types available in Processing*

The number and order of the vertices are very important when constructing a shape with beginShape/endShape. Figure 4-2 depicts how each vertex is incorporated into the shape, depending on the type. If we provide the vertices in a different order—for example, if we switch vertices 2 and 3 in a shape of type QUADS—then the resulting shape will look distorted. Also, each type (except for points and polygon) requires a specific number of vertices to construct an individual shape; for instance, 3 × N to draw N triangles, 4 × N to draw N quads, and so on. We must become familiar with these rules if we want to create complex shapes. Consider, for example, how the same disposition of vertices can lead to very different visual results under each shape type, as shown in Listing 4-2.

Listing 4-2. Drawing Different Shapes of Different Types Using beginShape() and endShape()

```
int[] types = {POINTS, LINES, TRIANGLES,
               TRIANGLE_STRIP, TRIANGLE_FAN,
               QUADS, QUAD_STRIP, POLYGON};
int selected = 0;

void setup() {
  size(300, 300);
  strokeWeight(2);
}

void draw() {
  background(150);
  beginShape(types[selected]);
  for (int i = 0; i <= 10; i++) {
    float a = map(i, 0, 10, 0, TWO_PI);
    float x0 = width/2  + 100 * cos(a);
    float y0 = height/2 + 100 * sin(a);
```

61

```
    float x1 = width/2  + 130 * cos(a);
    float y1 = height/2 + 130 * sin(a);
    vertex(x0, y0);
    vertex(x1, y1);
  }
  endShape();
}

void mousePressed() {
  selected = (selected + 1) % types.length;
  println("Drawing shape", selected);
}
```

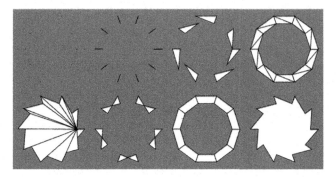

Figure 4-3. *Outputs for different shape types*

■ **Note**   The POLYGON type is the default argument of beginShape(), so if we don't provide any explicit type, we will be creating a polygonal shape. Also, polygons can be open or closed, and this can be controlled with endShape(mode), with mode being either OPEN or CLOSE.

Curve Shapes

The vertex() function we have been using so far allows us to add vertices to our shape that are then connected according to the type parameter we selected in beginShape(). This method is general enough to generate almost any shape we can think of, even curved ones. In such a case, we could compute the position of the vertices along a mathematical curve, then add those vertices to a polygonal shape. For example, in Listing 4-3 we use polar coordinates to generate a random, organic-looking shape.

Listing 4-3. Creating a Curved "Organic" Shape with Polar Coordinates

```
size(480, 480);
translate(width/2, height/2);
int numPoints = 100;
int degree = 5;
beginShape();
float[] coeffs = new float[degree];
for (int d = 0; d < degree; d++) {
  coeffs[d] = random(0, 1);
}
float phase = random(0, TWO_PI);
for (int i = 0; i <= numPoints; i++) {
  float theta = map(i, 0, numPoints, 0, TWO_PI);
  float rho = 5;
  for (int d = 1; d <= degree; d++) {
    rho += coeffs[d - 1] * sin(d*theta+phase);
  }
  float x = 30 * rho * cos(theta);
  float y = 30 * rho * sin(theta);
  vertex(x, y);
}
endShape();
```

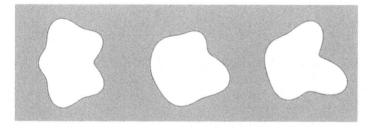

Figure 4-4. *Three shapes created by our "organic shape" example*

In this example, we used the variable numPoints to set the number of points to add to the shape. The higher this number is, the smoother the curve will look at the end. We could use Catmull-Rom splines and Bezier curves instead, with both giving us more intuitive control of the curve, as we will see next.

We add a Catmull-Rom spline inside a shape by repeatedly calling the curveVertex() function, once for each vertex the spline needs to go through, and by setting its *control points*. These control points determine the direction of the spline at its endpoints. A convenient aspect of Catmull-Rom splines is that they pass through all the control points, but the relationship between these points and the direction at the endpoints is not easy to visualize.

Let's look at the details of using splines. To make the code more readable, we will use the PVector class in Processing, which allows us to store 2D and 3D positions and carry out basic vector algebra. A PVector object has three float fields—x, y, z—and a number of methods to compute things like vector addition, subtraction, length, and heading angle. The Processing reference has a section detailing how to use this functionality (https://processing.org/reference/PVector.html), as well as a tutorial (https://processing.org/tutorials/pvector/). In Listing 4-4, we use an array of PVector objects to store all the points the spline passes through.

Listing 4-4. Creating Catmull-Rom Splines with curveVertex()

```
size(480, 480);

PVector[] points = new PVector[11];
for (int i = 0; i <= 10; i++) {
  if (i < 10) {
    float a = map(i, 0, 10, 0, TWO_PI);
    float r = random(100, 200);
    points[i] = new PVector(r * cos(a), r * sin(a));
  } else {
    points[10] = points[0].copy();
  }
}

translate(width/2, height/2);
fill(255);
beginShape();
for (int i = 0; i <= 10; i++) {
  if (i == 0 || i == 10) curveVertex(points[i].x, points[i].y);
  curveVertex(points[i].x, points[i].y);
}
endShape();

fill(0);
for (int i = 0; i <= 10; i++) {
  ellipse(points[i].x, points[i].y, 10, 10);
}
```

We first create an array of PVector objects where we store the positions along the curve. Since we are creating a closed shape, the last PVector is a copy of the first. Then, we just add the positions stored in the PVector array to the polygon shape as curve vertices. The line if (i == 0 || i == 10) curveVertex(points[i].x, points[i].y); adds the additional vertices corresponding to the control points, which are set to be the same as the first and last points in the curve. Even though the splines give us a smooth curve passing through all our points, we might get a sharp corner at the first point, as we can see in Figure 4-5.

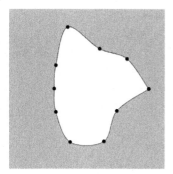

Figure 4-5. *Output of the Catmull-Rom spline example*

Bezier curves, on the other hand, allow for a more intuitive manipulation of the shape thanks to the control points that can be used to adjust the curvature between each pair of vertices along the curve. We applied Bezier curves in Chapter 2 to create shapes resembling flowers and leaves, and we can use them in many other situations. Similar to our earlier random blob, we can create a randomized shape using Bezier curves. We need to smoothly join pieces of Bezier curves; each one requires two control points and two vertices. Figure 4-6 shows how the vertices and control points of adjacent Bezier curves should be shared to ensure the overall curve does not contain sharp corners.

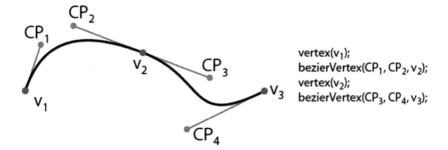

Figure 4-6. *Smoothly joining Bezier curves*

As with the splines, we can generate the points through which the Bezier curve will pass by moving around the entire perimeter of the shape at equally spaced intervals, then constructing the tangent directions along which we will place the control points to be shared among consecutive curves. This is what we have done in Listing 4-5.

Listing 4-5. Creating a Bezier Curve with Consecutive Vertices

```
size(480, 480);

PVector[] points = new PVector[11];
PVector[] directions = new PVector[11];
for (int i = 0; i <= 10; i++) {
  if (i < 10) {
    float a = map(i, 0, 10, 0, TWO_PI);
    float r = random(100, 200);
    points[i] = new PVector(r * cos(a), r * sin(a));
    directions[i] = PVector.fromAngle(points[i].heading() +
                    random(0, QUARTER_PI));
    directions[i].mult(60);
  } else {
    points[10] = points[0].copy();
    directions[10] = directions[0].copy();
  }
}

translate(width/2, height/2);
strokeWeight(2);
fill(255);
beginShape();
for (int i = 0; i < 10; i++) {
  vertex(points[i].x, points[i].y);
  PVector CP1 = PVector.add(points[i], directions[i]);
  PVector CP2 = PVector.sub(points[i+1], directions[i+1]);
  bezierVertex(CP1.x, CP1.y, CP2.x, CP2.y, points[i+1].x, points[i+1].y);
}
endShape();
```

Notice the use of PVector's fromAngle() method to generate a direction vector by rotating the position vector by a random amount between 0 and 90 degrees (QUARTER_PI) and then scaling it by a constant factor (60). Again, the position and direction of the final vector need to be copied from the first one so the shape is properly closed. Once all these vectors are computed and stored in the arrays, we just create the shape with the vertex() and bezierVertex() functions.

We can also add some extra code to our example to draw the vertices and control points. All we need to do is iterate over the points and directions arrays and then use ellipses and lines to show them in relation to the shape. Listing 4-6 contains this extra code, which we would paste at the end of the sketch from Listing 4-5 to get the output shown in Figure 4-7.

Listing 4-6. Drawing the Control Points and Tangent Directions to a Bezier Curve

```
strokeWeight(1);
for (int i = 0; i <= 10; i++) {
  PVector prevCP = PVector.sub(points[i], directions[i]);
  PVector nextCP = PVector.add(points[i], directions[i]);
  stroke(0);
  line(prevCP.x, prevCP.y, nextCP.x, nextCP.y);
  noStroke();
  fill(190, 30, 45);
  ellipse(points[i].x, points[i].y, 10, 10);
  fill(28, 117, 188);
  ellipse(prevCP.x, prevCP.y, 7, 7);
  ellipse(nextCP.x, nextCP.y, 7, 7);
}
```

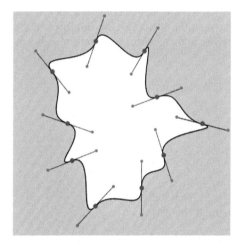

Figure 4-7. *Shape obtained by joining Bezier consecutive curves, with their control points*

It is possible to combine curve/Bezier vertices with regular vertices in the same shape. Let's use what we just learned to draw a simple seascape, making waves with Bezier curves. I sketched out this idea in Figure 4-8.

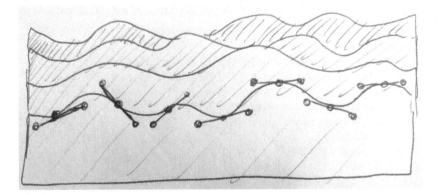

Figure 4-8. *Pen and paper sketch of a seascape using Bezier curves*

Since we will be drawing several shapes with the same code but different parameters, it can be convenient to store each shape inside a separate object. For this purpose, we will define a class holding a single wavy line, which we can then use to create several waves in the setup() function, as shown in Listing 4-7.

Listing 4-7. Seascape Sketch, Using Objects to Draw Several Shapes

```
void setup() {
  fullScreen();
  orientation(LANDSCAPE);
  colorMode(HSB, 360, 100,100);
  waves = new WavyLine[10];
  for (int i = 0; i < 10; i++) {
    float y = map(i, 0, 9, height * 0.85, height * 0.025);
    color c = color(225, map(i, 0, 10, 30, 100), 90);
    waves[i] = new WavyLine(y, c);
  }
}

void draw() {
  background(219, 240, 255);
  for (int i = waves.length - 1; i >= 0; i--) {
    waves[i].display();
  }
}

class WavyLine {
  int numDiv;
  color fillColor;
  PVector[] positions;
  PVector[] directions;
```

```
WavyLine(float y, color c) {
  numDiv = int(8 * displayDensity);
  positions = new PVector[numDiv];
  directions = new PVector[numDiv];

  fillColor = c;
  for (int i = 0; i < numDiv; i++) {
    float x = 0;
    if (0 < i) {
      if (i == numDiv - 1) x = width;
      else x = random(i/float(numDiv) * width * 1.2,
                   (i+1)/float(numDiv) * width * 0.8);
    }
    positions[i] = new PVector(x, y + random(-20, 20));
    directions[i] = PVector.fromAngle(random(-0.5 * HALF_PI,
                  +0.5 * HALF_PI));
    directions[i].mult(20 * displayDensity);
  }
}

void display() {
  noStroke();
  fill(fillColor);
  beginShape();
  for (int i = 0; i < numDiv - 1; i++) {
    vertex(positions[i].x, positions[i].y);
    PVector cp1 = PVector.add(positions[i], directions[i]);
    PVector cp2 = PVector.sub(positions[i+1], directions[i+1]);
    bezierVertex(cp1.x, cp1.y, cp2.x, cp2.y,
                positions[i+1].x, positions[i+1].y);
  }
  vertex(width, height);
  vertex(0, height);
  endShape();
}
}
```

In this example, we use the built-in displayDensity variable, which we already discussed in chapter 3, to make sure that the number of Bezier curve subdivisions and the length of the tangent vectors defined by the control points are scaled proportionally to the screen's DPI, so we can obtain a consistent output across different devices (Figure 4-9).

A few additional things we should note in this example are the orientation(LANDSCAPE) call in setup() to force the sketch to run in landscape orientation and the use of the HSB color space to implement the gradient from lighter to darker hues of blue more easily.

Figure 4-9. *Final result of the seascape sketch*

Shape Attributes

Processing allows us to set several attributes that determine the final appearance of shapes. We have been using the fill and stroke colors attributes, but there are several more. For example, we can set not only the color of a stroke line, but also its weight (how thick it is), endings caps, and joins connecting consecutive line segments, as demonstrated in Listing 4-8.

Listing 4-8. Setting Stroke Attributes

```
size(800, 480);
float x = width/2;
float y = height/2;
stroke(0, 150);
strokeWeight(10);
strokeJoin(ROUND);
strokeCap(ROUND);
beginShape(LINES);
for (int i = 0; i < 100; i++) {
  float px = x;
  float py = y;
  float nx = x + (random(0, 1) > 0.5? -1: +1) * 50;
  float ny = y + (random(0, 1) > 0.5? -1: +1) * 50;
  if (0 <= nx && nx < width && 0 <= ny && ny < height) {
    vertex(px, py);
    vertex(nx, ny);
    x = nx;
    y = ny;
  }
}
endShape();
```

Try this sketch with different values for the stroke joins (MITER, BEVEL, ROUND), caps (SQUARE, PROJECT, ROUND), and weight, and compare with the output shown in Figure 4-10.

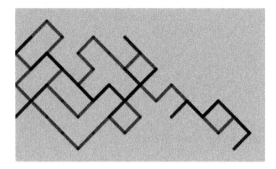

Figure 4-10. *Output of sketch demonstrating stroke attributes*

Even though these attributes are typically defined for the entire shape (i.e., they are applied to all the vertices in the shape), the P2D and P3D renderers allow you to define per-vertex attributes. For instance, the fill color can be set for each vertex separately, and then Processing will interpolate the color at intermediate positions. The output of the sketch in Listing 4-9 is similar to the HSB color wheel in Chapter 2, but here we do not need to set the intermediate colors since the P2D renderer does it automatically (Figure 4-11).

Listing 4-9. Using Color Interpolation in the P2D Renderer

```
size(300, 300, P2D);
colorMode(HSB, 360, 100, 100);
background(0, 0, 100);
translate(width/2, height/2);
noStroke();
beginShape(TRIANGLE_FAN);
    fill(TWO_PI, 0, 100);
    vertex(0, 0);
    for (int i = 0; i <= 10; i++) {
    float a = map(i, 0, 10, 0, 360);
    float x = 150 * cos(radians(a));
    float y = 150 * sin(radians(a));
    fill(a, 100, 100);
    vertex(x, y);
  }
endShape();
```

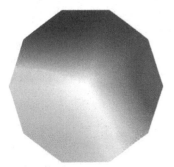

Figure 4-11. *Color wheel obtained by interpolation of the fill color*

Shape Styles

All the shape attributes that we can set with Processing determine the current "style." As we saw before, fill color, stroke color, weight, caps, and joins are all style attributes. As our sketches grow in complexity, especially with objects that set their own attributes when they are drawn, it can be easy to lose track of the current style.

Processing includes two functions, pushStyle() and popStyle(), that can be handy for managing the style of our shapes, especially in situations where we change many style attributes at different points of the execution of our sketch. pushStyle() saves the current values of all the style attributes, while popStyle() restores all the style attributes to the values we saved with the last call to pushStyle(). If we set a completely new style between consecutive pushStyle() and popStyle() calls, we can be certain that two different styles will not get mixed up. Listing 4-10 provides a simple example of this technique.

Listing 4-10. Saving and Restoring Styles with pushStyle() and popStyle()

```
Circle[] circles = new Circle[100];

void setup() {
  size(800, 800);
  for (int i = 0; i < circles.length; i++) {
    circles[i] = new Circle();
  }
}

void draw() {
  translate(width/2, height/2);
  rotate(frameCount * 0.01);
  for (int i = 0; i < circles.length; i++) {
    circles[i].display();
  }
}
```

```
class Circle {
  float x, y, r, w;
  color fc, sc;
  Circle() {
    x = random(-width/2, width/2);
    y = random(-height/2, height/2);
    r = random(10, 100);
    w = random(2, 10);
    fc = color(random(255), random(255), random(255));
    sc = color(random(255), random(255), random(255));
  }
  void display() {
    pushStyle();
    stroke(sc);
    strokeWeight(w);
    fill(fc);
    ellipse(x, y, r, r);
    popStyle();
  }
}
```

Shape Contours

Another useful feature in the Processing API is subtractive drawing using contours. All vertices that are enclosed between the beginContour() and endContour() functions define a negative shape that is removed from the larger shape, as shown in Listing 4-11, which generates the output seen in Figure 4-12.

Listing 4-11. Making Holes Inside a Shape with beginContour() and endContour()

```
void setup() {
  size(300, 300);
}

void draw() {
  background(190);
  translate(width/2, height/2);
  float r = width/2;
  beginShape();
  circleVertices(0, 0, r, 0, TWO_PI);
  makeContour(0, 0, r/4);
  makeContour(-r/2, -r/2, r/4);
  makeContour(+r/2, -r/2, r/4);
  makeContour(-r/2, +r/2, r/4);
  makeContour(+r/2, +r/2, r/4);
  endShape();
}
```

```
void makeContour(float xc, float yc, float r) {
  beginContour();
  circleVertices(xc, yc, r, TWO_PI, 0);
  endContour();
}

void circleVertices(float xc, float yc, float r, float a0, float a1) {
  for (int i = 0; i <= 30; i++) {
    float a = map(i, 0, 30, a0, a1);
    vertex(xc + r * cos(a), yc + r * sin(a));
  }
}
```

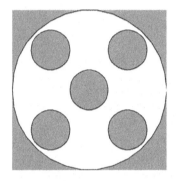

Figure 4-12. *Shape with holes created with beginContour/endContour*

■ **Note**   Contours can only be used with shapes of kind POLYGON. Also, the "winding" or direction of the vertices in the contour (clockwise or counterclockwise) must be opposite that of the containing shape.

The PShape Class

As we've seen so far, drawing shapes involves calling beginShape(), vertex(), and endShape() repeatedly in each frame. We can pre-calculate coordinates and put them inside a custom class like we did in the seascape example; however, Processing already offers a built-in class to hold shape data, appropriately called PShape. This class not only helps us keep the code more organized and readable, but also allows us to read shapes from vector graphics files (SVGs) and, when using the P2D renderer, increase the performance of our sketch.

Creating PShapes

An PShape object can be created with a call to the createShape() function, and we can pass the appropriate parameters to it in three different ways:

1. If no arguments are provided, createShape() returns an empty PShape, which we can use to construct a custom shape using beginShape(), vertex(), and endShape().

2. Providing a primitive type (ELLIPSE, RECT, etc.) and the additional parameters needed to initialize the primitive shape.

3. Specifying a single GROUP argument, which results in a PShape that can be used to contain other shapes, either custom or primitive.

Once we have created and properly initialized the PShape object, we can draw it as many times as we want using the shape() function, as shown in Listing 4-12 and Figure 4-13.

Listing 4-12. Creating and Drawing PShape Objects

```
size(650, 200, P2D);
PShape circle = createShape(ELLIPSE, 100, 100, 100, 100);
PShape poly = createShape();
poly.beginShape(QUADS);
poly.vertex(200, 50);
poly.vertex(300, 50);
poly.vertex(300, 150);
poly.vertex(200, 150);
poly.endShape();
PShape group = createShape(GROUP);
group.addChild(circle);
group.addChild(poly);
shape(circle);
shape(poly);
translate(300, 0);
shape(group);
```

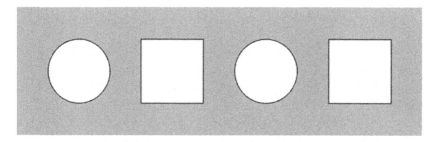

Figure 4-13. Primitive, custom, and group PShape objects

We can use all the shape-drawing functionality we learned in the first sections of this chapter to create custom shapes; the only difference is that we need to call the functions on the corresponding PShape object.

Group shapes are useful when we need to deal with a very large piece of geometry that does not change while the sketch is running. Without PShape, the vertices are copied to the GPU memory in each frame, which can slow down the framerate. However, if we pack all these vertices inside a PShape and use the P2D renderer, this copy happens just once, which results in better performance. This is particularly important for mobile devices, which are constrained by the use of battery power. As an example of this, let's consider the framerate of the CubicGridImmediate (no PShape) and CubicGridRetained (PShape) built-in examples under Demos|Performance in the mode examples. Both sketches create exactly the same geometry, a 3D grid of semi-transparent cubes; however, the first sketch barely exceeds 10 frames per second (fps), while the second will run at 60 fps on most devices.

Even though the PShape geometry must be, in principle, static to enable these performance improvements, it is still possible to modify vertex color and position to a certain extent without losing speed. If our modifications are only applied to a subset of children shapes inside a larger group, performance should remain high. Let's look at this scenario in Listing 4-13, which generates the output depicted in Figure 4-14.

Listing 4-13. Modifying Attributes of Child Shapes After Creation

```
PShape grid, sel;

void setup() {
  fullScreen(P2D);
  orientation(LANDSCAPE);
  grid = createShape(GROUP);
  for (int j = 0; j < 4; j++) {
    float y0 = map(j, 0, 4, 0, height);
    float y1 = map(j+1, 0, 4, 0, height);
    for (int i = 0; i < 8; i++) {
      float x0 = map(i, 0, 8, 0, width);
      float x1 = map(i+1, 0, 8, 0, width);
      PShape sh = createShape(RECT, x0, y0, x1 - x0, y1 - y0, 30);
      grid.addChild(sh);
    }
  }
}

void draw() {
  background(180);
  shape(grid);
}
```

```
void mousePressed() {
  int i = int(float(mouseX) / width * 8);
  int j = int(float(mouseY) / height * 4);
  int idx = j * 8 + i;
  sel = grid.getChild(idx);
  sel.setFill(color(#FA2D45));
}

void mouseReleased() {
  sel.setFill(color(#C252FF));
}
```

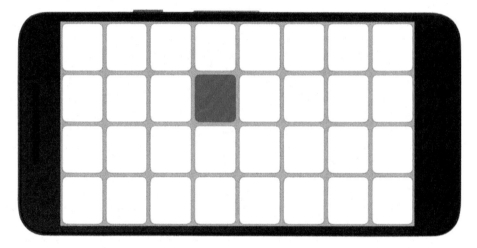

Figure 4-14. *Modifying the fill color of a child shape inside a group*

Here, only one child shape is modified at a time, getting a new fill color. Only the updated information is transferred to the GPU, keeping performance steady. However, this gain will diminish as more shapes are modified simultaneously, until performance becomes equivalent to drawing without any PShape objects.

■ **Note**   Most of the attributes of a PShape object can be modified after creating it. All the available setter functions can be found in the online reference at https://processing.org/reference/PShape.html.

Loading Shapes from SVG

We can also use a PShape object to load geometry stored in a file by using the loadShape() function. This function accepts the formats SVG and OBJ, the latter supported in the P3D renderer. SVG stands for scalable vector graphics, and a file in SVG format contains the specifications for a shape or group of shapes in a way that is very similar to how Processing handles geometry: as a list of vertices, splines, or Bezier curves.

In order to load an SVG file in our sketch, we first need to place it inside the data directory of the sketch. When we run the sketch on the device or emulator, all the contents of the data folder will be properly packaged so they can be accessed from the app.

■ **Note**   The data directory can be created manually inside the sketch's folder. It is also created automatically if one drags a media file into the PDE.

Once the SVG is loaded into a PShape object, we can apply transformations on it, like translations or rotations, or even change its style attributes, as we do in Listing 4-14, where we load three SVG files into separate shapes (Figure 4-15).

Listing 4-14. Load SVG Files into PShape Objects

```
size(450, 200, P2D);
PShape cc = loadShape("cc.svg");
PShape moz = loadShape("mozilla.svg");
PShape ruby = loadShape("ruby.svg");
translate(30, 50);
cc.setFill(color(170, 116, 0));
cc.setStroke(color(255, 155, 0));
shape(cc);
translate(cc.width + 30, 0);
shape(moz);
translate(moz.width + 30, 0);
shape(ruby);
```

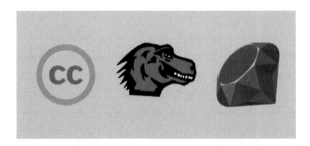

Figure 4-15. *Loading, modifying, and displaying SVGs*

SVG files can be useful for drawing complex geometry that would be hard to generate through code alone. Another advantage of complex SVGs is that they can be organized in a hierarchical fashion, with children shapes inside groups, allowing the manipulation of the subshapes individually. Let's look at an example that draws a world map SVG that also contains the names of countries (Listing 4-15). Running it should result in Figure 4-16.

Listing 4-15. Selecting a Child Shape by Name and Setting Its Attributes

```
PShape world;

void setup() {
  size(950, 620, P2D);
  world = loadShape("World-map.svg");
  for (PShape child: world.getChildren()) {
    if (child.getName().equals("algeria")) child.setFill(color(255, 0, 0));
  }
}

void draw() {
  background(255);
  shape(world);
}
```

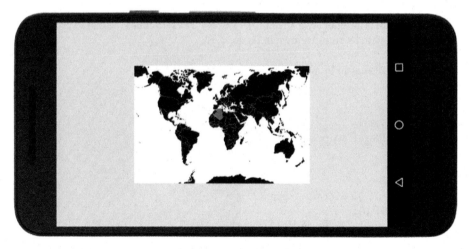

Figure 4-16. Loading a map from an SVG file and selecting a country by its name attribute

Note how we iterate over all the children shapes, which can be retrieved as an array of PShape objects from the containing group using the getChildren() function.

Drawing Images

Loading and displaying image files in our apps is a basic feature that Processing makes very easy. Processing supports GIF, JPG, TGA, and PNG image formats and includes a built-in class, PImage, to handle images inside a sketch. PImage encapsulates all the information of an image, including width, height, and individual pixels. Loading and displaying an image can be accomplished with two functions, loadImage() and image(), as shown in Listing 4-16.

Listing 4-16. Loading and Displaying an Image

```
fullScreen();
PImage img = loadImage("paine.jpg");
image(img, 0, 0, width, height);
```

The image() function accepts up to four parameters: the x and y coordinates of the image on the screen, and the width and height at which to display the image. These width and height parameters do not need to be the same as the original resolution of the image, which can be obtained from the PImage.width and PImage.height variables in the PImage object. Calling image() without width and height arguments results in the image being drawn at its source resolution, which would be equivalent to calling image(img, 0, 0, img.width, img.height).

We can apply a tint to the entire image using the tint() function and remove it afterward with noTint() (otherwise, all images displayed subsequently will have the same tint, as tint is another style attribute). Listing 4-17 exemplifies the use of tint() and noTint(), with its output shown in Figure 4-17.

Listing 4-17. Tinting an Image

```
PImage img;
void setup() {
  size(800, 533);
  img = loadImage("paine.jpg");
}

void draw() {
  image(img, 0, 0, width/2, height/2);
  tint(255, 0, 0);
  image(img, width/2, 0, width/2, height/2);
  tint(0, 255, 0);
  image(img, 0, height/2, width/2, height/2);
  tint(0, 0, 255);
  image(img, width/2, height/2, width/2, height/2);
  noTint();
}
```

■ **Note** When loading images or any other media files, such as SVGs, it is important to do so inside the setup() function, which is only called on app start. Otherwise, the images will be loaded repeatedly in each frame, slowing down the app to the point of making it unusable.

Figure 4-17. *Output of displaying an image with three different tints and no tinting*

Texturing Shapes

We can also use image files to texture shapes (only in the P2D/P3D renderers). Texturing essentially means wrapping an image around the shape so the shape is no longer drawn with a flat color. This process requires that we specify which parts of the image correspond to each vertex of the shape. Texturing can be quite involved, especially when dealing with irregular shapes in 3D. Listing 4-18 illustrates the simplest case—texturing a rectangular shape.

Listing 4-18. Texturing a Rectangle with an Image Loaded from a File

```
PImage img;
size(800, 533, P2D);
img = loadImage("paine.jpg");
beginShape();
texture(img);
vertex(100, 0, 0, 0);
vertex(width - 100, 0, img.width, 0);
vertex(width, height, img.width, img.height);
vertex(0, height, 0, img.height);
endShape();
```

As we see in this example, we need to provide two additional arguments to the vertex() function. These parameters in the vertex(x, y, u, v) call correspond to UV coordinates for texture mapping and indicate that pixel (u, v) in the image will go to the vertex (x, y) in the shape. The renderer will determine all the other pixel-vertex correspondences based on this information. In the case of our simple texturing code, the result is shown in Figure 4-18.

Figure 4-18. *Textured 2D shape*

Drawing Text

Text is another basic element of graphics programming. Processing offers several functions to draw text in our sketches and control its appearance by using different fonts and adjusting attributes such as size and alignment. We will look at some of these functions in the next few sections.

Loading and Creating Fonts

The first step in drawing text in a Processing sketch is to load a bitmap font. The font will be stored in a PFont variable, and we can switch between different PFont variables in the same sketch if we want to draw with different fonts at different times. The built-in font-creator tool (available under "Tools|Create Font...") allows us to create a new bitmap font from the fonts available on the PC or Mac computer on which we are running Processing. The interface of this tool is shown in Figure 4-19. Once we have selected the font, desired size, and filename, we hit OK, and the tool will generate a font file, with a .vlw extension, inside the data directory of our sketch, ready to use.

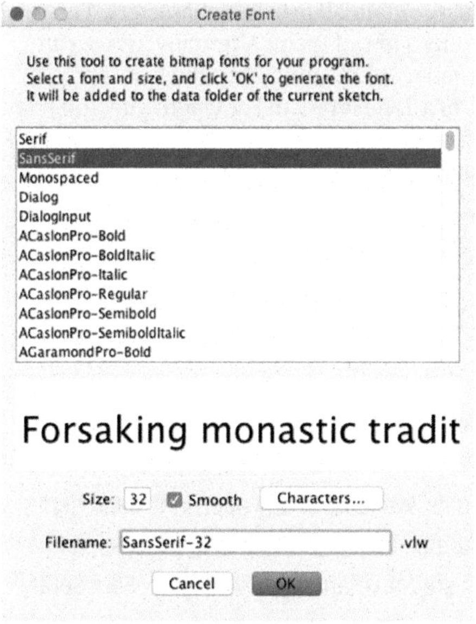

Figure 4-19. *Font-creator tool in the PDE*

To load our new font and set it as the current one, we use the loadFont() and textFont() functions, respectively. Once we have set the desired font, we can draw text anywhere on the screen using the text() function. All these functions are demonstrated in Listing 4-19.

Listing 4-19. Loading a bitmap font generated with the font creator tool

```
size(450, 100);
PFont font = loadFont("SansSerif-32.vlw");
textFont(font);
fill(120);
text("On Exactitude in Science", 40, 60);
```

The x and y arguments in the text(str, x, y) call let us set the screen location of the text. They represent, with the default text alignment options, the position of the lower-left corner of the first character. Figure 4-20 shows the output of our text-drawing sketch.

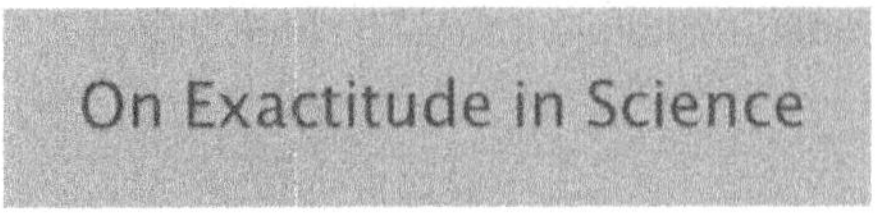

Figure 4-20. *Text output in Processing*

One disadvantage of creating a .vwl font file and then loading it into the sketch is that, since the font is created beforehand, it must contain all possible characters. This wastes memory, especially if we end up using only a few of them. Alternatively, we can create the font on the fly with the createFont(name, size) function, which accepts either a systemwide font name or the filename of a TrueType (.ttf) or OpenType (.otf) font located in the sketch's data folder, as well as a font size. Only the characters actually used in the sketch will be created and stored in memory. This is shown in Listing 4-20.

Listing 4-20. Creating a Font on the Fly

```
size(450, 100);
PFont font = createFont("SansSerif", 32);
textFont(font);
fill(120);
text("On Exactitude in Science", 40, 60);
```

■ **Note** Android provides three systemwide fonts available to any app: serif, sans-serif, and monospaced. Each one has four variants: normal, bold, italic, and bold italic, so, for example, the font names for the sans-serif fonts are SansSerif, SansSerif-Bold, SansSerif-Italic, and SansSerif-BoldItalic.

If we don't provide any other arguments to text(), the text string will continuously extend to the right until falling off of the screen or, if the string includes a line-break character (\n), going to the next line. We can set a rectangular area with four parameters, x, y, w, and h, and Processing will automatically accommodate the text within that rectangle by breaking it up into several lines if needed, as shown in Listing 4-21 and Figure 4-21.

Listing 4-21. Placing Text Inside a Rectangular Area

```
size(900, 300);
PFont font = createFont("Monospaced", 32);
textFont(font);
fill(120);
text("...In that Empire, the Art of Cartography attained such Perfection " +
    "that the map of a single Province occupied the entirety of a City, " +
    "and the map of the Empire, the entirety of a Province.", 20, 20,
    width - 40, height - 40);
```

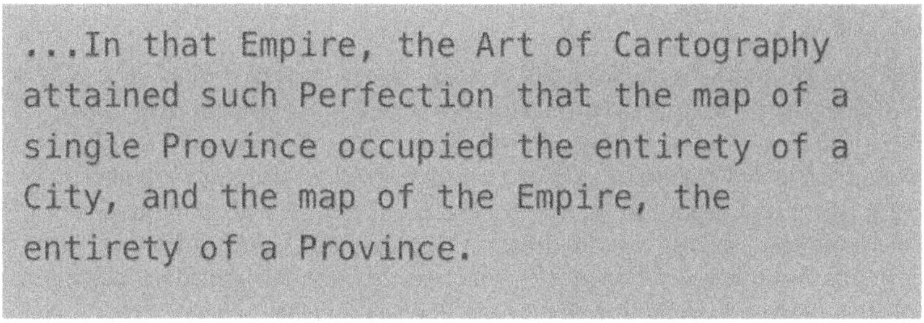

```
...In that Empire, the Art of Cartography
attained such Perfection that the map of a
single Province occupied the entirety of a
City, and the map of the Empire, the
entirety of a Province.
```

Figure 4-21. *Text output in Processing fitted inside a rectangular area*

Text Attributes

In addition to the font's name and size, we can control text alignment (LEFT, RIGHT, CENTER, BOTTOM, TOP) and the leading between lines of text (Listing 4-22). Figure 4-22 shows the result of setting these attributes. Even though in this example we set the alignment for only the horizontal direction, we can also set the vertical alignment by providing a second argument to textAlign()—CENTER, BOTTOM, or TOP.

Listing 4-22. Setting Text Alignment and Leading

```
size(900, 300);
PFont titleFont = createFont("Serif", 32);
PFont textFont = createFont("Serif", 28);
textFont(titleFont);
textAlign(CENTER);
fill(120);
text("On Exactitude in Science", width/2, 60);
textFont(textFont);
textAlign(RIGHT);
textLeading(60);
text("...In that Empire, the Art of Cartography attained such Perfection " +
    "that the map of a single Province occupied the entirety of a City, " +
    "and the map of the Empire, the entirety of a Province.",
    20, 100, width - 40, height - 20);
```

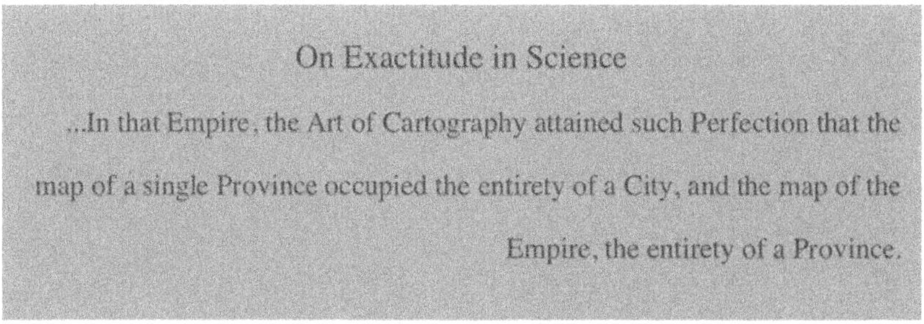

Figure 4-22. *Drawing text with different fonts and attributes*

Scaling Text

In Chapter 3, we saw how to scale the graphics in our sketch according to the device's DPI using the displayDensity variable. This technique allows us to maintain a consistent visual output across devices with different resolutions and screen sizes, and we can use it when drawing text as well. All we need to do is multiply the font size by displayDensity, as shown in Listing 4-23. We see in Figure 4-23 that the size of the text on the screen remains the same on three devices with different DPIs. An additional function we introduce in this example is loadStrings(), which reads a text file in the data folder and returns an array of strings containing all the lines of text in the file.

Listing 4-23. Scaling Font Size by the Display Density

```
fullScreen();
orientation(PORTRAIT);
PFont titleFont = createFont("Serif-Bold", 25 * displayDensity);
PFont bodyFont = createFont("Serif", 18 * displayDensity);
PFont footFont = createFont("Serif-Italic", 15 * displayDensity);
String[] lines = loadStrings("borges.txt");
String title = lines[0];
String body = lines[1];
String footer = lines[2];
textFont(titleFont);
textAlign(CENTER, CENTER);
fill(120);
text(title, 10, 10, width - 20, height * 0.1 - 20);
textFont(bodyFont);
text(body, 10, height * 0.1, width - 20, height * 0.8);
textAlign(RIGHT, BOTTOM);
textFont(footFont);
text(footer, 10, height * 0.9 + 10, width - 20, height * 0.1 - 20);
```

Figure 4-23. *From left to right, text output on a Samsung Galaxy Tab 4 (7", 1280 × 800 px, 216 dpi), Nexus 5X (5.2", 1920 × 800 px, 424 dpi), and a Moto E (4.3", 960 × 540 px, 256 dpi)*

Summary

This was a long chapter, but we covered a lot of important concepts and techniques! Building on the introduction to the Processing language we saw in Chapter 2, we've now learned the details of drawing shapes using various types of geometry, splines, and Bezier curves; adjusting their appearance with different attributes; and optimizing the code with the PShape class. In addition to all of that, we have also learned how to draw images and text in our sketches. By putting these resources into practice, we should be able to create virtually any visual composition we can think of and turn it into an Android app.

CHAPTER 5

▓ ▓ ▓

Touchscreen Interaction

This chapter will provide detailed coverage of the touchscreen support in Processing for Android. We will learn how to capture single and multi-touch events in our sketch, how to process these events to implement touch-based interactions such as selection, scrolling, swipe, and pinch, as well as how to use the virtual keyboard.

Touch Events in Android

With this chapter, we have reached a topic that is quite specific to mobile devices. Since the introduction of the iPhone in 2007, the touchscreen has become the main mechanism of interaction with smartphones, tablets, and wearable devices. Older phones often included a physical keyboard, but today those are very rare, and keyboard input is implemented through virtual or software keyboards.

Touchscreen interaction is very immediate and intuitive, and useful in applications that involve gesturing as a central part of the experience (e.g., note-taking and drawing apps). The physicality of touch makes it the ideal interaction for creative applications on mobile devices.

The Android system provides full support for touchscreen interaction, ranging from single-touch events, multi-touch gestures triggered with the fingers, to pen stylus input. Because of its generality, the touch API in Android can be hard to use, so Processing for Android wraps this complexity with a simpler API that, while it may not cover all touchscreen functions, makes it possible to create a wide range of touch-based interactions.

Basic Touch Events

Since its earliest versions, Java mode in Processing has included variables and functions to handle interaction with the mouse. All of these variables and functions are also available in Android mode, and they work very similarly to their original Java-mode counterparts, at least for single-touch events. The difference, of course, is that the events are triggered by our fingers pressing the touchscreen instead of by the movement of a mouse. We have used some of this mouse API in previous chapters—in particular, the mouseX and mouseY variables—to track the position of the touch point. Listing 5-1 shows a basic example of this API where we control the position of some shapes (Figure 5-1).

© Andrés Colubri 2017   89
A. Colubri, *Processing for Android*, https://doi.org/10.1007/978-1-4842-2719-0_5

Listing 5-1. Simple Touch Event Using the Mouse Variables

```
void setup() {
  fullScreen();
  strokeWeight(20);
  fill(#3B91FF);
}

void draw() {
  background(#FFD53B);
  stroke(#3B91FF);
  line(0, 0, mouseX, mouseY);
  line(width, 0, mouseX, mouseY);
  line(width, height, mouseX, mouseY);
  line(0, height, mouseX, mouseY);
  noStroke();
  ellipse(mouseX, mouseY, 200, 200);
}
```

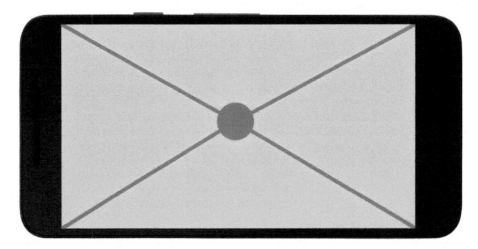

Figure 5-1. *Simple use of mouseX and mouseY variables to track touch position*

An important difference with an actual mouse is the existence of a "pressed" state: we can move the mouse without pressing any button, and when we do press it, a "drag" event is triggered until we release the button. With a touchscreen, the "mouse" is always in the "pressed" state while it is moving. This difference invalidates a typical mouse-based interaction, hovering, which occurs when we move the mouse inside a pre-defined area of the screen but without pressing any button.

We can perform specific tasks exactly when a touch starts/ends, or when a touch point changes position. The functions mousePressed(), mousedDragged(), and mouseReleased() are called automatically by Processing whenever any of these events take place, so we can implement our event-handling functionality in them. For example, in Listing 5-2, we draw a growing ellipse at the mouse position for as long as we drag the finger across the screen. Also, notice the use of displayDensity to scale the initial radius of the ellipse and its regular increments while dragging so that it appears the same size irrespective of the device's DPI.

Listing 5-2. Detecting Press, Drag, and Release "Mouse" Events

```
boolean drawing = false;
float radius;

void setup() {
  fullScreen();
  noStroke();
  fill(100, 100);
}

void draw() {
  background(255);
  if (drawing) {
    ellipse(mouseX, mouseY, radius, radius);
  }
}

void mousePressed() {
  drawing = true;
  radius = 70 * displayDensity;
}

void mouseReleased() {
  drawing = false;
}

void mouseDragged() {
  radius += 0.5 * displayDensity;
}
```

We can build on top of this simple example by keeping a list of all the ellipses created so far and assigning random RGB colors to them. For this purpose, we create a class to store the ellipses' position, size, and color, as shown in Listing 5-3.

Listing 5-3. Drawing Multiple Growing Ellipses with Mouse Events

```
ArrayList<Circle> circles;
Circle newCircle;

void setup() {
  fullScreen();
  circles = new ArrayList<Circle>();
  noStroke();
}

void draw() {
  background(255);
  for (Circle c: circles) {
    c.draw();
  }
  if (newCircle != null) newCircle.draw();
}

void mousePressed() {
  newCircle = new Circle(mouseX, mouseY);
}

void mouseReleased() {
  circles.add(newCircle);
  newCircle = null;
}

void mouseDragged() {
  newCircle.setPosition(mouseX, mouseY);
  newCircle.grow();
}

class Circle {
  color c;
  float x, y, r;
  Circle(float x, float y) {
    this.x = x;
    this.y = y;
    r = 70 * displayDensity;
    c = color(random(255), random(255), random(255), 100);
  }
  void grow() {
    r += 0.5 * displayDensity;
  }
  void setPosition(float x, float y) {
    this.x = x;
    this.y = y;
  }
```

```
  void draw() {
    fill(c);
    ellipse(x, y, r, r);
  }
}
```

In addition to the mouseX/Y variables, Processing also stores the previous position of the touch pointer in the pmouseX/Y variables. Using these variables, we can code a simple drawing sketch where we connect the previous and current mouse positions with a line segment, drawing a continuous path as long as the user keeps pressing the screen. We can determine if the user is pressing the screen with the built-in Boolean variable mousePressed. This sketch is shown in Listing 5-4, and a drawing made with it in Figure 5-2.

Listing 5-4. Simple Drawing Sketch Using Current and Previous Mouse Positions

```
void setup() {
  fullScreen();
  strokeWeight(10);
  stroke(100, 100);
}

void draw() {
  if (mousePressed) line(pmouseX, pmouseY, mouseX, mouseY);
}
```

Figure 5-2. *Generating a line drawing with our sketch*

The difference between the previous and current touch positions tells us how fast we are swiping the finger across the screen. The faster we swipe, the larger this difference will be, so we could use it to drive the motion of an object, like the circles we had in Listing 5-3. For example, the velocity of the circles could be proportional to the swipe speed. Let's implement this idea by adding a pair of velocity variables (vx for the x direction and vy for y) and a setVelocity() method to the Circle class, as shown in Listing 5-5.

Listing 5-5. Using the Difference Between Current and Previous Mouse Positions to Calculate the Velocity of Graphical Elements in Our Sketch

```
ArrayList<Circle> circles;
Circle newCircle;

void setup() {
  fullScreen();
  circles = new ArrayList<Circle>();
  noStroke();
}

void draw() {
  background(255);
  for (Circle c: circles) {
    c.draw();
  }
  if (newCircle != null) newCircle.draw();
}

void mousePressed() {
  newCircle = new Circle(mouseX, mouseY);
}

void mouseReleased() {
  newCircle.setVelocity(mouseX - pmouseX, mouseY - pmouseY);
  circles.add(newCircle);
  newCircle = null;
}

void mouseDragged() {
  newCircle.setPosition(mouseX, mouseY);
  newCircle.grow();
}

class Circle {
  color c;
  float x, y, r, vx, vy;
  Circle(float x, float y) {
    this.x = x;
    this.y = y;
```

```
    r = 70 * displayDensity;
    c = color(random(255), random(255), random(255), 100);
  }
  void grow() {
    r += 0.5 * displayDensity;
  }
  void setPosition(float x, float y) {
    this.x = x;
    this.y = y;
  }
  void setVelocity(float vx, float vy) {
    this.vx = vx;
    this.vy = vy;
  }
  void draw() {
    x += vx;
    y += vy;
    if (x < 0 || x > width) vx = -vx;
    if (y < 0 || y > height) vy = -vy;
    fill(c);
    ellipse(x, y, r, r);
  }
}
```

Whereas in the original version of this sketch the circles stopped moving immediately after we released the touch, they now continue their displacement along the swipe direction with a velocity proportional to the speed of the swipe, since we keep adding vx and vy to their current positions. Also, with the if (x < 0 || x > width) vx = -vx; and if (y < 0 || y > height) vy = -vy; lines we implement a very simple collision-detection algorithm, where if a circle moves past the edges of the screen, its velocity gets inverted so that its movement reverses toward the interior of the screen. In other words, the circle bounces against the edges of the screen.

As a final addition to this example, we will implement a Clear button. Since we keep adding circles every time we touch the screen, it eventually becomes cluttered. A button is just a rectangular area on the screen that triggers some action when pressed, which in this case would be removing all the circles we have added since the beginning. In fact, we don't need much additional code to implement this button. Listing 5-6 shows what we need to incorporate in draw() and mouseReleased() to draw and trigger the button (Figure 5-3).

Listing 5-6. Implementation of a Simple Clear Button

```
ArrayList<Circle> circles;
Circle newCircle;
float buttonHeight = 200 * displayDensity;
...
void draw() {
  background(255);
```

```
  for (Circle c: circles) {
    c.draw();
  }
  if (newCircle != null) newCircle.draw();
  fill(100, 180);
  rect(0, height - buttonHeight, width, buttonHeight);
  fill(80);
  text("Touch this area to clear", 0, height - buttonHeight, width,
  buttonHeight);
}
...
void mouseReleased() {
  newCircle.setVelocity(mouseX - pmouseX, mouseY - pmouseY);
  circles.add(newCircle);
  newCircle = null;
  if (height - buttonHeight < mouseY) circles.clear();
}
...
```

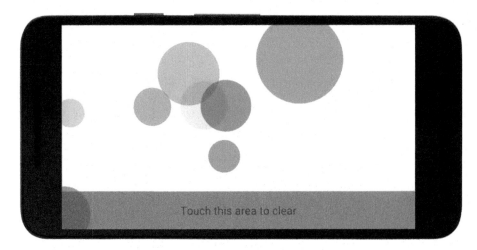

Figure 5-3. *Outcome of the circle-drawing sketch, complete with a Clear button*

This example shows us how far we can go with single-touch events and how to use them to control movement and interaction in our app. We can extend these techniques to much more complex situations with more interface actions and object behaviors.

Multi-touch Events

We have learned how to handle single-touch events using the mouse API inherited from Processing Java. However, touchscreens on Android devices can track several touch points at once, with a maximum determined by the capabilities of the screen. Some devices could track up to ten touch points simultaneously.

Processing includes the touches array to provide information about the touch points. Each element in this array contains a unique numerical identifier that allows us to track a pointer across successive frames and retrieve its current x and y coordinates, as well as the pressure and area of the pointer. The capacitive touchscreens on phones and tablets are capable of measuring not only the position of the touch point, but also how much pressure we apply to the screen. The area is an approximate measure of the size of the pointer, which is related to the pressure, since the harder we press our finger against the screen, the larger the contact area should be.

Every time a new touch point is detected, Processing will trigger the startTouch() function. Conversely, endTouch() will be called when a touch point is released. Similar to the mouseDragged() function for single-touch events, the touchMoved() function will be called every time any of the current touch points changes position. Also, analogous to mousePressed, there is a touchPressed logical variable that stores true or false depending on whether there is at least one touch point detected. All these functions are demonstrated in Listing 5-7, with its output in Figure 5-4 showing multiple touch points.

▪ **Note** Pressure and area are given as normalized values between 0 and 1 and need to be scaled according to the screen resolution (for the pressure) and the touchscreen calibration (for the area).

Listing 5-7. Accessing Properties of Multiple Touch Points

```
void setup() {
  fullScreen();
  noStroke();
  colorMode(HSB, 350, 100, 100);
  textFont(createFont("SansSerif", displayDensity * 24));
}

void draw() {
  background(30, 0, 100);
  fill(30, 0, 20);
  text("Number of touch points: " + touches.length, 20, displayDensity * 50);
  for (int i = 0; i < touches.length; i++) {
    float s = displayDensity * map(touches[i].area, 0, 1, 30, 300);
    fill(30, map(touches[i].pressure, 0.6, 1.6, 0, 100), 70, 200);
    ellipse(touches[i].x, touches[i].y, s, s);
  }
}

void touchStarted() {
  println("Touch started");
}
```

97

```
void touchEnded() {
  println("Touch ended");
}

void touchMoved() {
  println("Touch moved");
}
```

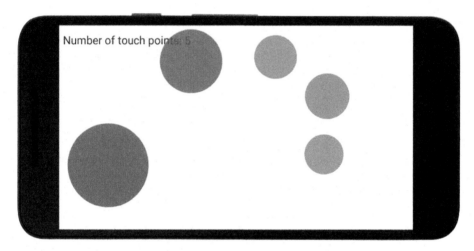

Figure 5-4. *Output of simple multi-touch example*

The mapping used to convert the normalized area and pressure values is device-specific. In this case, the size range goes from 0 to 1, which is the range observed in a Nexus 5X; however, other devices might have a different range. The situation is similar for the pressure, ranging from 0.6 to 1.6 on that same Nexus device.

Each touch point in the touches array has a unique ID that we can use to track its motion. The index of the touch point in the touches array must not be used as its identifier, since it may not be the same from one frame to the next (for example, a touch point could be element 0 in one frame and element 3 in the next). The touch ID, on the other hand, is unique for each touch point since it is pressed until finally released.

In the next example, Listing 5-8, we will use the touch ID to create a multi-touch painting sketch. Each finger will control a brush that draws a circle with an HSB color that is determined by the index of the touch point. The idea is to store these brush objects in a hash map, which is a data structure also known as a dictionary (https://developer. android.com/reference/java/util/HashMap.html) that we can use to associate values (in this case, brushes) to unique keys (touch IDs).

In this code, we add a new brush to the hash table when a touch is detected in the touchStarted() function, and we remove an existing brush when its key (ID) is not found in the touches array when touchEnded() is called. We update all brushes every time a movement triggers the touchMoved() function. A typical output of this sketch is shown in Figure 5-5.

Listing 5-8. Painting with Multiple Brushes

```java
import java.util.*;

HashMap<Integer, Brush> brushes;

void setup() {
  fullScreen();
  brushes = new HashMap<Integer, Brush>();
  noStroke();
  colorMode(HSB, 360, 100, 100);
  background(0, 0, 100);
}

void draw() {
  for (Brush b: brushes.values()) b.draw();
}

void touchStarted() {
  for (int i = 0; i < touches.length; i++) {
    if (!brushes.containsKey(touches[i].id)) {
      brushes.put(touches[i].id, new Brush(i));
    }
  }
}

void touchEnded() {
  Set<Integer> ids = new HashSet<Integer>(brushes.keySet());
  for (int id: ids) {
    boolean found = false;
    for (int i = 0; i < touches.length; i++) {
      if (touches[i].id == id) found = true;
    }
    if (!found) brushes.remove(id);
  }
}

void touchMoved() {
  for (int i = 0; i < touches.length; i++) {
    Brush b = brushes.get(touches[i].id);
    b.update(touches[i].x, touches[i].y, touches[i].area);
  }
}

class Brush {
  color c;
  float x, y, s;
  Brush(int index) {
    c = color(map(index, 0, 10, 0, 360), 60, 75, 100);
  }
```

```
void update(float x, float y, float s) {
  this.x = x;
  this.y = y;
  this.s = map(s, 0, 1, 50, 500);
}
void draw() {
  fill(c);
  ellipse(x, y, s, s);
}
}
```

Figure 5-5. *Multi-touch painting*

There are a couple of important things to pay attention to. First, we can be sure that touchStarted() and touchEnded() will be called only when a new touch point has gone down or up, respectively. So, all we need to do in these functions is identify which one is the incoming pointer and which is the outgoing pointer. In the case of a touch release, we iterate over all the current keys in the hash table until we find the one that does not correspond to a valid ID in the touches array. Since we are modifying the hash table as we iterate over its keys, we need to create a copy of the original set of keys with Set<Integer> ids = new HashSet<Integer>(brushes.keySet()); and only then perform the search and delete operation.

Touch-based Interaction

Creating an intuitive and engaging interface for a mobile app is not easy; it requires an understanding of user interface (UI) principles, practice, and a lot of iteration. Processing for Android does not provide any built-in UI functionality beyond the low-level single- and multiple-touch handling functions, so we have a lot of freedom to define how our app will manage interaction with the user. We will review a few basic techniques in this section, which we could apply in many different situations.

Shape Selection

Back in Chapter 4, we reviewed the use of PShape objects to store complex SVG shapes and increase the framerate with P2D or P3D renderers. Since SVG shapes are composed of subshapes that we may want to select individually with a touch, it is useful to know how to perform a test to determine if a touch point falls inside a PShape object. If we are dealing with a primitive shape, such as a rectangle or a circle, we can write a simple test specific for that shape; however, with irregular shapes, such as countries on a map, we need a more general approach. The PShape class has a function called getTessellation() that returns a new shape that is exactly the same as the source shape but is composed only of triangles (this collection of triangles determines what is called the "tessellation" of the more complex shape). Since it is easy to determine whether a point falls inside a triangle (http://blackpawn.com/texts/pointinpoly/default.html), we can check if the mouse or touch position falls inside any of the triangles of the tessellation, and, if it does, we can conclude that the larger shape has been selected. This is what we do in Listing 5-9, with its result shown in Figure 5-6.

Listing 5-9. Selecting a Child Shape Inside a Group Shape with Touch Events

```
PShape world, country;

void setup() {
  fullScreen(P2D);
  orientation(LANDSCAPE);
  world = loadShape("World-map.svg");
  world.scale(width / world.width);
}

void draw() {
  background(255);
  if (mousePressed) {
    if (country != null) country.setFill(color(0));
    for (PShape child: world.getChildren()) {
      if (child.getVertexCount() == 0) continue;
      PShape tess = child.getTessellation();
      boolean inside = false;
      for (int i = 0; i < tess.getVertexCount(); i += 3) {
        PVector v0 = tess.getVertex(i);
        PVector v1 = tess.getVertex(i + 1);
        PVector v2 = tess.getVertex(i + 2);
        if (insideTriangle(new PVector(mouseX, mouseY), v0, v1, v2)) {
          inside = true;
          country = child;
          break;
        }
      }
      if (inside) {
        country.setFill(color(255, 0, 0));
        break;
```

101

```
      }
    }
  }
  shape(world);
}

boolean insideTriangle(PVector pt, PVector v1, PVector v2, PVector v3) {
  boolean b1, b2, b3;
  b1 = sign(pt, v1, v2) < 0.0f;
  b2 = sign(pt, v2, v3) < 0.0f;
  b3 = sign(pt, v3, v1) < 0.0f;
  return ((b1 == b2) && (b2 == b3));
}

float sign (PVector p1, PVector p2, PVector p3) {
  return (p1.x - p3.x) * (p2.y - p3.y) - (p2.x - p3.x) * (p1.y - p3.y);
}
```

Figure 5-6. *Selecting a country inside an SVG shape with touch events*

Scrolling

Scrolling is another basic mode of interaction with mobile devices. Due to their small screen sizes relative to laptops and other computers, information often cannot be displayed all at once on one single page. A (horizontal or vertical) scroll bar controlled by touch displacement along the edges of the screen is the most common scrolling functionality.

The code example in Listing 5-10 includes a very simple vertical scrollbar class that keeps track of the displacement along the y axis in order to translate the graphical elements so the ones that should be visible are shown. The key part of this scrollbar implementation is to calculate the total height of all the elements and use that to determine how far down we can scroll with the bar until we reach the last element. The update() method in this class takes the amount of mouse/touch dragging and updates the variable translateY, which contains the vertical translation.

Listing 5-10. Implementing a Scrolling Bar

```
ScrollBar scrollbar;
int numItems = 20;

void setup() {
  fullScreen(P2D);
  orientation(PORTRAIT);
  scrollbar = new ScrollBar(0.2 * height * numItems, 0.1 * width);
  noStroke();
}

void draw() {
  background(255);
  pushMatrix();
  translate(0, scrollbar.translateY);
  for (int i = 0; i < numItems; i++) {
    fill(map(i, 0, numItems - 1, 220, 0));
    rect(20, i * 0.2 * height + 20, width - 40, 0.2 * height - 20);
  }
  popMatrix();
  scrollbar.draw();
}

public void mousePressed() {
  scrollbar.open();
}

public void mouseDragged() {
  scrollbar.update(mouseY - pmouseY);
}

void mouseReleased() {
  scrollbar.close();
}

class ScrollBar {
  float totalHeight;
  float translateY;
  float opacity;
  float barWidth;
```

```
ScrollBar(float h, float w) {
  totalHeight = h;
  barWidth = w;
  translateY = 0;
  opacity = 0;
}

void open() {
  opacity = 150;
}

void close() {
  opacity = 0;
}

void update(float dy) {
  if (totalHeight + translateY + dy > height) {
    translateY += dy;
    if (translateY > 0) translateY = 0;
  }
}

void draw() {
  if (0 < opacity) {
    float frac = (height / totalHeight);
    float x = width - 1.5 * barWidth;
    float y = PApplet.map(translateY / totalHeight, -1, 0, height, 0);
    float w = barWidth;
    float h = frac * height;
    pushStyle();
    fill(150, opacity);
    rect(x, y, w, h, 0.2 * w);
    popStyle();
  }
}
}
```

The condition totalHeight + translateY + dy > height makes sure that we don't scroll past the last element in our list, and translateY > 0 helps us avoid scrolling up past the top of the screen. We can use this class in any sketch so long as we can provide the total height of the elements we wish to display. Figure 5-7 shows our scrolling bar in action.

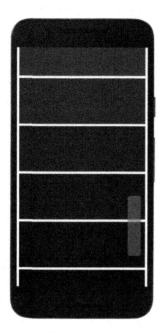

Figure 5-7. *Scrolling through a pre-defined list of elements*

Swipe and Pinch

The swipe and pinch gestures are two of the most characteristic touchscreen interactions on smartphones and tablets. We typically use the swipe or fling to flip between consecutive elements, such as pages or images, and the pinch or scale is the default gesture to zoom in and out on an image or part of the screen.

Although Processing for Android does not trigger calls similar to mousePressed() or touchMoved() when a swipe or a pinch takes place, we can use the Android API inside our Processing sketch to add support for these events. The official Android Developers site from Google has a very detailed section on how to use touch gestures (https://developer.android.com/training/gestures/index.html) via several gesture-detection classes.

Android offers a GestureDetector that needs to be combined with a listener class that contains a special "event handling" method that is called when a swipe or scaling event is detected. In order to use this functionality, we need to add a few imports from the Android SDK and then write the implementation for the gesture listener. The other important element when integrating event handling from Processing for Android is to pass the events objects from Processing to the gesture handler in the surfaceTouchEvent() function. This function is called every time there is a new touch event, but it also needs to call the parent implementation so Processing can carry out the default event handling (updating the mouse and touches variables and so forth). All of this is shown in Listing 5-11, where we do swipe detection, with its output shown in Figure 5-8.

Listing 5-11. Swipe Detection Using the Android API in Processing

```
import android.os.Looper;
import android.view.MotionEvent;
import android.view.GestureDetector;
import android.view.GestureDetector.OnGestureListener;

GestureDetector detector;
PVector swipe = new PVector();

void setup() {
  fullScreen();
  Looper.prepare();
  detector = new GestureDetector(surface.getActivity(),
                                 new SwipeListener());
  strokeWeight(20);
}

boolean surfaceTouchEvent(MotionEvent event) {
  detector.onTouchEvent(event);
  return super.surfaceTouchEvent(event);
}

void draw() {
  background(210);
  translate(width/2, height/2);
  drawArrow();
}

void drawArrow() {
  float x = swipe.x;
  float y = swipe.y;
  line(0, 0, x, y);
  swipe.rotate(QUARTER_PI/2);
  swipe.mult(0.85);
  line(x, y, swipe.x, swipe.y);
  swipe.rotate(-QUARTER_PI);
  line(x, y, swipe.x, swipe.y);
  swipe.rotate(QUARTER_PI/2);
  swipe.mult(1/0.85);
}

class SwipeListener extends GestureDetector.SimpleOnGestureListener {
  boolean onFling(MotionEvent event1, MotionEvent event2,
                  float velocityX, float velocityY) {
    swipe.set(velocityX, velocityY);
    swipe.normalize();
    swipe.mult(min(width/2, height/2));
    return true;
  }
}
```

Notice the call to Looper.prepare() in setup(). Android's Looper is a class that allows the main thread in an app to receive messages from other threads (https://developer. android.com/reference/android/os/Looper.html). In this particular case, we need the Looper to read the gesture events from our sketch.

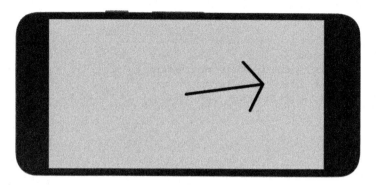

Figure 5-8. *Detecting swipe direction*

We can implement the scale detector in a similar way, and in Listing 5-12 we apply it to zoom in and out on an image.

Listing 5-12. Zooming In and Out with a Scale Detector

```
import android.os.Looper;
import android.view.MotionEvent;
import android.view.ScaleGestureDetector;
import android.view.ScaleGestureDetector.SimpleOnScaleGestureListener;

ScaleGestureDetector detector;
PImage img;
float scaleFactor = 1;

void setup() {
  fullScreen();
  img = loadImage("jelly.jpg");
  Looper.prepare();
  detector = new ScaleGestureDetector(surface.getActivity(),
                                      new ScaleListener());
  imageMode(CENTER);
}

boolean surfaceTouchEvent(MotionEvent event) {
  detector.onTouchEvent(event);
  return super.surfaceTouchEvent(event);
}
```

```
void draw() {
  background(180);
  translate(width/2, height/2);
  scale(scaleFactor);
  image(img, 0, 0);
}

class ScaleListener extends ScaleGestureDetector.
SimpleOnScaleGestureListener {
  public boolean onScale(ScaleGestureDetector detector) {
    scaleFactor *= detector.getScaleFactor();
    scaleFactor = constrain(scaleFactor, 0.1, 5);
    return true;
  }
}
```

Using the Keyboard

We conclude this chapter by describing some of the functions available in Processing for key input. Even though the keyboard and mouse are often distinct input devices on laptops and desktop computers, the touchscreen has largely absorbed the function of the keyboard by means of the "soft" or virtual keyboard.

Processing Java has several functions to handle keyboard events, and variables to inspect the last pressed key, as described in the online language reference (https://processing.org/reference/) and tutorials (https://processing.org/tutorials/interactivity/). All of these functions (with the exception of keyTyped) are available in Android mode as well.

If the device has a physical keyboard, there is nothing special to do in order to use the keyboard API, but in the case of virtual keyboards, we need to open it first, and close it once the user is done typing. Android mode adds two functions to do this, openKeyboard() and closeKeyboard(). The final example in this chapter, Listing 5-13, exemplifies their use, together with some of the other functions in the keyboard API.

Listing 5-13. Typing Text with the Virtual Keyboard

```
String text = "touch the screen to type something";
boolean keyboard = false;

void setup() {
  fullScreen();
  textFont(createFont("Monospaced", 25 * displayDensity));
  textAlign(CENTER);
  fill(100);
}

void draw() {
  background(200);
  text(text, 0, 20, width, height - 40);
}
```

```
void keyReleased() {
  if (key == DELETE || key == BACKSPACE) {
    text = text.substring(text.length() - 1);
  } else {
    text += key;
  }
}

void mouseReleased() {
  if (!keyboard) {;
    text = "";
    openKeyboard();
    keyboard = true;
  } else {
    closeKeyboard();
    keyboard = false;
  }
}
```

Summary

We have learned how to handle single- and multiple-touch events in Processing, and from there we moved on to examining different interaction techniques commonly used on mobile devices (selection, scroll, swipe, pinch, and zoom). With all of these tools at our disposal, we can implement user interfaces with the interaction type that best suits the needs of our users.

CHAPTER 6

Live Wallpapers

After going through the details of drawing and interaction with Processing for Android, we will conclude the second part of the book with this chapter on live wallpapers. We will learn how to load images from the camera to create a gallery wallpaper, and then how to use particle systems to implement an animated background for our phone or tablet.

Live Wallpapers

Live wallpapers are a special type of Android application that run as the background of the home and lock screens. They were introduced back in version 2.1 of Android, so the majority of today's devices support them. We can apply any of the drawing and interaction techniques we have seen so far to a live wallpaper. This enables us to create dynamic backgrounds for our devices while accessing sensor and network data and reacting to user input.

We can take any sketch from previous chapters and run it as a live wallpaper, but to design and implement a successful wallpaper, we have to take into consideration the specific characteristics and limitations of wallpaper apps, which we will discuss in the next sections.

Writing and Installing Live Wallpapers

Processing for Android lets us run our sketches as a live wallpaper very easily: all we need to do is select the "Wallpaper" option under the Android menu in the PDE. Once the sketch is installed as a wallpaper, it won't start running immediately. It needs to be selected through Android's wallpaper selector. To do so, long-press on any free area in the home screen and then choose the "Set Wallpaper" option in the pop-up menu that appears next, which might look different than the following screenshot depending on the Android or UI skin being used. The wallpaper will run first in a preview mode, where we can confirm the selection or continue browsing through the available wallpapers. Once selected, the wallpaper will be restarted to run in the background of the home screens, behind the launcher icons. Figure 6-1 shows these stages.

© Andrés Colubri 2017

A. Colubri, *Processing for Android*, https://doi.org/10.1007/978-1-4842-2719-0_6

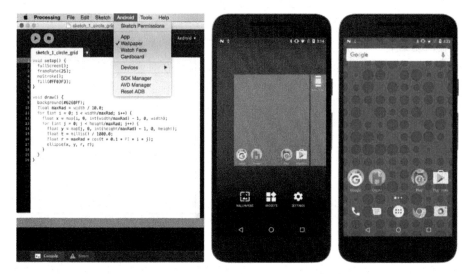

Figure 6-1. *Selecting the wallpaper option in the PDE (left), opening the wallpaper selector on the device (center), live wallpaper running in the home screen (right)*

Let's consider a couple of important aspects of live wallpapers. First, they cover the entire area of the screen, so we should initialize them with the fullScreen() function. Second, live wallpapers run continuously in the background, and thus they can drain the battery quickly. Because of this, it is a good idea to not use very heavy calculations in the sketches intended to be run as wallpapers. This recommendation is valid for all mobile apps in general, but even more so for wallpapers. A simple "trick" to decrease the battery use of a live wallpaper is to set a lower framerate via the frameRate() function. Using 30 or 25 instead of the default of 60 will keep the animation reasonably smooth without redrawing the screen at a very high rate and consuming more battery power.

The code in Listing 6-1 generates a grid of ellipses of variable sizes, and we use both fullScreen()—to ensure the wallpaper covers the entire screen—and frameRate(25), since the screen does not need be updated any faster.

Listing 6-1. Simple Live Wallpaper

```
void setup() {
  fullScreen();
  frameRate(25);
  noStroke();
  fill(#FF03F3);
}
```

```
void draw() {
  background(#6268FF);
  float maxRad = 50 * displayDensity;
  for (int i = 0; i < width/maxRad; i++) {
    float x = map(i, 0, int(width/maxRad) - 1, 0, width);
    for (int j = 0; j < height/maxRad; j++) {
      float y = map(j, 0, int(height/maxRad) - 1, 0, height);
      float t = millis() / 1000.0;
      float r = maxRad * cos(t + 0.1 * PI * i * j);
      ellipse(x, y, r, r);
    }
  }
}
```

To run a live wallpaper, we first need to open it in the selector. In fact, the selector shows us a preview instance of the wallpaper, which we can either set as the background or cancel in order to preview another one. Right after we set the wallpaper, the preview instance is shut down by the system, and a non-preview one is launched immediately. We can verify if the wallpaper is running in preview mode by calling the previewWallpaper() function, which returns true or false accordingly. This check gives us the opportunity to perform special customizations during the preview mode, such as loading fewer resources because the wallpaper will not run for long or showing a representative output of the wallpaper.

Using Multiple Home Screens

Before taking on more-advanced wallpaper examples, we will learn about a few important features of live wallpapers through a simpler application that shows a background image. We already saw how to load and display images in Processing. The same approach works for wallpapers: just copy an image file to the sketch's data folder, load it with loadImage(), and display it with image() so it covers the entire screen of the device, as shown in Listing 6-2.

Listing 6-2. Loading and Displaying an Image in Full-screen Mode

```
PImage pic;
fullScreen();
pic = loadImage("paine.jpg");
image(pic, 0, 0, width, height);
```

A problem with this code is that the image will look distorted if it does not have the same proportions as the screen. Also, the wallpaper is always displayed in portrait mode, so a picture taken in landscape orientation will appear stretched along the vertical direction. We could set the height in the image() function so that the width-to-height ratio of the displayed image is the same as its original ratio, like in Listing 6-3.

Listing 6-3. Keeping the Image Ratio

```
PImage pic;
fullScreen();
pic = loadImage("paine.jpg");
imageMode(CENTER);
float r = float(pic.width) / float(pic.height);
float h = width/r;
image(pic, width/2, height/2, width, h);
```

Here we set the image mode to CENTER, so the x and y arguments of the image() function are taken to be the center of the image, which makes it easy to center it on the screen. Since we are drawing it to be the width of the screen, we need to use a height of width/r, with r being the original width/height ratio of the image.

■ **Note**   The width and height variables in a PImage object are integer numbers, so we need to convert them into float numbers, using float(x) to obtain a correct ratio value with a decimal point, like 1.6 (the result of float(1280) / float(800)) or 0.561 (which is float(2576) / float(4592)).

However, with this approach we might end up wasting a lot of the screen space, especially if the image is very wide. Android offers a functionality that can help in this situation: multiple home screens. The user can move through these screens by swiping left and right, and the wallpaper will correspondingly shift to either side by the proper amount, which is determined based on the number of home screens and the width of those screens. Processing exposes this information through two functions: wallpaperHomeCount() and wallpaperOffset(). This first returns the current number of home screens (which could change during the lifetime of the wallpaper, as the user adds or removes home screens), while the second returns a float between 0 and 1 that corresponds to the horizontal displacement along the home screens: 0 when we are at the first screen, and 1 at the last. Listing 6-4 shows how we can use these functions to create the image-scroll interaction.

Listing 6-4. Image Scrolling Across Home Screens

```
PImage pic;
float ratio;

void setup() {
  fullScreen();
  pic = loadImage("paine.jpg");
  ratio = float(pic.width)/float(pic.height);
}
```

```
void draw() {
  background(0);
  float w = wallpaperHomeCount() * width;
  float h = w/ratio;
  float x = map(wallpaperOffset(), 0, 1, 0, -(wallpaperHomeCount()-1) *
width);
  image(pic, x, 0, w, h);
}
```

We use wallpaperHomeCount() * width as the display width of the image, spanning all the screens, and we translate the image to the left by the displacement x as the user swipes to the right. In this way, the correct portion of the image is displayed on the current screen, smoothly transitioning since wallpaperOffset() varies continuously between 0 and 1 (Figure 6-2).

Figure 6-2. *Interpretation of the offset function in live wallpapers*

■ **Note**   We may notice choppy animation when swiping across screens, especially on devices with high-resolution screens. This is likely the result of the default renderer not being able to draw in full-screen mode at smooth framerates. A solution is to switch to the P2D renderer, which uses the GPU for hardware-accelerated rendering.

Handling Permissions

We have learned to load an image and display it as a wallpaper across multiple home screens. We can build upon this technique to create a photo gallery wallpaper that browses through the photos that have been taken with the camera on the phone or tablet. But to load these photos, our sketch needs to access the external storage of the device, and permission for reading the external storage must be explicitly granted by the user. Although we will now look at permission requests in a wallpaper example, the functions can be used in any type of sketch.

Permissions are, in fact, a very important aspect of Android development since mobile devices handle several different kinds of personal data (contacts, location, messages), and unauthorized access of such data could lead to privacy breaches. The Android Operating System makes sure that every app is authorized to access only specific data and features in the device. Regular permissions (for instance, Wi-Fi and Bluetooth access) are granted once the user installs the app for the first time, while critical or "dangerous" permissions (such as access to camera, location, microphone, storage, and body sensors) need to be granted (on devices with Android 6.0 or newer) when the user opens the app (https://developer.android.com/guide/topics/permissions/index.html).

Any permissions required by our sketch, either regular or dangerous, have to be added to the sketch from the PDE by using the Android Permissions Selector, which is available from the "Sketch Permissions" option under the Android menu (see Figure 6-3).

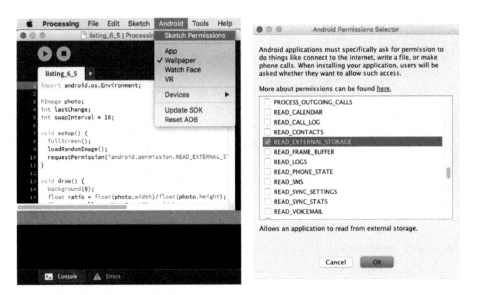

Figure 6-3. *"Sketch Permissions" option (left) and Android Permission Selector dialog (right)*

For normal permissions, all we need to do is select them with the Permissions Selector. However, for dangerous permissions, we also have to request them explicitly in the sketch code with the requestPermission() function. This function takes two arguments—the name of the permission to request (for example, android.permission.READ_EXTERNAL_STORAGE) and the name of a callback function in our sketch that will be called as soon as the user has granted (or denied) the permission. The callback function must have a Boolean argument, which is where it will receive the result of the permission request. This mechanism is illustrated in Listing 6-5, where the background color turns green when the permission is granted. The callback function is not necessarily called from setup(), because the Android system could show the permissions dialog when the sketch is already in the draw() function. So, we should be prepared to handle the lack of an expected permission in draw(). For this purpose, we can use the hasPermission() function to check whether the permission passed as an argument, i.e.: hasPermission("android.permission.READ_EXTERNAL_STORAGE"), has been granted or not, and run the appropriate code in each case.

Listing 6-5. Requesting a Dangerous Permission

```
color bckColor = #EA6411;

void setup() {
  fullScreen();
  requestPermission("android.permission.READ_EXTERNAL_STORAGE",
                    "handlePermission");
}

void draw() {
  background(bckColor);
}

void handlePermission(boolean granted) {
  if (granted) bckColor = #58EA11;
}
```

■ **Note**   A list of all permissions for each version of Android is available at https://developer.android.com/reference/android/Manifest.permission.html.

Returning to our image-gallery wallpaper sketch, besides requesting permission to read the external storage, it also needs to list all the photos stored in the external storage. This functionality is not part of the Processing API, but we can access the Android API from our sketch and import the Android packages that allow us to perform these more advanced tasks. In the case of listing files from the DCIM folder where pictures and videos taken with the camera are stored, we can use the getExternalStoragePublicDirectory() method from the android.os.Environment package (https://developer.android.com/reference/android/os/Environment.html). All we need to do to access this package is import it at the beginning of our sketch.

We now have all the pieces required for our image-gallery wallpaper, which is shown in Listing 6-6. We will now discuss the new code introduced in this example.

Listing 6-6. Image-Gallery Wallpaper

```
import android.os.Environment;

PImage defImage, currImage;
ArrayList<String> imageNames = new ArrayList<String>();
int lastChange;
int swapInterval = 10;

void setup() {
  fullScreen();
  defImage = loadImage("default.jpg");
  if (!wallpaperPreview()) {
    requestPermission("android.permission.READ_EXTERNAL_STORAGE",
                      "scanForImages");
  }
  loadRandomImage();
}

void draw() {
  background(0);
  float ratio = float(currImage.width)/float(currImage.height);
  float w = wallpaperHomeCount() * width;
  float h = w/ratio;
  if (h < height) {
    h = height;
    w = ratio * h;
  }
  float x = map(wallpaperOffset(), 0, 1, 0, -(wallpaperHomeCount()-1) *
  width);
  float y = (height - h)/2;
  image(currImage, x, y, w, h);
  int t = millis();
  if (swapInterval * 1000 < t - lastChange) {
    loadRandomImage();
```

```
    lastChange = t;
  }
}

void loadRandomImage() {
  if (imageNames.size() == 0) {
    currImage = defImage;
  } else {
    int i = int(random(1) * imageNames.size());
    String fn = imageNames.get(i);
    currImage = loadImage(fn);
  }
}

void scanForImages(boolean grantedPermission) {
  if (grantedPermission) {
    File dcimDir = Environment.getExternalStoragePublicDirectory(
                    Environment.DIRECTORY_DCIM);
    String[] subDirs = dcimDir.list();
    if (subDirs == null) return;
    for (String d: subDirs) {
      if (d.charAt(0) == '.') continue;
      File fullPath = new File (dcimDir, d);
      File[] listFiles = fullPath.listFiles();
      for (File f: listFiles) {
        String filename = f.getAbsolutePath().toLowerCase();
        if (filename.endsWith(".jpg")) imageNames.add(filename);
      }
    }
  }
}
```

The logic of this code is simple: we have current and default PImage variables (currImage and defImage) and a list of image file names (imageNames). This list is initialized in the scanForImages() function when the READ_EXTERNAL_STORAGE permission is granted. In this function, we obtain the File object representing the DCIM folder with getExternalStoragePublicDirectory(), which we then use to iterate over all its sub-folders, and finally we list the contents of each sub-folder. Files with the .jpg extension are added to the list. The loadRandomImage() is called every ten seconds and picks a random file name from the list to load a new PImage into currImage. If the list is empty, which will be the case if the permission is not granted, the sketch just uses the default image that we should have added to the data folder before running the sketch.

As we discussed at the beginning of this chapter, we don't want to present the user with the permission dialog when just previewing the wallpaper, which is why we only call requestPermission() if we are not in preview mode. The preview will show the default image, so that the user will still be able to see an image while previewing the wallpaper.

Particle Systems

App developers often use live wallpapers to create animated graphics that offer an alternative to static background images. However, these graphics cannot be too overpowering, since they might distract the user from the relevant information presented on the device's screen (calls, messages, alerts from other apps).

How can we create a visually interesting wallpaper that is not distracting? A possible concept is a fluid simulation where a swarm of particles move "organically" in the background and leave some kind of trace behind. The organic movement would help to keep the wallpaper subdued, but still attractive, with the added component of random variation. We could also incorporate touch interaction to drive the particle movements in some form, since the touch API we saw in the previous chapter is available for wallpapers. With these ideas in mind, this may be a good moment to find visual inspiration in existing works, from paintings to code-based projects (Figure 6-4).

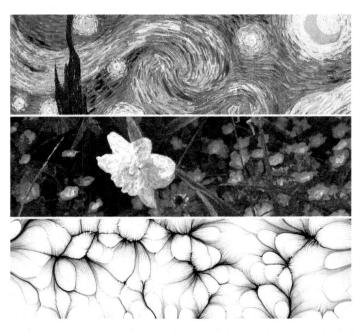

Figure 6-4. From top to bottom: "Starry Night," by Vincent van Gogh (1889), Plate from "Processing Images and Video for An Impressionist Effect" by Peter Litwinowicz (1997), Drawing Machine #10 by Ale Gonzalez (https://www.openprocessing.org/sketch/34320).

We can now start sketching out some ideas with pen and paper (Figure 6-5). One idea: individual particles move between touch points following a curved path. The question is, how can we simulate these smooth paths? In the next section, we will go over some techniques that would allow us to implement a system like this.

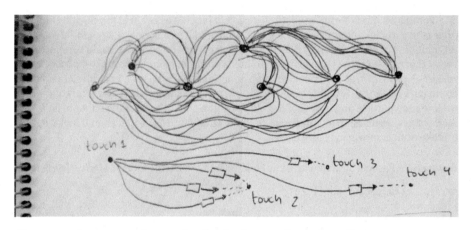

Figure 6-5. *Some pen and paper sketches for the particle-system wallpaper*

Autonomous Agents

The problem of creating natural-feeling particle systems has been investigated for many years. The book *The Nature of Code* by Daniel Shiffman (available online at http://natureofcode.com/) gives excellent coverage of the topic (in particular, chapters 4 and 6). Particle systems allow us to simulate the emerging behavior of large swarms of individual entities, each one following a simple (or more complex) movement rule.

A swarm where the particles have some degree of autonomous behavior, determined by forces acting upon them, could be useful in our project since we don't need to specify the exact movement of each particle, only the overall forces. Craig Reynolds (http://www.red3d.com/cwr/steer/) proposed algorithms that generate steering behaviors. In one such algorithm, called flow field following, a field of target velocities (a "flow field") can direct the particles' movements toward specific locations without it looking forced or artificial. In this algorithm, each particle has a dynamic state determined by its acceleration, velocity, and position, and a force acts upon the particle based on the difference between the current velocity and a target velocity defined at each point of the screen space, as illustrated in Figure 6-6.

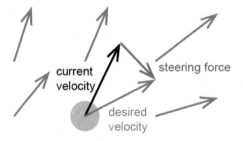

Figure 6-6. *Diagram of the steering force (red) that is applied on a particle moving on a flow field of velocities (blue)*

For this method to work properly, we need to provide a flow field of velocities that drives the particles' motion. We were considering touch interaction as a potential source of this motion. For example, every time the pointer changes position, we could compute the vector that measures the change in the pointer's position, namely (mouseX - pmouseX, mouseY - pmouseY), as the "velocity" at position (mouseX, mouseY). Let's implement this approach in Listing 6-7. In this example, we will use two classes to organize the code—one to store each particle and the other to hold the entire field. We can run it either in Java mode or as a regular app on our device or in the emulator. The output should look more or less like what is shown in Figure 6-7.

Listing 6-7. Particle System with Flow Field Calculated from Touch or Mouse Events

```
ArrayList<Particle> particles;
Field field;

void setup() {
  size(1200, 600);
  field = new Field();
  particles = new ArrayList<Particle>();
}

void draw() {
  background(255);
  field.display();
  for (int i = particles.size() - 1; i >= 0; i--) {
    Particle p = particles.get(i);
    p.update(field);
    p.display();
    if (p.dead()) particles.remove(i);
  }
}

void mouseDragged() {
  field.update(mouseX, mouseY, mouseX - pmouseX, mouseY - pmouseY);
  particles.add(new Particle(mouseX, mouseY));
}

class Particle {
  PVector position;
  PVector velocity;
  PVector acceleration;
  float size;
  int life;
  float maxAccel;
  float maxSpeed;
  int maxLife;
```

```
Particle(float x, float y) {
  position = new PVector(x, y);
  size = random(15, 25);
  velocity = new PVector(0, 0);
  acceleration = new PVector(0, 0);
  maxSpeed = random(2, 5);
  maxAccel = random(0.1, 0.5);
  maxLife = int(random(100, 200));
}

boolean dead() {
  return maxLife < life;
}

public void setPosition(float x, float y) {
  position.set(x, y);
}

void update(Field flow) {
  PVector desired = flow.lookup(int(position.x), int(position.y));
  acceleration.x = maxSpeed * desired.x - velocity.x;
  acceleration.y = maxSpeed * desired.y - velocity.y;
  acceleration.limit(maxAccel);
  velocity.add(acceleration);
  velocity.limit(maxSpeed);
  position.add(velocity);
  life++;
}

void display() {
  noStroke();
  fill(180, 150);
  ellipse(position.x, position.y, size, size);
}
}

class Field {
  PVector[][] field;

  Field() {
    field = new PVector[width][height];
    for (int i = 0; i < width; i++) {
      for (int j = 0; j < height; j++) {
        field[i][j] = new PVector(0, 0);
      }
    }
  }
```

123

```
  void update(int x, int y, float vx, float vy) {
    for (int i = max(0, x - 20); i < min(x + 20, width); i++) {
      for (int j = max(0, y - 20); j < min(y + 20, height); j++) {
        PVector v = field[i][j];
        v.set(vx, vy);
        v.normalize();
      }
    }
  }

  PVector lookup(int x, int y) {
    return field[x][y];
  }

  void display() {
    int resolution = 20;
    int cols = width / resolution;
    int rows = height / resolution;
    for (int i = 1; i < cols; i++) {
      for (int j = 1; j < rows; j++) {
        int x = i * resolution;
        int y = j * resolution;
        PVector v = lookup(x, y);
        pushMatrix();
        translate(x, y);
        stroke(28, 117, 188);
        strokeWeight(2);
        rotate(v.heading());
        float len = v.mag() * (resolution - 2);
        if (0 < len) {
          float arrowsize = 8;
          line(0, 0, len, 0);
          line(len, 0, len-arrowsize, +arrowsize/2);
          line(len, 0, len-arrowsize, -arrowsize/2);
        }
        popMatrix();
      }
    }
  }
}
```

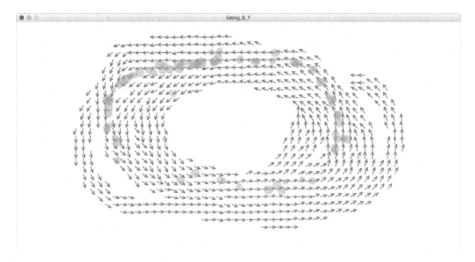

Figure 6-7. *Particle movement steered by a flow field derived from changes in touch position*

There are several things happening in this code, so let's review it step by step. In the draw( ) function, we first display the flow field, and then iterate over the list of particles to update their positions based on the current field. We display them and eventually remove those marked as "dead." Notice that we iterate the list in reverse order, because we are removing elements from it as we iterate. If we do a normal forward loop, we could end up stepping over the end of the list (because its size when we started the loop is smaller than its size at the end), causing a runtime error. In mouseDragged( ), we update the field at the current pointer position, using the difference between the current and last positions, and also add a new particle.

The Particle class keeps track of the dynamic state of the particle, including its position, velocity, and acceleration, as well as its "lifetime." Every time we call the update( ) method, we obtain the desired velocity from the flow field at the particle's current position and then compute the acceleration resulting from the steering force, which, following Reynolds' formula, is the difference between the desired and current velocities. The maxSpeed factor allows us to have variation in the movement of the particles, since it's determined randomly in the Particle constructor and results in some particles moving faster and others slower.

The Field class has an array of PVector objects, with width×height elements, containing the value of the flow field at each pixel of the screen. The field is initially zero everywhere, but we use the update( ) method to set it to the values derived from the touch or mouse events. Note that in this method, we don't set the field vector only at the (x, y) position, but rather in a rectangle centered around (x, y), because otherwise the changes in the vector field would affect just a very small area—not enough to steer the particles across the screen. Finally, the display( ) method also needs some attention, since we cannot draw the field vectors for all pixels on the screen. We use a larger grid so we can draw one vector per each rectangle of size resolution. The methods in the PVector class, such as heading( ), become handy here to draw the vectors as little arrows, which helps to visualize the direction of the flow.

Although this example is a simple application of steering behaviors that we can refine in many different ways, one problem is that it requires constant touch input to keep the system evolving. While this is okay for a regular app, depending so much on touch interaction in a wallpaper can be problematic because touches on the home screen are primarily used to drive the interactions with the UI. A drag to create a movement in the particles could be mistaken for a swipe to change the home screen, and vice versa. We will see in the next section how to generate a flow field that does not require touch interaction.

Image Flow Field

There are several ways we can generate a smooth flow field that gives enough visual variability to our particle system. One possibility is to use a field generated with Perlin noise (mrl.nyu.edu/~perlin/doc/oscar.html), which is a synthetically-generated random noise that changes smoothly and results in more organic-looking patterns. Another possibility is to use images. As it turns out, we can convert the color information at each pixel position in an image to compute a velocity vector for our flow field.

More specifically, if we compute the brightness of a color with the brightness() function, we obtain a number between 0 (black) and 1 (white), which we can use as the angle of our velocity vector with respect to the x axis. This results in a smooth velocity flow field that follows the image's features (edges, swirls of color, etc.). We can use the fromAngle(theta) function in Processing's PVector class to easily calculate the vectors. Another piece of functionality that is very important when generating our velocity field from an image is the ability to access the individual pixels in an image. We can do this with the pixels array that any PImage object has available once we call the loadPixels() function. We combine all of this in Listing 6-8, which loads an image and generates the associated flow field, shown in Figure 6-8.

Listing 6-8. Code That Generates a Flow Field from an Image

```
PImage img;

void setup() {
  fullScreen();
  img = loadImage("jupiter.jpg");
  img.loadPixels();
}

void draw() {
  image(img, 0, 0, width, height);
  int resolution = 30;
  int cols = width / resolution;
  int rows = height / resolution;
  for (int i = 1; i < cols; i++) {
    for (int j = 1; j < rows; j++) {
      int x = i * resolution;
      int y = j * resolution;
```

```
      int ix = int(map(x, 0, width, 0, img.width - 1));
      int iy = int(map(y, 0, height, 0, img.height - 1));
      int idx = ix + iy * img.width;
      int c = img.pixels[idx];
      float theta = map(brightness(c), 0, 255, 0, TWO_PI);
      PVector v = PVector.fromAngle(theta);
      drawArrow(x, y, v, resolution-2);
    }
  }
}

void drawArrow(float x, float y, PVector v, float l) {
  pushMatrix();
  float arrowsize = 8;
  translate(x, y);
  strokeWeight(2);
  stroke(28, 117, 188);
  rotate(v.heading());
  float len = v.mag() * l;
  line(0, 0, len, 0);
  line(len, 0, len-arrowsize, +arrowsize/2);
  line(len, 0, len-arrowsize, -arrowsize/2);
  popMatrix();
}
```

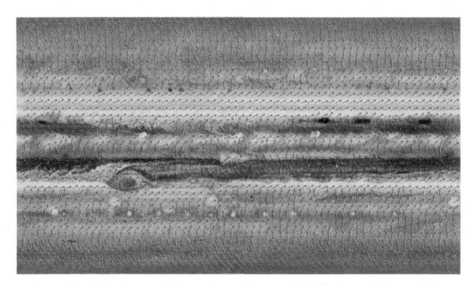

Figure 6-8. *Flow field generated from an image*

In this example, we need to access the individual pixels in the image. We do this by first calling the method loadPixels() in setup(), which initializes the pixels array we use later in draw(). This is a one-dimensional array where each row of pixels from the image is stored one after another, so that pixel (ix, iy) corresponds to element idx in the array, as illustrated in Figure 6-9. However, there is another transformation in the code, since we are stretching the image to cover the entire screen. So, we first need to map the screen coordinates (x, y) to pixel indices (ix, iy) by using the map() function. Then, we can apply the correspondence between the indices of the pixels in the image and the indices in the array.

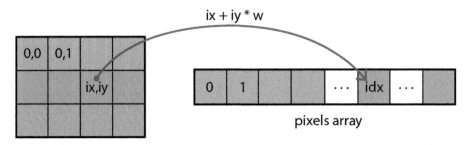

Figure 6-9. *Correspondence between pixels in an image and elements in the pixels array*

An Image-flow Wallpaper

We now know how to generate a smooth vector field from any image. We could add a fixed list of images to our sketch and cycle through them to produce variable motion patterns. But better still, we can apply the technique we learned with the photo gallery example to load pictures taken with the device's camera and use them as the source of our flow fields. This will add unique and endless variability to our wallpaper. However, there are still some important details to solve in order to implement this wallpaper, which we will consider in the following sections.

Loading, Resizing, and Cropping Images

One problem we might face is that the device's camera, especially for recent Android phones, can take pictures at very high resolutions. When we load these pictures into a PImage object and then load the pixels array with loadPixels(), we might run out of memory (wallpapers have fewer resources allocated to them to avoid affecting other apps in the system). However, we don't need an image at full high resolution in order to compute the flow field. We can, in fact, load a picture into a temporary bitmap object and then resize and crop it to the desired size before loading it into the PImage object in our sketch. In Listing 6-9, we add the croppedBitmap() function to the image gallery example from Listing 6-6.

Listing 6-9. Cropping and Loading Images

```
import android.os.Environment;
import java.io.FileOutputStream;
import android.graphics.Bitmap;
import android.graphics.BitmapFactory;
...
void loadRandomImage() {
  if (imageNames.size() == 0) {
    currImage = defImage;
  } else {
    int i = int(random(1) * imageNames.size());
    String sourceFn = imageNames.get(i);
    try {
      File destFile = sketchFile("cropped.jpg");
      Bitmap bitmap = croppedBitmap(sourceFn);
      OutputStream fout = new FileOutputStream(destFile);
      bitmap.compress(Bitmap.CompressFormat.JPEG, 85, fout);
      currImage = loadImage("cropped.jpg");
    } catch (Exception ex) {
      println("An error while cropping has occurred");
      currImage = defImage;
    }
  }
}
...
Bitmap croppedBitmap(String sourceFile) {
  BitmapFactory.Options options = new BitmapFactory.Options();
  options.inJustDecodeBounds = false;
  options.inSampleSize = 4;
  Bitmap src = BitmapFactory.decodeFile(sourceFile, options);
  int srcW = options.outWidth;
  int srcH = options.outHeight;
  float ratio = float(width)/float(height);
  float srcRatio = float(srcW)/float(srcH);
  int cropX, cropY, cropW, cropH;
  if (ratio < srcRatio) {
    cropH = srcH;
    cropW = int(ratio * cropH);
  } else {
    cropW = srcW;
    cropH = int(cropW / ratio);
  }
  cropX = (srcW - cropW)/2;
  cropY = (srcH - cropH)/2;
  return Bitmap.createBitmap(src, cropX, cropY, cropW, cropH);
}
```

Here, after selecting the image file, we apply the resize/cropping, where we make use of the Bitmap class to decode an image while at the same time downsampling it (in this case, reducing its original width and height by a factor of four), and then we determine the crop area so that a correctly proportioned area of the image is shown in full-screen mode. We save the cropped image to a new file inside the sketch's folder, called cropped. jpg, which we then load with loadImage() as before. We should be able to see the pixelation of the images shown in the background.

Putting Everything Together

After going through the preceding sections to create a flow field from an image (Listing 6-8) and crop and load images from the external storage (Listing 6-9), we are ready to put together our image-flow wallpaper. We can follow the structure of the touch-based particle system, with separate Particle and Field classes, to arrive at Listing 6-10.

Listing 6-10. Image-flow Wallpaper

```
import android.os.Environment;
import java.io.FileOutputStream;
import android.graphics.Bitmap;
import android.graphics.BitmapFactory;

int maxParticles = 200;
int swapInterval = 10;
Field field;
ArrayList<Particle> particles;
ArrayList<String> imageNames = new ArrayList<String>();
int lastChange;

void setup() {
  fullScreen(P2D);
  frameRate(25);
  field = new Field();
  if (!wallpaperPreview()) {
    requestPermission("android.permission.READ_EXTERNAL_STORAGE",
                      "scanForImages");
  }
  particles = new ArrayList<Particle>();
  for (int i = 0; i < maxParticles; i++) {
    particles.add(new Particle(random(width), random(height)));
  }
  loadRandomImage();
  background(255);
}
```

```
void draw() {
  for (Particle b: particles) {
    b.update(field);
    b.display();
  }
  int t = millis();
  if (swapInterval * 1000 < t - lastChange) {
    loadRandomImage();
    lastChange = t;
  }
}

void loadRandomImage() {
  if (imageNames.size() == 0) {
    field.update("default.jpg");
  } else {
    int i = int(random(1) * imageNames.size());
    String sourceFn = imageNames.get(i);
    try {
      File destFile = sketchFile("cropped.jpg");
      Bitmap bitmap = croppedBitmap(sourceFn);
      OutputStream fout = new FileOutputStream(destFile);
      bitmap.compress(Bitmap.CompressFormat.JPEG, 85, fout);
      field.update("cropped.jpg");
    } catch (Exception ex) {
      println("An error while cropping has occurred");
      field.update("default.jpg");
    }
  }
}

void scanForImages(boolean grantedPermission) {
  if (grantedPermission) {
    File dcimDir = Environment.getExternalStoragePublicDirectory(
                   Environment.DIRECTORY_DCIM);
    String[] subDirs = dcimDir.list();
    if (subDirs == null) return;
    for (String d: subDirs) {
      if (d.charAt(0) == '.') continue;
      File fullPath = new File (dcimDir, d);
      File[] listFiles = fullPath.listFiles();
      for (File f: listFiles) {
        String filename = f.getAbsolutePath().toLowerCase();
        if (filename.endsWith(".jpg")) imageNames.add(filename);
      }
    }
  }
}
```

```
Bitmap croppedBitmap(String sourceFile) {
  BitmapFactory.Options options = new BitmapFactory.Options();
  options.inJustDecodeBounds = false;
  options.inSampleSize = 4;
  Bitmap src = BitmapFactory.decodeFile(sourceFile, options);
  int srcW = options.outWidth;
  int srcH = options.outHeight;
  float ratio = float(width)/float(height);
  float srcRatio = float(srcW)/float(srcH);
  int cropX, cropY, cropW, cropH;
  if (ratio < srcRatio) {
    cropH = srcH;
    cropW = int(ratio * cropH);
  } else {
    cropW = srcW;
    cropH = int(cropW / ratio);
  }
  cropX = (srcW - cropW)/2;
  cropY = (srcH - cropH)/2;
  return Bitmap.createBitmap(src, cropX, cropY, cropW, cropH);
}

class Field {
  PImage flowImage;

  void update(String fn) {
    flowImage = loadImage(fn);
    flowImage.loadPixels();
  }

  PVector lookupVector(PVector v) {
    if (flowImage == null) return PVector.random2D();
    color c = flowImage.pixels[getPixelIndex(v.x, v.y)];
    float theta = map(brightness(c), 0, 255, 0, TWO_PI);
    return PVector.fromAngle(theta);
  }

  color lookupColor(PVector v) {
    if (flowImage == null) return color(0, 0, 100, 0);
    return flowImage.pixels[getPixelIndex(v.x, v.y)];
  }
```

```
  int getPixelIndex(float x, float y) {
    int ix = int(map(x, 0, width, 0, flowImage.width - 1));
    int iy = int(map(y, 0, height, 0, flowImage.height - 1));
    return constrain(ix + iy * flowImage.width, 0, flowImage.pixels.length
    - 1);
  }
}

class Particle {
  PVector position;
  PVector velocity;
  PVector acceleration;
  float size;
  color color;
  int life;
  float maxAccel;
  float maxSpeed;
  int maxLife;

  Particle(float x, float y) {
    position = new PVector(x, y);
    size = random(2, 4) * displayDensity;
    velocity = new PVector(0, 0);
    acceleration = new PVector(0, 0);
    maxSpeed = random(2, 5);
    maxAccel = random(0.1, 0.5);
    maxLife = int(random(5, 20));
  }

  void update(Field flow) {
    if (life == 0) {
      color = flow.lookupColor(position);
    } else if (life > frameRate * maxLife) {
      position.x = random(width);
      position.y = random(height);
      life = 0;
      color = flow.lookupColor(position);
    }

    PVector desired = flow.lookupVector(position);
    acceleration.x = maxSpeed * desired.x - velocity.x;
    acceleration.y = maxSpeed * desired.y - velocity.y;
    acceleration.limit(maxAccel);
    velocity.add(acceleration);
    velocity.limit(maxSpeed);
    position.add(velocity);
```

```
    if (position.x < -size) position.x = width + size;
    if (position.y < -size) position.y = height + size;
    if (position.x > width + size) position.x = -size;
    if (position.y > height + size) position.y = -size;

    life++;
  }

  void display() {
    float theta = velocity.heading();
    noStroke();
    pushMatrix();
    translate(position.x,position.y);
    rotate(theta);
    fill(color);
    beginShape(QUADS);
    vertex(-2*size, -size);
    vertex(+2*size, -size);
    vertex(+2*size, +size);
    vertex(-2*size, +size);
    endShape();
    popMatrix();
  }
}
```

The Field class contains the PImage object holding the image to derive the flow field from, the update() method to set a new image by passing in its file name, and two look-up methods, lookupVector() and lookupColor(), which return the field vector and the image color at the given position, respectively. It is important to notice the use of the getPixelIndex() method, used internally by the class to convert a screen position (x, y) into a valid pixel index, irrespective of the resolution of the current flow image.

The Particle class is very similar to that seen in Listing 6-7, with a few key additions: at the beginning of each update, we compute the particle color at the beginning of its "lifetime" and restart its position when the life variable reaches the maximum value; at the end of the update, we check if the particle is outside of the screen, and, if so, we wrap it around so it emerges from the opposite side of the screen to ensure that our particles don't wander away.

Using Threads

As explained in the online reference, Processing sketches follow a specific sequence of steps: setup() first, followed by draw() over and over and over again in a loop. A thread is also a series of steps with a beginning, a middle, and an end. A Processing sketch is a single thread, often referred to as the "Animation" thread (https://processing.org/reference/thread_.html). While a single thread is enough in most situations, sometimes we need a separate thread to perform extra calculations. For example, a problem with our image-flow wallpaper is that it pauses for a short while when a new image is resized and loaded. The reason is that the resizing/loading process currently happens in the Animation thread, blocking the rendering of the subsequent frames, hence the delay. The solution is to run the loadRandomImage() function in a separate thread so the image can be resized and loaded in parallel without obstructing the rendering. This can be done by replacing the call to loadRandomImage() in draw() with thread("loadRandomImage").

Because threads run independently of each other, we might face the problem of multiple threads calling the update() method in the Field class concurrently, or particles looking up field data from the Animation thread while it is being updated by another thread. This concurrent access can lead to unexpected errors if not handled properly. A solution is to mark all the methods in the Field class that access flowImage as "synchronized." Synchronized methods cannot be called from one thread while they are being called from another. The changes in the wallpaper code required to use threads and handle concurrency are shown in Listing 6-11.

Listing 6-11. Running the Image-loading Function in a Separate Thread

```
void draw() {...
  if (swapInterval * 1000 < t - lastChange) {
    thread("loadRandomImage");
    lastChange = t;
  }
}
...
class Field {
  PImage flowImage;

  synchronized void update(String fn) {
    flowImage = loadImage(fn);
    flowImage.loadPixels();
  }

  synchronized PVector lookupVector(PVector v) {
    if (flowImage == null) return PVector.random2D();
    color c = flowImage.pixels[getPixelIndex(v.x, v.y)];
    float theta = map(brightness(c), 0, 255, 0, TWO_PI);
    return PVector.fromAngle(theta);
  }

  synchronized color lookupColor(PVector v) {
    if (flowImage == null) return color(0, 0, 100, 0);
    return flowImage.pixels[getPixelIndex(v.x, v.y)];
  }
...
}
```

Controlling the Hue

As we discussed earlier, a live wallpaper should be visually attractive but not overpower the UI. In our case, the colors of the particles could be too bright or saturated, making it hard to see the icons in the foreground. One solution to this issue could be to use the HSB color space in our sketch and then adjust the brightness of the color when it is obtained from the pixels array. Listing 6-12 includes a modified lookupColor() method that applies Processing's hue() and saturation() functions to extract these properties and then reconstructs the final color with color() so the particle keeps its original hue and saturation but lowers its brightness and opacity.

Listing 6-12. Using the HSB Color Space

```
void setup() {
  ...
  colorMode(HSB, 360, 100, 100, 100);
  background(0, 0, 100);
}
...
class Field {
  ...
  synchronized color lookupColor(PVector v) {
    if (flowImage == null) return color(0, 0, 100, 0);
    color c = flowImage.pixels[getPixelIndex(v.x, v.y)];
    float h = hue(c);
    float s = saturation(c);
    float b = 50;
    return color(h, s, b, 70);
  }
  ...
}
```

In order to use the HSB color space, we need to set the color mode in setup() using the colorMode() function, which we saw already in Chapter 4. Our image-flow wallpaper should display more muted colors after this modification, as suggested by Figure 6-10.

Figure 6-10. *Final version of the image-flow wallpaper running in the background*

Wrapping the Project Up

As a final stage in this project, we should create icons for all the required resolutions (36 × 36, 48 × 48, 72 × 72, 96 × 96, 144 × 144, and 192 × 192 pixels) and set a unique package name and version number for our wallpaper in the manifest file. See Figure 6-11.

Figure 6-11. *Icon set for the image flow wallpaper.*

The manifest file will already have most of the required values already filled in if the sketch has been run at least once on the device or in the emulator. We should set a unique pacakge name, and also the android:label attribute in both the application and service tags so the wallpaper is identified with a more readable title in the wallpaper selector and app listing. A complete manifest file with all these values is show below:

```xml
<?xml version="1.0" encoding="UTF-8"?>
<manifest xmlns:android="http://schemas.android.com/apk/res/android"
        android:versionCode="1"android:versionName="1.0"
        package="com.example.image_flow">
    <uses-sdk android:minSdkVersion="17" android:targetSdkVersion="25"/>
    <uses-feature android:name="android.software.live_wallpaper"/>
    <application android:icon="@drawable/icon"
                android:label="Image Flow">
        <service android:label="Image Flow"
                android:name=".MainService"
                android:permission="android.permission.BIND_WALLPAPER">
            <intent-filter>
                <action
                android:name="android.service.wallpaper.WallpaperService"/>
            </intent-filter>
            <meta-data android:name="android.service.wallpaper"
                    android:resource="@xml/wallpaper"/>
        </service>
        <activity android:name="processing.android.PermissionRequestor"/>
    </application>
    <uses-permission android:name="android.permission.READ_EXTERNAL_STORAGE"/>
</manifest>
```

After editing the manifest, we are ready to export the sketch as a signed package for uploading to the Google Play Store, as we discussed in Chapter 3.

Summary

Live wallpapers give us a unique medium to create animated graphics that users can experience as dynamic backgrounds on their devices. We can apply the entire drawing API in Processing to create original wallpapers, and, as we learned in this chapter, it is also possible to import the Android API to carry out more advanced tasks, such as reading files from external storage or resizing images. This chapter also introduced the concept of normal and dangerous permissions and how to request them from our sketches, which we will revisit many times in next chapters.

PART III

Sensors

CHAPTER 7

Reading Sensor Data

Android devices read data from the physical world around us using numerous sensors, such as accelerometers, gyroscopes, and magnetometers. In this chapter, we will learn how to access this data from our Processing sketch using the Android SDK and the Ketai library.

Sensors in Android Devices

Nowadays, almost every mobile device, from smartphones to activity trackers, is equipped with a wide range of hardware sensors to capture data about the movement, environment, and location of the device (and, by extension, of ourselves). Android devices commonly contain accelerometers, gyroscopes, magnetometers, and location sensors. These sensors give us access to a large amount of information we can use in our Processing sketches in multiple ways, from controlling the behavior of graphical elements on the screen and creating user interfaces that are not limited to the touch gestures, to inferring and visualizing our own patterns of motion.

Let's begin this chapter by going over the most typical sensors available on an Android phone, tablet, or watch (check Google's official developer guide for more details: https://developer.android.com/guide/topics/sensors/sensors_overview.html).

Accelerometer

An accelerometer sensor is able to measure acceleration along three coordinate axes placed as shown in Figure 7-1. Acceleration is measured in meters/second^2, and Android includes in this measurement acceleration resulting from the force of gravity. Acceleration data has many uses; for example, it can be the basis for determining orientation in space, and it can also aid in detecting sudden motions, such as shocks or vibrations.

© Andrés Colubri 2017

A. Colubri, *Processing for Android*, https://doi.org/10.1007/978-1-4842-2719-0_7

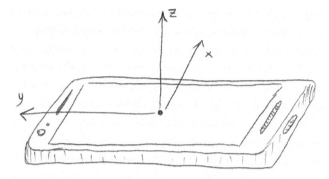

Figure 7-1. *Physical axes that Android uses to describe acceleration and other sensor data*

Gyroscope

The gyroscope measures the angular velocity of the device; that is, the rate of rotation (in radians/second) around each of the same three axes as defined for the accelerometer sensor in Figure 7-1. Although it is similar to the accelerometer in that both can be used to determine the position of orientation of the device, the gyroscope can sense rotation, whereas the accelerometer cannot. Because of this, the gyroscope is very useful when we need to measure rotational movement, such as spinning, turning, and so on.

Magnetometer

The magnetometer is a sensor that measures the strength and direction of the geomagnetic field—also using the coordinate system described in Figure 7-1—by providing the raw components of the field along each axis in μT (microtesla). A typical application of this sensor, which we will examine in more detail in the next chapter, is to implement a compass to show the angle of the device with respect to the magnetic North.

Location

This is not an actual sensor, but rather a combination of data collected from different sources (Global Positioning System, or GPS, cell-ID, and Wi-Fi) that allows us to determine the device's geographical location (in latitude/longitude) at different levels of resolution (coarse or fine). GPS data is obtained from a network of satellites orbiting Earth and has an accuracy of around 4.9 meters (16 feet) under open sky (http://www.gps.gov/systems/gps/performance/accuracy/). Location information derived from cellular tower or Wi-Fi access point IDs has much lower accuracy (between 5,300 feet and 1 mile), but uses very little energy as it works passively, in contrast to the active location-fixing done by GPS.

Accessing Sensors from Processing

The Processing language does not have specialized functions to read sensor data, but there are two easy ways to access this data from our code. The first is to rely on the Android API, which we can call from Processing by importing all the relevant Android packages, as we did in Chapter 4 to read files from external storage. The second way is to use a contributed library that extends the functionality of Android mode. We will learn both ways of accessing sensor data, starting with using the Android SDK from our sketch.

Creating a Sensor Manager

The first step to using the Android sensor API is to obtain the "context" of the app containing the sketch. We can think of this context as an interface that allows us to access useful information about our app. For instance, once we get a hold of the context, we can create a sensor manager from it. This manager will create any sensor we need in our sketch.

Let's look at a concrete example that reads accelerometer data. We put the initialization of the sensor manager inside the setup() function, as shown in Listing 7-1, where we also create the sensor object for the accelerometer.

Listing 7-1. Accessing the Accelerometer

```
import android.content.Context;
import android.hardware.Sensor;
import android.hardware.SensorManager;

Context context;
SensorManager manager;
Sensor sensor;

void setup() {
  fullScreen();
  context = getContext();
  manager = (SensorManager)context.getSystemService(Context.SENSOR_SERVICE);
  sensor = manager.getDefaultSensor(Sensor.TYPE_ACCELEROMETER);
}

void draw() {
}
```

In this code, we had to import several packages from the Android SDK to gain access to the Context, SensorManager, and Sensor classes.

Adding a Sensor Listener

In the next step (Listing 7-2), we add a listener object that will notify the sketch that new data is available from the sensor. We derive the listener class specific to our sketch from the base SensorEventListener class in the Android API by implementing two methods, onSensorChanged() and onAccuracyChanged(). The former is called when new data is available, and the latter when the accuracy of the sensor changes. Once we obtain an instance of the listener class, we must register it with the manager so it's ready to produce data.

Listing 7-2. Creating a Listener

```
import android.content.Context;
import android.hardware.Sensor;
import android.hardware.SensorManager;
import android.hardware.SensorEvent;
import android.hardware.SensorEventListener;

Context context;
SensorManager manager;
Sensor sensor;
AccelerometerListener listener;

void setup() {
  fullScreen();
  context = getActivity();
  manager = (SensorManager)context.getSystemService(Context.SENSOR_SERVICE);
  sensor = manager.getDefaultSensor(Sensor.TYPE_ACCELEROMETER);
  listener = new AccelerometerListener();
  manager.registerListener(listener, sensor,
                      SensorManager.SENSOR_DELAY_NORMAL);
}

void draw() {
}

class AccelerometerListener implements SensorEventListener {
  public void onSensorChanged(SensorEvent event) {
  }
  public void onAccuracyChanged(Sensor sensor, int accuracy) {
  }
}
```

You may have noticed the SensorManager.SENSOR_DELAY_NORMAL argument in the listener registration. This argument sets the rate at which the sensor is updated with new data. Faster rates mean more responsiveness, but also more battery consumption. The default SENSOR_DELAY_NORMAL sets a rate fast enough for screen orientation changes, while SENSOR_DELAY_GAME and SENSOR_DELAY_UI are suitable for use in games and user interfaces, respectively. Finally, SENSOR_DELAY_FASTEST allows us to get sensor data as fast as possible.

Reading Data from the Sensor

As we just mentioned, the event listener has two methods, onSensorChanged() and onAccuracyChanged(). We only need to use onSensorChanged() to get the data from the sensor. In the case of the accelerometer, the data consist of three float numbers, which represent the acceleration along the x, y, and z axes of the device.

In Listing 7-3, we simply print these values to the screen. We can verify that if we place the phone flat on the table with the screen facing up, we should see a Z acceleration of 9.81 m/s^2 (the actual acceleration will fluctuate around this value, since the accelerometer data is noisy), which corresponds to the acceleration of gravity.

Listing 7-3. Reading the Accelerometer

```
import android.content.Context;
import android.hardware.Sensor;
import android.hardware.SensorManager;
import android.hardware.SensorEvent;
import android.hardware.SensorEventListener;

Context context;
SensorManager manager;
Sensor sensor;
AccelerometerListener listener;
float ax, ay, az;

void setup() {
  fullScreen();
  context = getContext();
  manager = (SensorManager)context.getSystemService(Context.SENSOR_SERVICE);
  sensor = manager.getDefaultSensor(Sensor.TYPE_ACCELEROMETER);
  listener = new AccelerometerListener();
  manager.registerListener(listener, sensor,
                           SensorManager.SENSOR_DELAY_NORMAL);

  textFont(createFont("SansSerif", displayDensity * 24));
  textAlign(CENTER, CENTER);
}

void draw() {
  background(157);
  text("X: " + ax + "\n" + "Y: " + ay + "\n" + "Z: " + az, width/2,
height/2);
}
```

147

```
public void resume() {
  if (manager != null) {
    manager.registerListener(listener, sensor,
                             SensorManager.SENSOR_DELAY_NORMAL);
  }
}

public void pause() {
  if (manager != null) {
    manager.unregisterListener(listener);
  }
}
class AccelerometerListener implements SensorEventListener {
  public void onSensorChanged(SensorEvent event) {
    ax = event.values[0];
    ay = event.values[1];
    az = event.values[2];
  }
  public void onAccuracyChanged(Sensor sensor, int accuracy) {
  }
}
```

Additionally, we unregister the listener when the sketch is paused and reregister when it resumes. Figure 7-2 shows the output of our first sensor sketch, which is just a printout of the X, Y, and Z acceleration values.

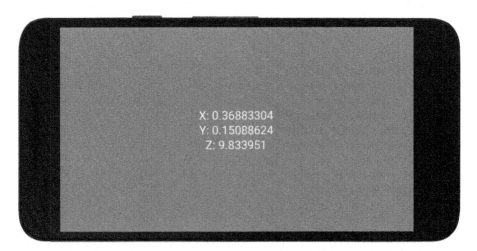

Figure 7-2. *Output of the accelerometer sensor example*

> ■ **Note** As a best practice for using sensors, we should unregister the associated listeners when the sketch's activity is paused to reduce battery usage, then register it again when the activity resumes.

Reading from Other Sensors

The structure we put together in the previous example can be reused with almost no changes for other types of sensors. For example, if we want to read the rotation angle around each axis using the gyroscope, all we need to do is request a TYPE_GYROSCOPE sensor, which is demonstrated in Listing 7-4.

Listing 7-4. Reading the Gyroscope

```
import android.content.Context;
import android.hardware.Sensor;
import android.hardware.SensorManager;
import android.hardware.SensorEvent;
import android.hardware.SensorEventListener;

Context context;
SensorManager manager;
Sensor sensor;
GyroscopeListener listener;
float rx, ry, rz;

void setup() {
  fullScreen();
  context = getContext();
  manager = (SensorManager)context.getSystemService(Context.SENSOR_SERVICE);
  sensor = manager.getDefaultSensor(Sensor.TYPE_GYROSCOPE);
  listener = new GyroscopeListener();
  manager.registerListener(listener, sensor,
                           SensorManager.SENSOR_DELAY_NORMAL);

  textFont(createFont("SansSerif", displayDensity * 24));
  textAlign(CENTER, CENTER);
}

void draw() {
  background(157);
  text("X: " + rx + "\n" + "Y: " + ry + "\n" + "Z: " + rz, width/2, height/2);
}
```

```
public void resume() {
  if (manager != null) {
    manager.registerListener(listener, sensor,
                             SensorManager.SENSOR_DELAY_NORMAL);
  }
}

public void pause() {
  if (manager != null) {
    manager.unregisterListener(listener);
  }
}

class GyroscopeListener implements SensorEventListener {
  public void onSensorChanged(SensorEvent event) {
    rx = event.values[0];
    ry = event.values[1];
    rz = event.values[2];
  }
  public void onAccuracyChanged(Sensor sensor, int accuracy) {
  }
}
```

The Ketai Library

We have learned to access sensor data by calling the Android API directly from our sketch. The advantage of this approach is that we can always access the Android API, but a downside is the additional code we need in order to create sensor managers and listeners. This extra code does not follow the conventions of the Processing API, so it may be difficult for new users to understand it.

We had to use Android sensor APIs because Processing for Android does not include one. However, we can add new functionality to Processing through the use of contributed libraries. As we saw in Chapter 1, contributed libraries are modules that package extra functions and classes that are not part of the Processing core. We can import these libraries into our sketch to use their features and functionality. It turns out that there is a library aimed precisely at working with Android sensors in a simplified, Processing-like manner. It is called Ketai (http://ketai.org/) and was created by Daniel Sauter and Jesus Duran.

Installing Ketai

Contributed libraries, such as Ketai, can be easily installed in Processing using the Contributions Manager, or CM. To open the CM, we go to the Sketch menu and then select "Import Library|Add Library..." We already used the CM to install Android mode, but it is also the main interface to install libraries, tools, and examples.

After opening the CM, we select the Libraries tab; there we can search for the library of interest by either scrolling down the list or searching by name. Once we find the entry for Ketai, all we need to do is click on the Install button (Figure 7-3).

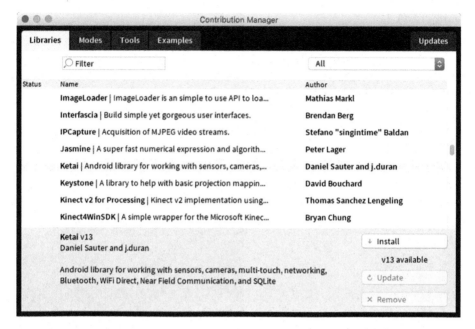

Figure 7-3. *Installing the Ketai library through the Contributions Manager*

Using Ketai

The Ketai library provides a simple interface to the sensors in our Android device, following the style of the core Processing API. Ketai requires some initialization code to import the library and create a KetaiSensor object, but reading sensor values is very easy. We only have to add an "event handler" function to our sketch, which will get called every time there is a new value from the sensor (similar to how the built-in mousePressed() or touchMoved() functions work).

A simple sketch that reads the accelerometer and shows the values as text, like we did in Listing 7-3, is presented in Listing 7-5. Its output is shown in Figure 7-4.

Listing 7-5. Reading the Accelerometer with Ketai

```
import ketai.sensors.*;

KetaiSensor sensor;
float accelerometerX, accelerometerY, accelerometerZ;

void setup() {
  fullScreen();
  sensor = new KetaiSensor(this);
  sensor.start();
  textAlign(CENTER, CENTER);
  textSize(displayDensity * 36);
}
```

```
void draw() {
  background(78, 93, 75);
  text("Accelerometer: \n" +
    "x: " + nfp(accelerometerX, 1, 3) + "\n" +
    "y: " + nfp(accelerometerY, 1, 3) + "\n" +
    "z: " + nfp(accelerometerZ, 1, 3), 0, 0, width, height);
}

void onAccelerometerEvent(float x, float y, float z) {
  accelerometerX = x;
  accelerometerY = y;
  accelerometerZ = z;
}
```

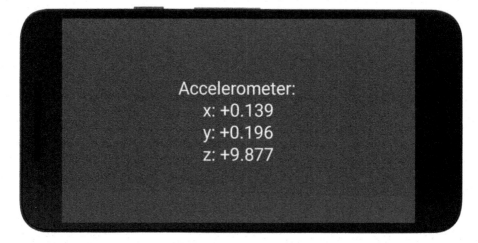

Figure 7-4. *Output of Ketai accelerometer example*

Data from other sensors is accessed in the same way; we only need to add a different event handler. For example, to read the values from the gyroscope, we use onGyroscopeEvent (Listing 7-6).

Listing 7-6. Reading the Gyroscope with Ketai

```
import ketai.sensors.*;

KetaiSensor sensor;
float rotationX, rotationY, rotationZ;

void setup() {
 fullScreen();
  sensor = new KetaiSensor(this);
```

```
  sensor.start();
  textAlign(CENTER, CENTER);
  textSize(displayDensity * 24);
}

void draw() {
  background(78, 93, 75);
  text("Gyroscope: \n" +
    "x: " + nfp(rotationX, 1, 3) + "\n" +
    "y: " + nfp(rotationY, 1, 3) + "\n" +
    "z: " + nfp(rotationZ, 1, 3), 0, 0, width, height);
}

void onGyroscopeEvent(float x, float y, float z) {
  rotationX = x;
  rotationY = y;
  rotationZ = z;
}
```

Event Handlers in Ketai

With Ketai, we indicate what sensor data to read by adding the corresponding event handler function. Some handlers supported by Ketai are shown here, and the complete list is available in the reference of the library (http://ketai.org/reference/sensors). *Rapid Android Development* by Daniel Sauter, available online at https://www. mobileprocessing.org, is also a good resource to learn all the details about Ketai.

- void onSensorEvent(SensorEvent e): This handler returns a "raw" Android sensor event object that contains all the relevant information describing the event, including type, values, and so on. The SensorEvent class is fully documented in the official Android reference, found here: https://developer.android. com/reference/android/hardware/SensorEvent.html

- void onAccelerometerEvent(float x, float y, float z, long a, int b): We receive accelerometer data, with x, y, z being the acceleration along the three axes in m/s^2, a the timestamp of the event (in nanoseconds), and b the current accuracy level.

- void onAccelerometerEvent(float x, float y, float z): Same as before, but does not give the timestamp or the accuracy

- void onGyroscopeEvent(float x, float y, float z, long a, int b): Provides the x, y, z angular velocity in radians/second, the event timestamp a, and the accuracy level b

- void onGyroscopeEvent(float x, float y, float z): Only angular velocity

153

- void onPressureEvent(float p): Current ambient pressure p in hectopascals (hPa)

- void onTemperatureEvent(float t): Current temperature t in degrees Celsius

We can use several sensors at once just by adding all the required event handlers. However, a device might not include a specific sensor. In order to handle such situations properly, we can check the availability of any supported sensors using the isXXXAvailable() functions in KetaiSensor. Let's combine our previous examples into a single sketch that reads and displays accelerometer and gyroscope data, but only if the device has these sensors. Generally, almost all Android phones come with an accelerometer, but cheaper entry-level devices often lack a gyro.

Listing 7-7 includes the sensor availability code in the setup() function and displays the accelerometer and gyroscope values graphically using bars whose length represents the magnitude of the sensor values (Figure 7-5). It is inspired by a more comprehensive example created by Tiago Martins, who also wrote several other sketches illustrating the use of sensors in Processing (https://github.com/tms-martins/processing-androidExamples).

Listing 7-7. Checking Sensor Availability with Ketai

```
import ketai.sensors.*;

KetaiSensor sensor;
boolean hasAccel = false;
boolean hasGyro = false;
PVector dataAccel = new PVector();
PVector dataGyro = new PVector();

void setup() {
  fullScreen();
  sensor = new KetaiSensor(this);
  sensor.start();

  if (sensor.isAccelerometerAvailable()) {
    hasAccel = true;
    println("Device has accelerometer");
  }
  if (sensor.isGyroscopeAvailable()) {
    hasGyro = true;
    println("Device has gyroscope");
  }

  noStroke();
}
```

```
void draw() {
  background(255);
  float h = height/6;
  float y = 0;
  translate(width/2, 0);
  if (hasAccel) {
    fill(#C63030);
    rect(0, y, map(dataAccel.x, -10, +10, -width/2, +width/2), h);
    y += h;
    rect(0, y, map(dataAccel.y, -10, +10, -width/2, +width/2), h);
    y += h;
    rect(0, y, map(dataAccel.z, -10, +10, -width/2, +width/2), h);
    y += h;
  }
  if (hasGyro) {
    fill(#30C652);
    rect(0, y, map(dataGyro.x, -10, +10, -width/2, +width/2), h);
    y += h;
    rect(0, y, map(dataGyro.y, -10, +10, -width/2, +width/2), h);
    y += h;
    rect(0, y, map(dataGyro.z, -10, +10, -width/2, +width/2), h);
  }
}

void onAccelerometerEvent(float x, float y, float z) {
  dataAccel.set(x, y, z);
}

void onGyroscopeEvent(float x, float y, float z) {
  dataGyro.set(x, y, z);
}
```

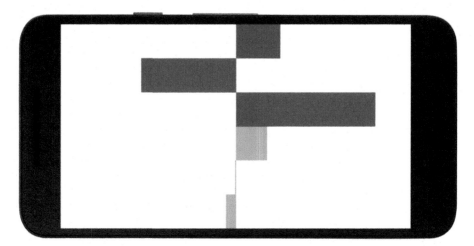

Figure 7-5. *Showing values from the accelerometer and the gyroscope*

Summary

This chapter gave us a foundation for using sensor data in our Processing sketches, either through the Android API or with the Ketai library. In the next chapters, we will build on these techniques to create graphics and interactions that are driven by the movement or location of our device.

CHAPTER 8

■ ■ ■

Driving Graphics and Sound with Sensor Data

With the basics of reading sensor data already covered in the previous chapter, we will now see how to use data from the accelerometer, magnetometer, and gyroscope to generate interactive graphics and sound in our Processing sketches.

Using Ketai to Read Sensor Data

The sensors available in an Android device give us plenty of data about the surroundings of the device. We saw how we can retrieve this data by using either the Android API or the Ketai library, the latter of which makes sensor handling easier. Once the data is available as numerical values inside our sketch, we can use it in any way we want to drive the animations and interactions in the code.

In this chapter, we will focus on three specific sensors that provide immediate feedback on the movement and position state of our device: the accelerometer (and the derived step counter), the magnetic field sensor, and the gyroscope. With the data from these sensors, our Android sketches will be able to react to a wide range of movements detected by the device: sudden shaking, walking, rotation in space, and orientation with respect to the Earth's magnetic field.

We will use Ketai to read the sensor data, since it simplifies the code by eliminating the need to define event listeners and sensor managers. However, all the examples in this chapter can be adapted to use the Android API without much difficulty.

Measuring Acceleration

Acceleration is the rate of change of velocity with respect to time, but the acceleration values returned by Android also include acceleration due to gravity, which is directed toward the ground and has a magnitude of 9.8 m/s^2. If our phone is placed completely at rest on a table, with its screen facing up, its acceleration would read a = (0, 0, -9.8), since it includes gravity along the negative direction of the z-axis (remember Figure 7-1). But if we rotate our phone around, the acceleration from gravity will be projected along the three axes, depending on the orientation of the phone with respect to the vertical direction.

© Andrés Colubri 2017
A. Colubri, *Processing for Android*, https://doi.org/10.1007/978-1-4842-2719-0_8

Shake Detection

When we shake the phone, we make its velocity change quickly from zero to a high value in a very short time. Consequently, acceleration will be high during that time. We can detect this situation by calculating the magnitude of the acceleration vector and triggering a "shake event" if it is large enough. However, we also need to take into consideration that gravity is already in the acceleration, so its magnitude needs to be at least larger than gravity's magnitude, $9.8 \, m/s^2$. We can do this by comparing the magnitude of the acceleration vector as obtained from Ketai with gravity's constant, deciding that a shake takes place if the former is larger by a pre-defined threshold. This is what we will do in Listing 8-1.

Listing 8-1. Simple Shake-Detection Code

```
import ketai.sensors.*;
import android.hardware.SensorManager;

KetaiSensor sensor;
PVector accel = new PVector();
int shakeTime;

color bColor = color(78, 93, 75);

void setup() {
  fullScreen();
  sensor = new KetaiSensor(this);
  sensor.start();
  textAlign(CENTER, CENTER);
  textSize(displayDensity * 36);
}

void draw() {
  background(bColor);
  text("Accelerometer: \n" +
    "x: " + nfp(accel.x, 1, 3) + "\n" +
    "y: " + nfp(accel.y, 1, 3) + "\n" +
    "z: " + nfp(accel.z, 1, 3), 0, 0, width, height);
}

void onAccelerometerEvent(float x, float y, float z) {
  accel.set(x, y, z);
  int now = millis();
  if (now - shakeTime > 250) {
    if (1.2 * SensorManager.GRAVITY_EARTH < accel.mag()) {
      bColor = color(216, 100, 46);
      shakeTime = now;
    } else {
      bColor = color(78, 93, 75);
    }
  }
}
```

The condition that checks for a shake is 1.2 * SensorManager.GRAVITY_EARTH < accel.mag()). Here, we are using 1.2 as the threshold for the shake detection, and we can use a smaller or larger value to detect weaker or stronger shakes. The SensorManager class from the Sensor API in Android becomes handy as it contains a constant, GRAVITY_ EARTH, that represents Earth's gravity acceleration (there are similar constants for all the planets in the solar system, plus the moon, the sun, and the fictional Death Star). The time condition is in place so our app cannot trigger more than one shake every 250 milliseconds.

Step Counter

With the case of shake detection, we only had to recognize a single event characterized by the magnitude of the acceleration. In the case of detecting steps when walking or running, the problem is harder: it is not enough to recognize a single change in acceleration when we make one step, but rather we need to note a regular pattern through time, as shown in Figure 8-1.

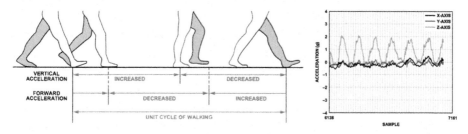

Figure 8-1. *Acceleration pattern during the walking stages (left), and acceleration data corresponding to a series of steps (right). Reproduced with permission from Neil Zhao*

However, this pattern does not follow a perfect curve, because it is affected by signal noise and irregularities in the walking pace. Furthermore, it is different from person to person, depending on their gait. While it is not too hard to figure out an algorithm capable of detecting steps from the raw accelerometer data, Android takes care of this problem by providing a new type of sensor in version 4.4 (KitKat): the step counter. This sensor does the analysis of the accelerometer input for us. It triggers an new event with each step, so we can count steps in any interval of time we wish. A very simple step of a step-detection sketch in Processing is described in Listing 8-2.

Listing 8-2. Using Android's Step Counter

```
import ketai.sensors.*;

KetaiSensor sensor;
color bColor = color(78, 93, 75);
int stepTime = 0;
int stepCount = 0;

void setup() {
  fullScreen();
  orientation(PORTRAIT);
  sensor = new KetaiSensor(this);
  sensor.start();
  textAlign(CENTER, CENTER);
  textSize(displayDensity * 24);
}

void draw() {
  if (millis() - stepTime > 500) {
    bColor = color(78, 93, 75);
  }
  background(bColor);
  text("Number of steps = " + stepCount, 0, 0, width, height);
}

void onStepDetectorEvent() {
  bColor = color(216, 100, 46);
  stepTime = millis();
  stepCount++;
}
```

Ketai has another function, onStepCounterEvent(float s), where we receive in the variable s, the total number of steps since the device was rebooted. This can be useful if we need to track the total number of steps throughout the day without missing the activity while the app is not running.

Audio-Visual Mapping of Step Data

As we just saw, it is very easy to count individual steps using the step-detector event in Ketai. How to use this step-count data in our Processing sketch is a question that we can answer only after considering what our final goal is; for example, showing a "utilitarian" visualization of physical activity, creating a more abstract representation of this activity, driving some background graphics (and/or audio) that we can use as a live wallpaper, and so on.

It is up to us to determine how we would map the sensor data into visual or sound elements. For the purpose of illustrating how to carry out this mapping, we will work on a sketch where each new step triggers a simple animation of a colored circle showing up on the screen and fading back into the background, so the end result would be a geometric pattern that responds to our walk.

We could start writing some initial sketches in Java mode to refine the visual concept before moving on to Android mode. One possible approach would be to work with a rectangular grid on which we place the colored dots at random. It could be useful to define a class to hold the animation logic of the dots, as well as to use an array list to keep track of a variable number of dots while the sketch is running. All of these ideas are implemented in Listing 8-3.

Listing 8-3. Random Colored Dots

```
float minSize = 50;
float maxSize = 100;
ArrayList<ColorDot> dots;

void setup() {
  size(800, 480);
  colorMode(HSB, 360, 100, 100, 100);
  noStroke();
  dots = new ArrayList<ColorDot>();
}

void draw() {
  background(0, 0, 0);

  if (random(1) < 0.1) {
    dots.add(new ColorDot());
  }

  for (int i = dots.size() - 1; i >= 0 ; i--) {
    ColorDot d = dots.get(i);
    d.update();
    d.display();
    if (d.colorAlpha < 1) {
      dots.remove(i);
    }
  }
}

class ColorDot {
  float posX, posY;
  float rad, maxRad;
  float colorHue, colorAlpha;
```

```
ColorDot() {
  posX = int(random(1, width/maxSize)) * maxSize;
  posY = int(random(1, height/maxSize)) * maxSize;
  rad = 0.1;
  maxRad = random(minSize, maxSize);
  colorHue = random(0, 360);
  colorAlpha = 70;
}

void update() {
  if (rad < maxRad) {
    rad *= 1.5;
  } else {
    colorAlpha -= 0.3;
  }
}

void display() {
  fill(colorHue, 100, 100, colorAlpha);
  ellipse(posX, posY, rad, rad);
  }
}
```

Here, we used the HSB space to pick a random color from along the entire spectrum while keeping the saturation and brightness fixed. The dots animate by growing in size quickly (with the rad *= 1.5 update of the radius) and then fade out by decreasing the alpha with colorAlpha -= 0.3 until they become completely transparent, which is when they are removed. New dots are added with a probability of 0.1 in each frame. After tweaking these values, we should get an output similar to Figure 8-2.

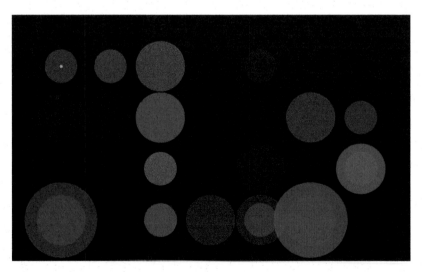

Figure 8-2. *Output of the initial sketch that generates random dots, running from Java mode*

The next step is connecting the dot animation with the step detection. An easy way to achieve this could be to create a new dot every time a step-detector event is triggered. So, we would need to add the Ketai library to our previous code and then create the dots in the onStepDetectorEvent() event, which is shown in Listing 8-4.

Listing 8-4. Using Steps to Animate the Dots

```
import ketai.sensors.*;

KetaiSensor sensor;

float minSize = 150 * displayDensity;
float maxSize = 300 * displayDensity;
ArrayList<ColorDot> dots;

void setup() {
  fullScreen();
  orientation(LANDSCAPE);
  colorMode(HSB, 360, 100, 100, 100);
  noStroke();
  dots = new ArrayList<ColorDot>();
  sensor = new KetaiSensor(this);
  sensor.start();
}

void draw() {
  background(0, 0, 0);
  for (int i = dots.size() - 1; i >= 0 ; i--) {
    ColorDot d = dots.get(i);
    d.update();
    d.display();
    if (d.colorAlpha < 1) {
      dots.remove(i);
    }
  }
}

class ColorDot {
  float posX, posY;
  float rad, maxRad;
  float colorHue, colorAlpha;

  ColorDot() {
    posX = int(random(1, width/maxSize)) * maxSize;
    posY = int(random(1, height/maxSize)) * maxSize;
    rad = 0.1;
    maxRad = random(minSize, maxSize);
```

```
    colorHue = random(0, 360);
    colorAlpha = 70;
  }

  void update() {
    if (rad < maxRad) {
      rad *= 1.5;
    } else {
      colorAlpha -= 0.1;
    }
  }

  void display() {
    fill(colorHue, 100, 100, colorAlpha);
    ellipse(posX, posY, rad, rad);
  }
}

void onStepDetectorEvent() {
  dots.add(new ColorDot());
}
```

Notice how the minimum and maximum sizes of the dots are now scaled by displayDensity, so the output of our sketch preserves its proportions irrespective of the DPI of the screen's device. We can run this sketch as either a regular app or a live wallpaper, in case we want to have it running the entire time and driving the background image in our home screen.

It is possible to refine this sketch in different ways. For example, we could decrease randomness in the size and color of the dots by linking these parameters to the time and the walking speed. To calculate the latter, we could reset the step-count variable to zero at some fixed interval—say, every five seconds—and divide the count value by the time elapsed since the last reset (since speed=difference in value /difference in time). Listing 8-5 includes the additional variables we need to store the current walking speed, the time of the last update, and the step count, as well as the differences in the calculation of the dot radius and hue (the rest being identical to Listing 8-4).

Listing 8-5. Using Time and Walking Speed to Control Animation

```
import ketai.sensors.*;

KetaiSensor sensor;

float minSize = 150 * displayDensity;
float maxSize = 300 * displayDensity;
ArrayList<ColorDot> dots;
```

```
int stepCount = 0;
int updateTime = 0;
float walkSpeed = 0;
...
class ColorDot {
  float posX, posY;
  float rad, maxRad;
  float colorHue, colorAlpha;

  ColorDot() {
    posX = int(random(1, width/maxSize)) * maxSize;
    posY = int(random(1, height/maxSize)) * maxSize;
    rad = 0.1;
    float speedf = constrain(walkSpeed, 0, 2)/2.0;
    maxRad = map(speedf, 1, 0, minSize, maxSize);
    colorHue = map(second(), 0, 60, 0, 360);
    colorAlpha = 70;
  }
  ...
}

void onStepDetectorEvent() {
  int now = millis();
  stepCount++;
  if (5000 < now - updateTime) {
    walkSpeed = stepCount/5.0;
    stepCount = 0;
    updateTime = now;
  }
  dots.add(new ColorDot());
}
```

If we inspect the calculation of the radius in the constructor of the ColorDot class, we can see that the value in walkSpeed is not used directly, but rather is first constrained to the 0-2 steps/second range with the function constrain() and then normalized so we have a value between 0 and 1 that we can consistently map onto the radius range maxSize-minSize. This implies that the faster we walk, the smaller the dots should appear. The hue of the dots is also the result of a mapping, in this case the current second obtained with the second() function to the 0-360 hue range.

Playing Audio

So far, all the examples in this book have been purely visual, with no audio component. However, the dots sketch could make use of sound to complement the walk-driven animation. One option is to just play random audio clips each time a step is detected, but perhaps we can do something a little more interesting by playing notes from a musical scale.

To keep things simple, let's consider a pentatonic scale (http://www.musictheoryis.com/pentatonic-scale/) with notes A, G, E, D, and C. If we always play these notes in their natural order, we will hear the original scale over and over again, and the result would be fairly repetitive. At the other extreme, choosing a note at random would be too chaotic. So, we could try an intermediate solution that has enough variability while retaining the harmony of the scale; for example, by playing either the previous or next note to the current one, giving each choice a predefined probability. How do we go about implementing this idea?

First of all, as with sensors, Processing does not include any built-in functions for audio playback. However, we can use the Android API to create a minimal AudioPlayer class that extends Android's MediaPlayer. We then need to obtain audio clips for our five notes and copy them into the sketch's data folder.

■ **Note** Android supports several audio formats, including MP3, WAVE, MIDI, and Vorbis. Refer to the media formats page on the development site for a full list of media formats and codecs: https://developer.android.com/guide/topics/media/media-formats.html.

Listing 8-6 combines our previous colored dot sketch with an AudioPlayer class and the simple logic we discussed previously to pick which note to play (only the parts of the code that differ from Listing 8-5 are shown).

Listing 8-6. Playing a Pentatonic Scale by Walking

```
import ketai.sensors.*;
import android.media.MediaPlayer;
import android.content.res.AssetFileDescriptor;
import android.media.AudioManager;

KetaiSensor sensor;
...
int numNotes = 5;
AudioPlayer [] notes = new AudioPlayer[numNotes];
int lastNote = int(random(1) * 4);

void setup() {
  fullScreen();
  orientation(LANDSCAPE);
  colorMode(HSB, 360, 100, 100, 100);
  noStroke();
  for (int i = 0; i < numNotes; i++) notes[i] = new AudioPlayer();
  notes[0].loadFile(this, "5A.wav");
  notes[1].loadFile(this, "4G.wav");
  notes[2].loadFile(this, "4E.wav");
  notes[3].loadFile(this, "4D.wav");
  notes[4].loadFile(this, "4C.wav");
```

```
  dots = new ArrayList<ColorDot>();
  sensor = new KetaiSensor(this);
  sensor.start();
}
...
class ColorDot {
  float posX, posY;
  float rad, maxRad;
float colorHue, colorAlpha;
int note;

  ColorDot() {
    posX = int(random(1, width/maxSize)) * maxSize;
    posY = int(random(1, height/maxSize)) * maxSize;
    rad = 0.1;
    float speedf = constrain(walkSpeed, 0, 2)/2.0;
    maxRad = map(speedf, 1, 0, minSize, maxSize);
    selectNote();
    colorHue = map(note, 0, 4, 0, 360);
    colorAlpha = 70;
  }

  void selectNote() {
    float r = random(1);
    note = lastNote;
    if (r < 0.4) note--;
    else if (r > 0.6) note++;
    if (note < 0) note = 1;
    if (4 < note) note = 3;
    notes[note].play();
    lastNote = note;
  }
  ...
}
...
class AudioPlayer extends MediaPlayer {
  boolean loadFile(PApplet app, String fileName) {
    AssetFileDescriptor desc;
    try {
      desc = app.getActivity().getAssets().openFd(fileName);
    } catch (IOException e) {
      println("Error loading " + fileName);
      println(e.getMessage());
      return false;
    }
```

```
    if (desc == null) {
      println("Cannot find " + fileName);
      return false;
    }

    try {
      setDataSource(desc.getFileDescriptor(), desc.getStartOffset(),
                    desc.getLength());
      setAudioStreamType(AudioManager.STREAM_MUSIC);
      prepare();
      return true;
    } catch (IOException e) {
      println(e.getMessage());
      return false;
    }
  }

  void play() {
    if (isPlaying()) seekTo(0);
    start();
  }
}
```

We load each note in a separate instance of the AudioPlayer class and store the five AudioPlayer objects in the notes array. We initialize this array in setup(), then implement the selection logic in the new selectNote() method in the ColorDot class, using 0.4 as the probability for selecting the preceding note in the scale, and 0.6 for selecting the next. Figure 8-3 shows the output of this sketch, but, of course, we need to run it on an actual device to appreciate its audio component as we walk around.

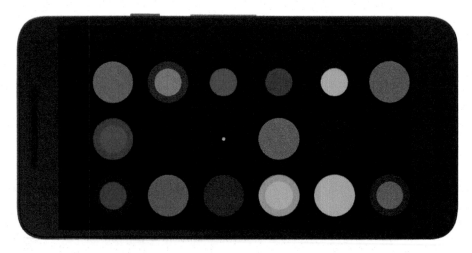

Figure 8-3. *Dots sketch running on the device*

Using the Magnetic Sensor

The magnetic sensor (or magnetometer) is another very common sensor we find in Android devices, which is useful for several applications. For example, Listing 8-7 shows how we can use it to detect the proximity of a metal object by comparing the measured magnitude of the magnetic field with the expected magnitude of Earth's magnetic field at our present location. If we ran this sketch on our phone, we would be effectively turning it into a metal detector!

Listing 8-7. Detecting the Strength of the Magnetic Field

```
import ketai.sensors.*;
import android.hardware.GeomagneticField;

KetaiSensor sensor;
float expMag, obsMag;

void setup() {
  fullScreen();
  sensor = new KetaiSensor(this);
  sensor.start();
  GeomagneticField geoField = new GeomagneticField(14.0093, 120.996147, 300,
                              System.currentTimeMillis());
  expMag = geoField.getFieldStrength()/1000;
}

void draw() {
  println(obsMag, expMag);
  if (obsMag < 0.7 * expMag || 1.3 * expMag < obsMag) {
    background(255);
  } else {
    background(0);
  }
}

void onMagneticFieldEvent(float x, float y, float z) {
  obsMag = sqrt(sq(x) + sq(y) + sq(z));
}
```

Note that we have to provide the geographical coordinates of our current location expressed as latitude and longitude in degrees and altitude in meters, as well as the so-called Epoch Time (current time expressed as milliseconds since January 1, 1970), to the GeomagneticField() constructor in order to obtain the field due solely to the Earth's magnetic field. We can then perform the comparison with the actual magnetic field measured by the device.

Creating a Compass App

Besides being used to implement a handy metal detector, combining the magnetic field data with the acceleration can be used to determine the orientation of the device with respect to Earth's magnetic North Pole. In other words, a compass.

The gravity and geomagnetic vectors encode all the information required to determine the orientation of the device in relation to Earth's surface. Using Ketai, we can get the components of the acceleration and magnetic field vectors and, with those, obtain the rotation matrix that transforms coordinates from the device system (Figure 7-1) to a world coordinate system that we can imagine attached to our location on the surface of Earth, as illustrated in Figure 8-4.

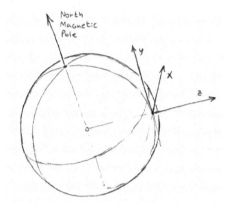

Figure 8-4. *World coordinate system, with x pointing east, y pointing north, and z away from Earth's center*

The final step is to derive, from the rotation matrix, the orientation angles with respect to these xyz axes: azimuth (the angle around –z), pitch (the angle around x), and roll (the angle around y). For the purpose of implementing a compass, we only need the azimuth angle, since it gives us the deviation with respect to the y-axis pointing north at our location. The SensorManager class from the Android API contains several convenient methods to carry out all these calculations, which we perform in Listing 8-8.

Listing 8-8. A Compass Sketch

```
import ketai.sensors.*;
import android.hardware.SensorManager;

KetaiSensor sensor;

float[] gravity = new float[3];
float[] geomagnetic = new float[3];
float[] I = new float[16];
float[] R = new float[16];
float orientation[] = new float[3];
```

```
float easing = 0.05;
float azimuth;

void setup() {
  fullScreen(P2D);
  orientation(PORTRAIT);
  sensor = new KetaiSensor(this);
  sensor.start();
}

void draw() {
  background(255);

  float cx = width * 0.5;
  float cy = height * 0.4;
  float radius = 0.8 * cx;

  translate(cx, cy);

  noFill();
  stroke(0);
  strokeWeight(2);
  ellipse(0, 0, radius*2, radius*2);
  line(0, -cy, 0, -radius);

  fill(192, 0, 0);
  noStroke();
  rotate(-azimuth);
  beginShape();
  vertex(-30, 40);
  vertex(0, 0);
  vertex(30, 40);
  vertex(0, -radius);
  endShape();
}

void onAccelerometerEvent(float x, float y, float z) {
  gravity[0] = x; gravity[1] = y; gravity[2] = z;
  calculateOrientation();
}

void onMagneticFieldEvent(float x, float y, float z) {
  geomagnetic[0] = x; geomagnetic[1] = y; geomagnetic[2] = z;
  calculateOrientation();
}
```

```
void calculateOrientation() {
  if (SensorManager.getRotationMatrix(R, I, gravity, geomagnetic)) {
    SensorManager.getOrientation(R, orientation);
    azimuth += easing * (orientation[0] - azimuth);
  }
}
```

By providing the acceleration and magnetic field vectors to the getRotationMatrix() and getOrientation() methods in SensorManager, we will obtain an orientation vector containing the azimuth, pitch, and roll angles. In this example, we only use the azimuth to draw the compass, which we can install as a live wallpaper so it is always available in the background (shown in Figure 8-5).

Figure 8-5. *Compass sketch running as a live wallpaper*

The values from both the accelerometer and the magnetometer are noisy, so that's the reason we apply some "easing" of the values with the line azimuth += easing * (orientation[0] - azimuth). With this formula, we update the current azimuth value with a fraction of the new value so changes are softer and noise is smoothed out. The closer to 0 the easing constant is, the stronger the smoothing and more dampened the movement of the compass' hand. On the other end, an easing value of 1 will result in no smoothing at all, since it is equivalent to assigning the new sensor value azimuth = orientation[0].

Alternatively, we can get the orientation vector directly from Ketai without having to rely on the SensorManager class from Android. To do so, we first have to enable the accelerometer and magnetic field sensors explicitly in setup() (since we will not be using Ketai's event functions), and we can then just call getOrientation() from the KetaiSensor object in draw(), as shown in Listing 8-9. The output of this modified version of the sketch should be the same as before.

Listing 8-9. Using Ketai's getOrientation() Function

```
import ketai.sensors.*;

float orientation[] = new float[3];
float easing = 0.05;
float azimuth;

KetaiSensor sensor;

void setup() {
  fullScreen(P2D);
  orientation(PORTRAIT);
  sensor = new KetaiSensor(this);
  sensor.enableAccelerometer();
  sensor.enableMagenticField();
  sensor.start();
}

void draw() {
  ...
  ellipse(0, 0, radius*2, radius*2);
  line(0, -cy, 0, -radius);

  sensor.getOrientation(orientation);
  azimuth += easing * (orientation[0] - azimuth);

  fill(192, 0, 0);
  noStroke();
  ...
}
```

The Gyroscope

The gyroscope can complement the accelerometer and magnetometer, but could also be applied in situations that are not handled by those sensors. The accelerometer and magnetometer give us data about the movement and orientation of the device in space; however, they have limitations. The accelerometer, on one hand, is not able to detect movements at constant speed, since in such cases the acceleration is zero, while the magnetic sensor, on the other hand, only gives a very coarse variable related to the location (i.e., orientation with respect to Earth's magnetic field). Also, both sensors return values with a significant amount of noise.

The gyroscope, in contrast, gives us a precise reading of the angular velocity at which the device is rotating in space. With this velocity, it is possible to infer the orientation of the device with respect to an arbitrary initial state. This is to say, it cannot give us an absolute description of its orientation with respect to a system such as the world coordinates we discussed before. However, this information can be inferred with help from the accelerometer and magnetometer.

Let's look at a few simple examples to get a sense of how the gyroscope works. Since it provides values that we apply use to control 3D movement in our Processing sketch, it makes sense to write a very simple 3D sketch. With Ketai, it is easy to obtain the rotational angles from the gyroscope, as we did for the other sensors earlier. We will use the P3D renderer in Listing 8-10 to draw a simple 3D scene with a cube that rotates around its center according to the angular velocity measured by the gyroscope.

Listing 8-10. Rotating a Box with the Gyroscope

```
import ketai.sensors.*;

KetaiSensor sensor;
float rotationX, rotationY, rotationZ;

void setup() {
  fullScreen(P3D);
  orientation(LANDSCAPE);
  sensor = new KetaiSensor(this);
  sensor.start();
  rectMode(CENTER);
  fill(180);
}

void draw() {
  background(255);
  translate(width/2, height/2);
  rotateZ(rotationZ);
  rotateY(rotationX);
  rotateX(rotationY);
  box(height * 0.3);
}
```

```
void onGyroscopeEvent(float x, float y, float z) {
    rotationX += 0.1 * x;
    rotationY += 0.1 * y;
    rotationZ += 0.1 * z;
}
```

Since the x, y, and z values are (angular) velocities, we cannot use them directly as the rotation angles of the objects in our scene, but we should instead add them to the rotation variables (scaled by a constant that in this case is 0.1, but can be adjusted to make the movement slower or faster). Moreover, we apply the rotationX angle with the rotateY() function (meaning that we are rotating the cube around the y-axis), and rotationY with rotateX(). The reason for this switch is that the orientation of the device is locked in LANDSCAPE, meaning that the x-axis in the Processing screen corresponds to the horizontal direction of the device, which runs along the y-axis of the device's coordinate system, which we saw in Figure 7-1.

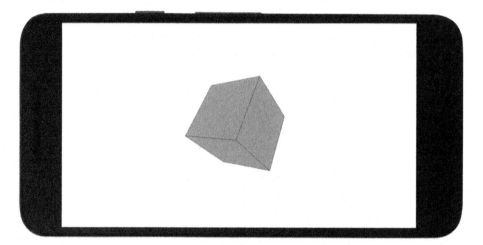

Figure 8-6. *Sketch using the gyroscope to control rotation of a cube*

Another important aspect of using the gyroscope is that any rotation involving the device will be measured by the sensor; for example, it will detect when the person holding the phone turns around while walking (even if the relative orientation of the phone with respect to the user does not change). In such cases, we can keep the initial orientation by subtracting an offset value any time we want to "re-center" the scene on our phone. For instance, we can store the current rotation angles as our offset when touching the screen, as is done in Listing 8-11 (only showing the parts that are different from Listing 8-10).

Listing 8-11. Recentering the Gyroscope Data

```
...
void draw() {
  background(255);
  translate(width/2, height/2);
  rotateZ(rotationZ - offsetZ);
  rotateY(rotationX - offsetX);
  rotateX(rotationY - offsetY);
  box(height * 0.3);
}
...
void mousePressed() {
  offsetX = rotationX;
  offsetY = rotationY;
  offsetZ = rotationZ;
}
```

We are not limited to working with 3D geometry when using the gyroscope. If we are drawing in 2D, all we need to do is keep track of the z rotation, like in Listing 8-12.

Listing 8-12. Gyroscope Rotation in 2D

```
import ketai.sensors.*;

KetaiSensor sensor;
float rotationZ, offsetZ;

void setup() {
  fullScreen(P2D);
  orientation(LANDSCAPE);
  sensor = new KetaiSensor(this);
  sensor.start();
  rectMode(CENTER);
  fill(180);
}

void draw() {
  background(255);
  translate(width/2, height/2);
  rotate(rotationZ - offsetZ);
  rect(0, 0, height * 0.3, height * 0.3);
}

void onGyroscopeEvent(float x, float y, float z) {
  rotationZ += 0.1 * z;
}

void mousePressed() {
  offsetZ = rotationZ;
}
```

The gyroscope can be useful for implementing input in a game app. We will see how to do that in the final section of this chapter.

Controlling Navigation with the Gyroscope

In the previous examples, we used the rotation angles to control 2D and 3D shapes that remained fixed in the center of the screen. This would be enough if we needed to control only the rotation of the shapes, but if we want to determine their translation as well, we need to come up with other methods.

In fact, one approach is to not translate the shapes we want to control with the gyro, but rather to translate the rest of the scene in the opposite direction. The diagram in Figure 8-7 helps to visualize this idea. Here, we will write a sketch to navigate a "spaceship" (just a triangle shape) through an endless field of asteroids (ellipses). The key is to properly code for the translation of all the ellipses, in order to convey the relative movement of the spaceship with respect to the asteroids.

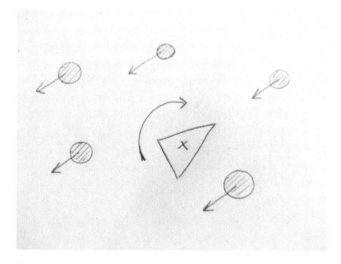

Figure 8-7. *Diagram on relative translations of moving objects*

The math to achieve this effect is not difficult: if our shape is initially moving toward the top edge of the screen, the forward vector describing this movement would be v = new PVector(0, -1), since the y-axis in Processing points down. We can calculate a matrix that represents the rotation that should be applied on this vector. The resulting vector can be used to translate all the other shapes in the scene to create the relative motion.

The Processing API includes a PMatrix2D class that encapsulates these calculations. If our rotation angle is, for example, QUARTER_PI, we can generate a rotation matrix corresponding to this rotation by doing mat.rotate(QUARTER_PI), with mat being an object of type PMatrix3D. Once we have done this, we can apply the matrix to the PVector object representing the translation; e.g., mat.mult(v, rv), where v is the original PVector and rv is the resulting rotated PVector. Let's see this API in Listing 8-13.

Listing 8-13. Controlling a Spaceship with the Gyroscope

```
import ketai.sensors.*;

KetaiSensor sensor;
float rotationZ, offsetZ;
PMatrix2D rotMatrix = new PMatrix2D();
PVector forward = new PVector(0, -1);
PVector forwardRot = new PVector();
ArrayList<Asteroid> field;
float speed = 2;

void setup() {
  fullScreen(P2D);
  orientation(LANDSCAPE);
  sensor = new KetaiSensor(this);
  sensor.start();
  ellipseMode(CENTER);
  noStroke();
  field = new ArrayList<Asteroid>();
  for (int i = 0; i < 100; i++) {
    field.add(new Asteroid());
  }
}

void draw() {
  background(0);

  boolean hit = false;
  float angle = rotationZ - offsetZ;
  rotMatrix.reset();
  rotMatrix.rotate(angle);
  rotMatrix.mult(forward, forwardRot);
  forwardRot.mult(speed);
  for (Asteroid a: field) {
    a.update(forwardRot);
    a.display();
    if (a.hit(width/2, height/2)) hit = true;
  }
```

```
  pushMatrix();
  translate(width/2, height/2);
  rotate(angle);
  if (hit) {
    fill(252, 103, 43);
  } else {
    fill(67, 125, 222);
  }
  float h = height * 0.2;
  triangle(0, -h/2, h/3, +h/2, -h/3, +h/2);
  popMatrix();
}

void onGyroscopeEvent(float x, float y, float z) {
  rotationZ += 0.1 * z;
}

void mousePressed() {
  offsetZ = rotationZ;
}

class Asteroid {
  float x, y, r;
  color c;
  Asteroid() {
    c = color(random(255), random(255), random(255));
    r = height * random(0.05, 0.1);
    x = random(-2 * width, +2 * width);
    y = random(-2 * height, +2 * height);
  }
  void update(PVector v) {
    x -= v.x;
    y -= v.y;
    if (x < -2 * width || 2 * width < x ||
        y < -2 * height || 2 * height < y) {
      x = random(-2 * width, +2 * width);
      y = random(-2 * height, +2 * height);
    }
  }
  void display() {
    fill(c);
    ellipse(x, y, r, r);
  }
  boolean hit(float sx, float sy) {
    return dist(x, y, sx, sy) < r;
  }
}
```

As we can see in this code, the spaceship is always drawn at the center of the screen, and it is the asteroids that are translated by the rotated forward vector, as we discussed earlier. The Asteroid class contains all the logic that handles placing each asteroid at a random position, updating its position using the rotated forward vector, displaying it at the current position, and determining if it is hitting the spaceship by checking if it is close enough to the center of the screen.

Each asteroid is placed in a rectangular area of dimensions [-2 * width, +2 * width] × [-2 * height, +2 * height], and as soon as it moves out of this area (which is determined by the boundary check in the update() function), it's placed back inside again. Also, notice the minus sign in the translations along x and y, -v.x, and -v.y, which ensures the correct relative motion. We can think of the forward vector as the velocity of our spaceship, and in fact by scaling it by the speed factor (set to 2 in this sketch), we can make the spaceship move faster or slower.

Finally, we implemented a simple collision detection element so that the spaceship changes color when an asteroid gets close to its position at the center of the screen. We can imagine multiple ways to turn this early prototype into a more engaging game by adding interaction to control the speed, better graphics with images and SVG shapes, and so on. In its initial form, the output should look similar to Figure 8-8.

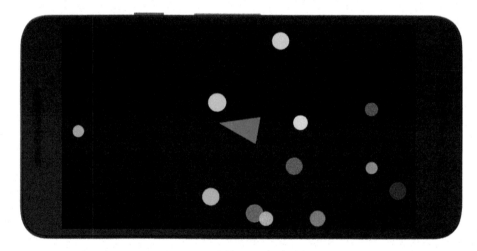

Figure 8-8. *Controlling the navigation through a field of obstacles with the gyroscope*

Summary

Building upon the basic techniques to read sensor data in Processing, we have now learned some advanced applications of three common hardware sensors: the accelerometer, the magnetometer, and the gyroscope. These sensors are particularly important because they provide instant feedback on the movement and position of our device and so enable us to create interactive apps based on physical gestures and actions. We will find these interactions very useful in a wide range of projects, from visualizing physical activity to coding our own game experiences with graphics and sound.

CHAPTER 9

Geolocation

The geolocation sensors in our Android devices give us the ability to know where we are with high accuracy, and we can use this information in location-aware apps. In this chapter, we will see how to create this type of app in Processing, and we will develop a final project combining location with images from Google Street View.

Location Data in Android

We use location-aware apps in our smartphones on a daily basis to find places of interest around us, to plan travel directions in advance, or to play location-based games, like Turf and Pokémon GO. All these uses are made possible by the same underlying geolocation technology, mainly the global positioning system (GPS), but also cell-tower triangulation, Bluetooth proximity detection, and Wi-Fi access points. GPS is the technology that most people immediately associate with geolocation: it is based on a network of satellites owned by the United States and operated by the United States Air Force that send geolocation information to GPS receivers on Earth's surface, including those in a mobile phone.

 Note   Other countries have also developed similar systems, such as GLONASS (Russia), BeiDou (China), NAVIC (India), and Galileo (Europe). By default, the Android system only uses GPS satellites, but some manufacturers introduced changes to get geolocation data from these other systems as well, which can provide better coverage and accuracy. The GPS Test app, available in the Play Store, shows the systems in use by the phone.

One drawback of using GPS or a comparable navigation satellite system to get location data is that it draws a lot of battery to power the GPS antenna. Also, the phone needs to have an unobstructed line of sight to the sky. To deal with these issues, we can take advantage of other location sources, such as Cell-ID, Bluetooth, and Wi-Fi, which are less precise but consume less energy. As a reference, the accuracy of GPS location is around 16 feet (4.9 meters), while Wi-Fi is accurate to within 130 feet (40 meters). Cell-ID has a much higher degree of variability, depending on cell size, which can range from a few feet to miles.

© Andrés Colubri 2017
A. Colubri, *Processing for Android*, https://doi.org/10.1007/978-1-4842-2719-0_9

However, we don't need to worry about when and how to choose a particular location system, as Android will automatically switch between the best location provider given a general configuration in the settings of the phone, seen in Figure 9-1. In Android 7 and higher, all we have to do is to set whether we want high-accuracy location by combining all possible sources, battery saving without GPS, or GPS only.

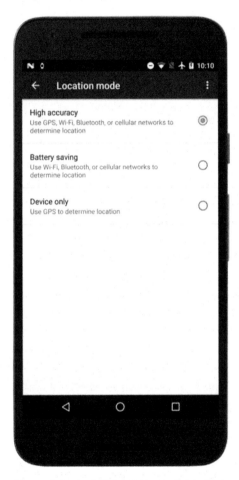

Figure 9-1. *Android settings to choose the location mode*

Using Location API in Processing

Android provides a comprehensive API to access the location services available in the system (https://developer.android.com/guide/topics/location/index.html). We can also use the Ketai library to get location values without having to worry about this API, as we did for motion sensors. However, in this chapter we will use the location API directly from our Processing sketch because there are a number of important aspects to consider when using location services, specifically permission handling and concurrency, and it is a good idea to familiarize ourselves with them even if we later use Ketai.

■ **Note** Google Play Services location APIs (`https://developer.android.com/training/location/index.html`) are a newer and more feature-rich alternative to the standard Android location API we will learn in this chapter. However, Processing only supports the latter when coding from the PDE. We can export our sketch as an Android project and then import it from Android Studio to use Google Play Services (see Appendix A for details).

Location Permissions

The use of specific functionality in our Android app, such as accessing the Internet, requires adding the appropriate permissions to our sketch using the Android Permissions Selector. However, we saw in Chapter 6 that this is not enough for dangerous permissions, which need an additional explicit request during runtime in devices running Android 6 or newer. The permissions to access location data fall within this category, and they are ACCESS_COARSE_LOCATION and ACCESS_FINE_LOCATION. The first grants access to an approximate location derived from cell towers and Wi-Fi, while the second enables obtaining location from the GPS. In order to use these permissions in our sketch, we need to check them in the Permissions Selector (Figure 9-2) and then use the requestPermission() function in the code of our sketch.

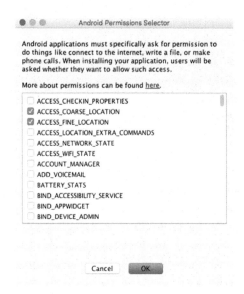

Figure 9-2. *Selecting coarse and fine location permissions*

Listing 9-1 demonstrates the basic setup of a location-enabled sketch, where we define a location manager and the associated listener in a similar manner as we did with other sensors earlier, including setting up the permissions required by the sketch.

Listing 9-1. Getting Location Data

```
import android.content.Context;
import android.location.Location;
import android.location.LocationListener;
import android.location.LocationManager;
import android.os.Bundle;

LocationManager manager;
SimpleListener listener;
String provider;

double currentLatitude;
double currentLongitude;
double currentAltitude;

void setup () {
  fullScreen();
  textFont(createFont("SansSerif", displayDensity * 24));
  textAlign(CENTER, CENTER);
  requestPermission("android.permission.ACCESS_FINE_LOCATION",
  "initLocation");
}

void draw() {
  background(0);
  if (hasPermission("android.permission.ACCESS_FINE_LOCATION")) {
    text("Latitude: " + currentLatitude + "\n" +
         "Longitude: " + currentLongitude + "\n" +
         "Altitude: " + currentAltitude, width, height);
  } else {
    text("No permissions to access location", 0, 0, width, height);
  }
}

void initLocation(boolean granted) {
  if (granted) {
    Context context = getContext();
    listener = new SimpleListener();
    manager = (LocationManager)
                context.getSystemService(Context.LOCATION_SERVICE);
```

```
    provider = LocationManager.NETWORK_PROVIDER;
    if (manager.isProviderEnabled(LocationManager.GPS_PROVIDER)) {
      provider = LocationManager.GPS_PROVIDER;
    }
    manager.requestLocationUpdates(provider, 1000, 1, listener);
  }
}

public void resume() {
  if (manager != null) {
    manager.requestLocationUpdates(provider, 1000, 1, listener);
  }
}

public void pause() {
  if (manager != null) {
    manager.removeUpdates(listener);
  }
}

class SimpleListener implements LocationListener {
  public void onLocationChanged(Location loc) {
    currentLatitude = loc.getLatitude();
    currentLongitude = loc.getLongitude();
    currentAltitude = loc.getAltitude();
  }
  public void onProviderDisabled(String provider) { }
  public void onProviderEnabled(String provider) { }
  public void onStatusChanged(String provider, int status, Bundle extras) {
}
}
```

The location object received in onLocationChanged() contains several pieces of information, the most important of which are the latitude and longitude values that indicate the phone's position on Earth's surface, along the lines parallel to the Equator and the meridian lines that connect the geographical poles.

■ **Note**   Android provides latitude and longitude as double-precision numbers, and the significant digits reflect the precision of the location reading: five significant digits are needed for meter precision, while six or more are required for sub-meter detail.

There are a few more things that are important to note. First, we requested the fine location permission, which will give us the highest resolution available as well as access to less-accurate sources, so there is no need to request separate permission for coarse location. Second, we configured the location manager with requestLocationUpdates()

185

by indicating our preferred provider (network or GPS). Android will determine the actual provider by considering the combination of requested permissions, the location mode of the device, and the available source of location data at each moment. In the code, we set the network provider as the default, which determines location using data from cell towers and Wi-Fi access points, and switch to the more accurate GPS if the corresponding provider is enabled. We also set the minimum time interval between location updates in milliseconds (here 1000 means that updates cannot happen more often than once every second) and the minimum distance, in meters, at which to trigger location updates.

Finally, we implemented the resume and pause events as we did with other sensors, so no location updates are generated while the app is paused, and the app requests them again after resuming. This is very important in order to save battery when the app is running in the background.

Event Threads and Concurrency

In all sensor examples we saw earlier, we read the sensor data in the corresponding listener without major difficulties. As long as we are just storing the last-received data in float variables, we should be fine. However, problems will start as soon as we save sensor information in data structures such as an array or an array list to keep track of previous values. The problem originates from the fact that the draw() function in Processing is called from the animation thread (take a look at the "Using Threads" section in Chapter 6), while the event handling methods, like onLocationChanged() in the case of location, are called from another thread, the app's main thread. Since these threads run in parallel, conflicts could happen when they try to access the same data concurrently; that is, at the same time. This can lead to unexpected behaviors in our app, and even crashes.

As we discussed in Chapter 6, solving concurrency issues requires some extra work. One solution is to store the location data obtained in each call of onLocationChanged() in a "queue" and then retrieve the events from the queue during drawing. The queue is "synchronized" so that when new data is being added or existing data is removed in one thread, any other thread must wait until the operation is concluded. This particular technique would not fix all concurrency problems, but it should be enough in our case. Listing 9-2 shows how we can implement a queue of latitude/longitude locations.

Listing 9-2. Storing Locations in a Queue

```
import android.content.Context;
import android.location.Location;
import android.location.LocationListener;
import android.location.LocationManager;
import android.os.Bundle;

LocationManager manager;
SimpleListener listener;
String provider;
LocationQueue queue = new LocationQueue();
ArrayList<LocationValue> path = new ArrayList<LocationValue>();
```

```
void setup () {
  fullScreen();
  textFont(createFont("SansSerif", displayDensity * 24));
  textAlign(CENTER, CENTER);
  requestPermission("android.permission.ACCESS_FINE_LOCATION",
  "initLocation");
}

void draw() {
  background(0);
  while (queue.available()) {
    LocationValue loc = queue.remove();
    path.add(0, loc);
  }
  String info = "";
  for (LocationValue loc: path) {
    info += loc.latitude + ", " + loc.longitude + "\n";
  }
  text(info, 0, 0, width, height);
}

void initLocation(boolean granted) {
  if (granted) {
    Context context = getContext();
    listener = new SimpleListener();
    manager = (LocationManager)
              context.getSystemService(Context.LOCATION_SERVICE);
    provider = LocationManager.NETWORK_PROVIDER;
    if (manager.isProviderEnabled(LocationManager.GPS_PROVIDER)) {
      provider = LocationManager.GPS_PROVIDER;
    }
    manager.requestLocationUpdates(provider, 1000, 1, listener);
  }
}

class SimpleListener implements LocationListener {
  public void onLocationChanged(Location loc) {
    queue.add(new LocationValue(loc.getLatitude(), loc.getLongitude()));
  }
  public void onProviderDisabled(String provider) { }
  public void onProviderEnabled(String provider) { }
  public void onStatusChanged(String provider, int status, Bundle extras) {
}
}
```

```
public void resume() {
  if (manager != null) {
    manager.requestLocationUpdates(provider, 1000, 1, listener);
  }
}

public void pause() {
  if (manager != null) {
    manager.removeUpdates(listener);
  }
}

class LocationValue {
  double latitude;
  double longitude;
  LocationValue(double lat, double lon) {
    latitude = lat;
    longitude = lon;
  }
}

class LocationQueue {
  LocationValue[] values = new LocationValue[10];
  int offset, count;

  synchronized void add(LocationValue val) {
    if (count == values.length) {
      values = (LocationValue[]) expand(values);
    }
    values[count++] = val;
  }

  synchronized LocationValue remove() {
    if (offset == count) {
      return null;
    }
    LocationValue outgoing = values[offset++];
    if (offset == count) {
      offset = 0;
      count = 0;
    }
    return outgoing;
  }

  synchronized boolean available() {
    return 0 < count;
  }
}
```

The permission and listener setup code is the same as in Listing 9-1, but now we have two new classes, LocationValue and LocationQueue. LocationValue is very simple, it just stores a single pair of latitude/longitude values in double precision. Let's look at LocationQueue more closely. It has three methods: add(), remove(), and available(), all of which are synchronized so they cannot be called simultaneously from different threads. When a new location is received in onLocationChanged(), we create a new LocationValue and add it to the queue. As new locations keep coming in from the event thread, they get stored in the values array inside the queue, which is expanded by doubling its size if needed. On the animation thread, we remove locations from the queue and add them to the path array list so we can print in every frame all the latitude/longitude values received so far, in reverse order from last to first. Notice that we remove the locations from the queue not using how many are to be left, since this number could change if new locations arrive while we are still drawing a new frame, but simply by checking if the queue has available elements.

■ **Note**   We may experience a delay until the app starts receiving location values. This delay is caused by the device's search for a signal from a GPS satellite or from a local cell tower or Wi-Fi access point.

We can now draw the path as a line strip connecting the successive locations. Listing 9-3 shows the new draw() function that does this, with the rest of the sketch being the same. Since we map the latitude and longitude values to positions on the screen, we have to determine the minimum and maximum values to define the mapping. Also, we convert the double-precision values into single-precision floats we can use as arguments in the min(), max(), and map() functions. Figure 9-3 shows a typical output of this sketch as one walks around.

Listing 9-3. Drawing the Locations Along a Line Strip

```
float minLat = 90;
float maxLat = -90;
float minLon = 180;
float maxLon = -180;
...
void draw() {
  background(255);
  while (queue.available()) {
    LocationValue loc = queue.remove();
    minLat = min(minLat, (float)loc.latitude);
    maxLat = max(maxLat, (float)loc.latitude);
    minLon = min(minLon, (float)loc.longitude);
    maxLon = max(maxLon, (float)loc.longitude);
    path.add(0, loc);
  }
```

```
  stroke(70, 200);
  strokeWeight(displayDensity * 4);
  beginShape(LINE_STRIP);
  for (LocationValue loc: path) {
    float x = map((float)loc.longitude, minLon, maxLon,
                                  0.1 * width, 0.9 * width);
    float y = map((float)loc.latitude, minLat, maxLat,
                                  0.1 * height, 0.9 * height);
    vertex(x, y);
  }
  endShape();
}
```

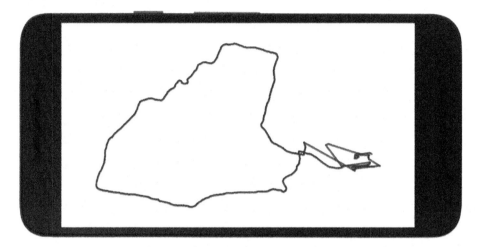

Figure 9-3. *Path-tracking sketch running*

Location with Ketai

The advantage of using Ketai is that all the details we discussed in the previous section (permissions, concurrency) are automatically taken care of, so we can focus on using the location values. The previous example, rewritten using Ketai, is much shorter, as we can see in Listing 9-4.

Listing 9-4. Getting Location Data with Ketai

```
import ketai.sensors.*;

KetaiLocation location;
ArrayList<LocationValue> path = new ArrayList<LocationValue>();

float minLat = 90;
float maxLat = -90;
float minLon = 180;
float maxLon = -180;

void setup () {
  fullScreen();
  location = new KetaiLocation(this);
}

void draw() {
  background(255);
  stroke(70, 200);
  strokeWeight(displayDensity * 4);
  beginShape(LINE_STRIP);
  for (LocationValue loc: path) {
    float x = map((float)loc.longitude, minLon, maxLon,
                                    0.1 * width, 0.9 * width);
    float y = map((float)loc.latitude, minLat, maxLat,
                                    0.1 * height, 0.9 * height);
    vertex(x, y);
  }
  endShape();
}

void onLocationEvent(double lat, double lon) {
  path.add(new LocationValue(lat, lon));
  minLat = Math.min(minLat, (float)lat);
  maxLat = Math.max(maxLat, (float)lat);
  minLon = Math.min(minLon, (float)lon);
  maxLon = Math.max(maxLon, (float)lon);
}

class LocationValue {
  double latitude;
  double longitude;
  LocationValue(double lat, double lon) {
    latitude = lat;
    longitude = lon;
  }
}
```

The onLocationEvent() is triggered by Ketai in the same thread as the draw() function, so there is no risk of running into concurrency issues.

Using Additional Location Data

When our location listener receives a new location in the onLocationChanged() handler method, it is not only the latitude and longitude of the location that become available to us, but also other relevant information, such as altitude, accuracy, and bearing (https://developer.android.com/reference/android/location/Location.html). The accuracy value is important as it reflects the location precision of the current provider. In particular, it would not make sense to store consecutive location values if they differ by less than the current accuracy. We can modify our previous location queue example (Listing 9-3) to incorporate this check. The changes are shown in Listing 9-5.

Listing 9-5. Using Location Accuracy

```
void draw() {
  background(255);
  while (queue.available()) {
    LocationValue loc = queue.remove();
    minLat = min(minLat, (float)loc.latitude);
    maxLat = max(maxLat, (float)loc.latitude);
    minLon = min(minLon, (float)loc.longitude);
    maxLon = max(maxLon, (float)loc.longitude);
    if (0 < path.size()) {
      LocationValue last = path.get(path.size() - 1);
      if (last.distanceTo(loc) < loc.accuracy + last.accuracy) continue;
    }
    path.add(0, loc);
  }
  stroke(70, 200);
  strokeWeight(displayDensity * 4);
  beginShape(LINE_STRIP);
  for (LocationValue loc: path) {
    float x = map((float)loc.longitude, minLon, maxLon,
                                      0.1 * width, 0.9 * width);
    float y = map((float)loc.latitude, minLat, maxLat,
                                      0.1 * height, 0.9 * height);
    vertex(x, y);
  }
  endShape();
}
...
class SimpleListener implements LocationListener {
  public void onLocationChanged(Location loc) {
    queue.add(new LocationValue(loc.getLatitude(), loc.getLongitude(),
                              loc.getAccuracy()));
  }
```

```
  ...
}
...
class LocationValue {
  double latitude;
  double longitude;
  double accuracy;

  LocationValue(double lat, double lon, double acc) {
    latitude = lat;
    longitude = lon;
    accuracy = acc;
  }

  double distanceTo(LocationValue dest) {
    double a1 = radians((float)latitude);
    double a2 = radians((float)longitude);
    double b1 = radians((float)dest.latitude);
    double b2 = radians((float)dest.longitude);

    double t1 = Math.cos(a1) * Math.cos(a2) * Math.cos(b1) * Math.cos(b2);
    double t2 = Math.cos(a1) * Math.sin(a2) * Math.cos(b1) * Math.sin(b2);
    double t3 = Math.sin(a1) * Math.sin(b1);
    double tt = Math.acos(t1 + t2 + t3);

    return 6366000 * tt;
  }
}
```

We obtain the location accuracy from the Location argument in the onLocationChanged() event and store it in the LocationValue object alongside its latitude and longitude. Then, we use the accuracy of the latest and previous location to determine if the latest is different enough to be added to the path. This involves calculating the distance between two locations, which is the length of the arc connecting them on Earth's surface. There are several formulas to approximate this distance (https://en.wikipedia.org/wiki/Great-circle_distance#Computational_formulas); in the code, we used the so-called Law of Cosines that assumes a perfectly spherical Earth (not perfectly accurate, since our planet is slightly flattened along its South-North axis, but good enough for this simple application).

A Street View Collage

At this point, we have several techniques at our disposal to create a more elaborate geolocation project. As mentioned at the beginning, we use location-aware apps on a daily basis, probably dozens or even hundreds of times a day. Tools such as Google Street View are so popular that we often first see a new place not when we visit it in person, but when we view it on Google Maps. Our experience in the city is so mediated by these apps that it could be worth trying to use imagery from Street View in combination with the locations we visit during the day to create some kind of non-functional visual collage. In fact, this idea is not new, and many artists have been working with it before, transforming the everyday urban landscape into compositions that are at the same time familiar and strange and disorienting. Figure 9-4 reproduces a panoramic photo collage by artist Masumi Hayashi (http://masumimuseum.com/), who used a custom-made system for capturing 360° strips of scenery that later combined into collages. More recently, Annalisa Casini (http://www.annalisacasini.com/project-withtools-google-maps/) has been creating surreal photo collages of urban landscapes from Street View images.

Thanks to the always-on nature of the smartphone and the possibility of real-time location updates, we could build a dynamic collage that uses Street View images downloaded from the Internet as we move around. From the point of view of the visual output, the most important question to solve is how to combine urban imagery into an engaging composition. Of course, there are many (infinite!) ways we could do this, and work from artists like Hayashi and Casini gives us some references to inspire our own.

We will start by solving the problem of retrieving Street View images via our Processing sketch, as this step is a prerequisite for any further work to realize our concept. Once we are able to solve this technical issue, we will consider automated ways to create the collage.

Figure 9-4. Top: OSERF Building Broad Street View, Columbus, Ohio, by Masumi Hayashi (2001). Reproduced with permission from the Estate of Masumi Hayashi.

Using Google Street View Image API

Google Street View is a popular feature of Google Maps and Google Earth that provides panoramic views of many places around the world, primarily streets in cities and towns, but which now also includes sites like building interiors, coral reefs, and even space! Street View can be accessed from Android apps using different APIs, one of which allows you to create interactive panoramas inside a specialized view component. However, this API is not suitable for use in our Processing sketch, since the panorama view cannot be integrated with Processing's drawing surface.

Fortunately, Google also offers an image API via which one can download Street View static images corresponding to a latitude/longitude coordinate using an HTTP request (https://developers.google.com/maps/documentation/streetview/intro). To use this API, we first have to enable the Google Street View Image API under the Google Maps APIs and create a Google API project in the Developer's Console (https://console.developers.google.com/apis/dashboard). Then, we must obtain an API key (https://developers.google.com/maps/documentation/android-api/signup) to add to the project. These steps are very important, or our applications will not be able to request Street View images. We can test if everything is working as expected by creating a request in the web browser. Google Street View Image API requests have the following format:

```
http://maps.googleapis.com/maps/api/streetview?size=WIDTHxHEIGHT&location=
LAT,LONG&sensor=SENSOR_STATUS&heading=HEADING&fov=FOV&pitch=PITCH&key=GOOG
LE_API_CONSOLE_KEY
```

Most of the parameters in the request are optional, with the exception of the location, size, and, of course, API key. The Google Street View Image API page linked to in the previous paragraph describes all these URL parameters in detail. The request should return an image that we can then save on our computer.

We can use exactly the same request syntax in a Processing sketch to request a PImage. This is achieved with the simple code in Listing 9-6, where you have to provide your own API key and also add the Internet permission to the sketch.

Listing 9-6. Requesting a Street View Image

```
PImage street;
String apiKey = "<your API key>";

void setup() {
  size(512, 512);
  street = requestImage("http://maps.googleapis.com/maps/api/streetview?" +
                 "location=42.383401,-71.116110&size=512x512&" +
                 "fov=90&pitch=-10&key=" + apiKey);
}

void draw() {
  if (0 < street.width && 0 < street.height) {
    image(street, 0, 0, width, height);
  }
}
```

The requestImage() function returns a PImage object that will be downloaded in a separate thread to avoid hanging our sketch while the image data is transferred. We will know that the image is ready when its width and height are greater than zero. If for some reason the request failed, the width and height will both be set to -1. This is why have the if (0 < street.width && 0 < street.height) condition in draw().

By combining the ability to request images from the Google Street View Image API with our previous path-tracking sketch from Listing 9-5, we will be able to display a street image of the latest position received from the location services. Let's see how to do this in Listing 9-7.

Listing 9-7. Showing Street View of Our Last Location

```
...
ArrayList<LocationValue> path = new ArrayList<LocationValue>();
ArrayList<PImage> street = new ArrayList<PImage>();
String apiKey = "<your API key>";
...
void draw() {
  background(255);
  while (queue.available()) {
    LocationValue loc = queue.remove();
    minLat = min(minLat, (float)loc.latitude);
    maxLat = max(maxLat, (float)loc.latitude);
    minLon = min(minLon, (float)loc.longitude);
    maxLon = max(maxLon, (float)loc.longitude);
    if (0 < path.size()) {
      LocationValue last = path.get(path.size() - 1);
      if (last.distanceTo(loc) < loc.accuracy + last.accuracy) continue;
    }
    path.add(0, loc);
    String url = "http://maps.googleapis.com/maps/api/streetview?location=" +
                 loc.latitude + "," + loc.longitude +
                 "&size=512x512&fov=90&pitch=-10&sensor=false&key=" +
                 apiKey;
    street.add(requestImage(url));
  }
  if (0 < street.size()) {
    PImage img = street.get(street.size() - 1);
    if (0 < img.width && 0 < img.height) {
      image(img, 0, 0, width, height);
    }
  }
}
...
```

We add the requested images for each new location to the street array list and then select the last one in the list when it has finished downloading, like we did in Listing 9-6.

> ■ **Note** If you use a version-control service, such as GitHub, to store your code projects, be careful to not upload your API keys to public repositories that anyone can access. If you committed sensitive data into a public Git repository, this article explains how to completely remove it: `https://help.github.com/articles/removing-sensitive-data-from-a-repository/`.

Voronoi Tessellations

We now face the challenge of creating a visually interestingly collage through code. One way of thinking about this problem is by contemplating how we could divide the screen into non-overlapping regions, each one corresponding to a location and its associated image. This partition is technically called a *tessellation*. A tessellation using rectangles will be easy to implement, but will probably look too simple. However, there is a well-known partition called a Voronoi tessellation. To create a Voronoi tessellation, we start with a set of arbitrary 2D points. Next, if we are at position (x, y) in the 2D plane, we find the point p in the set that is the closest to (x, y). We say (x, y) belongs to the region determined by p. We then paint all such positions (x, y) associated with p using the same color. Following this simple algorithm, we will reach a partition of the plane into regions that look more or less like in the left panel of Figure 9-5.

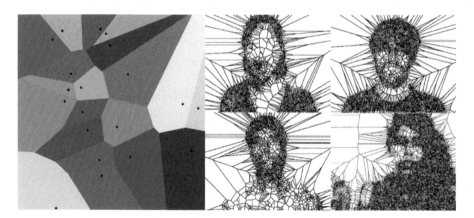

Figure 9-5. *Left: Voronoi tessellation with 20 regions. Right: Voronoi portraits by Mark Kleback and Sheiva Rezvani*

Voronoi tessellations have applications in fields as diverse as biology, geography, mathematics, meteorology, and robotics, where there is a need to conduct spatial data analysis. Voronoi tessellations are capable of dividing space into regions that make it easier to manipulate data. Artists have also used it as the basic technique to create pieces where some underlying dataset (like the portraits in the right panel of Figure 9-5) is processed to generate a "natural" partition of the data while also being visually attractive.

There are many algorithms with which to generate the Voronoi tessellation given a point set—some very efficient but also complicated to implement. The simplest algorithm, but also the least efficient, is the one that literally translates our textual description of the Voronoi tessellation into code. It is very inefficient because we need to compare each pixel (x, y) in the screen with all the points in the set, and so its execution time grows as the square of the number of pixels in the screen, which in turn is the product of the width and height. This implies that the algorithm slows down very quickly as the screen resolution increases.

However, if the screen resolution is not too high, this simple algorithm is still fast enough to be run interactively. In Listing 9-8, we add a new point to the Voronoi set every time we press the mouse (or touch the screen). We set the maximum number of "Voronoi points" to 10 and the resolution to 512 × 512. This sketch can be run from either Java or Android modes without any modifications. The key element that makes possible an easy implementation of this algorithm in Processing is the pixels array, which we discussed back in Chapter 6. This array contains the color of each pixel in the screen, arranged as consecutive values so that, if the resolution of the screen is W × H, the first W elements in the pixels array correspond to the first row in the screen, the next W elements to the second, etc. We can also use the pixels array to set the color of any pixel in the screen. We do so in Listing 9-8.

Listing 9-8. Generating a Voronoi Tessellation

```
int lastPoint = 0;
int maxPoints = 10;
VoronoiPoint[] points = new VoronoiPoint[maxPoints];
boolean updated = false;

void setup () {
  size(512, 512);
}

void draw() {
  if (updated) {
    updateColors();
    drawPoints();
    updated = false;
  }
}
```

```
void mousePressed() {
  points[lastPoint] = new VoronoiPoint(mouseX, mouseY, color(random(255),
  random(255), random(255)));
  lastPoint = (lastPoint + 1) % maxPoints;
  updated = true;
}

void updateColors() {
  int idx = 0;
  loadPixels();
  for (int y = 0; y < height; y++) {
    for (int x = 0; x < width; x++) {
      int closest = findClosestPoint(x, y);
      if (-1 < closest) pixels[idx] = points[closest].getColor();
      idx++;
    }
  }
  updatePixels();
}

void drawPoints() {
  strokeWeight(10);
  stroke(0, 50);
  for (int i = 0; i < points.length; i++) {
    VoronoiPoint p = points[i];
    if (p == null) break;
    point(p.x, p.y);
  }
}

int findClosestPoint(float x, float y) {
  int minIdx = -1;
  float minDist = 1000;
  for (int i = 0; i < points.length; i++) {
    VoronoiPoint p = points[i];
    if (p == null) break;
    float d = dist(x, y, p.x, p.y);
    if (d < minDist) {
      minIdx = i;
      minDist = d;
    }
  }
  return minIdx;
}
```

```
class VoronoiPoint {
  float x, y;
  color c;
  VoronoiPoint(float x, float y, color c){
    this.x = x;
    this.y = y;
    this.c = c;
  }
  color getColor() {
    return c;
  }
}
```

We set the color of each screen pixel in the updateColors() function by locating the point in the Voronoi list that is closest to it. For this to work, we need to call loadPixels() first to make sure that the pixels array is initialized, and then updatePixels()so the pixels are drawn to the screen. The findClosestPoint() function finds the closest point to a screen position (x, y); it works by setting an large initial distance (1000), then iterating over all points, saving in the variable minIdx the index of the point with a distance to (x, y) smaller than the previous one.

If we run this sketch, either on the computer or on the Android device, we will create new Voronoi regions until a maximum of ten, with each region being assigned a random color. Once we go over ten, the sketch cycles over the points array, and the new mouse/touch positions will replace the original ones. Figure 9-6 shows a typical output.

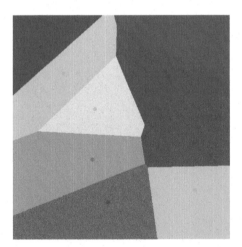

Figure 9-6. *A typical Voronoi tessellation*

In this interactive tessellation, we assigned a solid color to each point. However, we could use an image instead so that the pixels in the corresponding region are painted with the colors from the image's pixels. In this way, each region would show a portion of a different image. If all images have the same size as the screen resolution, it will be easy to modify the previous listing to use images. This is what we do in Listing 9-9. Here, we use a set of ten images generated with Street View at 512 × 512 resolution, streetview0.jpg through streetview9.jpg, and stored in the data folder of the sketch.

Listing 9-9. Painting a Voronoi Tessellation with Images

```
...
void mousePressed() {
  points[lastPoint] = new VoronoiPoint(mouseX, mouseY, lastPoint);
  lastPoint = (lastPoint + 1) % maxPoints;
  updated = true;
}

void updateColors() {
  int idx = 0;
  loadPixels();
  for (int y = 0; y < height; y++) {
    for (int x = 0; x < width; x++) {
      int closest = findClosestPoint(x, y);
      if (-1 < closest) pixels[idx] = points[closest].getColor(idx);
      idx++;
    }
  }
  updatePixels();
}
...
class VoronoiPoint {
  float x, y;
  PImage img;
  VoronoiPoint(float x, float y, int i) {
    this.x = x;
    this.y = y;
    img = loadImage("streetview" + i + ".jpg");
    img.loadPixels();
  }
  color getColor(int idx) {
    return img.pixels[idx];
  }
}
```

This listing only shows the few parts of the code that need changes. Now, we use the point index to load the image object we store inside each VoronoiPoint class. The PImage class also has a pixels array, and from it we can retrieve the colors of the image at each one of its pixels. Using ten images from Google Street View, our new example should generate a collage similar to the one shown in Figure 9-7.

Figure 9-7. *Painting the regions in a Voronoi tessellation using Street View images*

Using an Offscreen Drawing Surface

A limitation of our Voronoi tessellation code is that it should be used only at low resolutions, making it unsuitable for full-screen apps. We could apply offscreen drawing to address this issue. The idea is to draw the tessellation onto a smaller drawing surface and then render the contents of this surface on the screen at full resolution. Processing allows us to create an offscreen drawing surface with the createGraphics(width, height) function, which returns a PGraphics object (https://processing.org/reference/PGraphics.html) encapsulating a surface with the requested resolution. We can use all the APIs we have learned so far to draw into a PGraphics object. One important thing to keep in mind is to enclose all PGraphics drawing calls between beginDraw() and endDraw(). Listing 9-10 shows the changes needed to make the image tessellation sketch into a full-screen app using offscreen rendering.

Listing 9-10. Drawing into an Offscreen Pgraphics Object

```
...
PGraphics canvas;

void setup () {
  fullScreen();
  canvas = createGraphics(512, 512);
}

void draw() {
  ...
  image(canvas, 0, 0, width, height);
}

void mousePressed() {
  float x = map(mouseX, 0, width, 0, canvas.width);
  float y = map(mouseY, 0, height, 0, canvas.height);
  points[lastPoint] = new VoronoiPoint(x, y, lastPoint);
  lastPoint = (lastPoint + 1) % maxPoints;
  updated = true;
}

void updateColors() {
  int idx = 0;
  canvas.beginDraw();
  canvas.loadPixels();
  for (int y = 0; y < canvas.height; y++) {
    for (int x = 0; x < canvas.width; x++) {
      int closest = findClosestPoint(x, y);
      if (-1 < closest) canvas.pixels[idx] = points[closest].getColor(idx);
      idx++;
    }
  }
  canvas.updatePixels();
  canvas.endDraw();
}

void drawPoints() {
  canvas.beginDraw();
  canvas.strokeWeight(10);
  canvas.stroke(0, 50);
  for (int i = 0; i < points.length; i++) {
    VoronoiPoint p = points[i];
    if (p == null) break;
    canvas.point(p.x, p.y);
  }
  canvas.endDraw();
}
```

Also, remember that, while the (x, y) coordinates in the main screen surface range from (0, 0) to (width, height), the PGraphics resolution is (PGraphics.width, PGraphics.height), meaning that we might need to map coordinates from one surface to the other. For instance, (mouseX, mouseY) coordinates always refer to the screen, so we should map them to the width and height of the PGraphics object so the interactions work properly on the offscreen surface.

Putting Everything Together

Thus far, we have managed to generate the collage with a set of predefined Street View images. So, it is time to combine that code with our earlier sketches that retrieved the device's location from the available location services. We will use the latitude and longitude values to assemble the HTTPS request to obtain a new Street View image, as we did in Listing 9-7, and assign it to a random Voronoi point.

However, we should consider a couple of important technical aspects. First, we want to draw the collage at full-screen resolution, and to do this we could use an offscreen PGraphics object at a lower resolution, e.g., 512 × 512, and then scale it up to cover the entire screen, as we did in Listing 9-10, although preserving the original square ratio of the image.

The second aspect concerns the frequency of the location updates. Requesting updates very often, especially in high-accuracy mode (i.e., GPS), will drain the battery faster, but we actually don't need very frequent updates, since the app should wait long enough to ensure that there are noticeable differences in the surroundings. The granularity of the location updates are set in the call to requestLocationUpdates(), where we have been using 1 second and 1 meters as minimum time and distance for the updates. These values are too small for the purpose of our collage, and we can increase them quite a bit—for example, to 30 seconds and 20 meters, respectively. With these considerations in mind, let's take a look at the full code in Listing 9-11.

Listing 9-11. Street View Collage

```
import android.content.Context;
import android.location.Location;
import android.location.LocationListener;
import android.location.LocationManager;
import android.os.Bundle;

LocationManager manager;
SimpleListener listener;
String provider;
LocationQueue queue = new LocationQueue();
ArrayList<LocationValue> path = new ArrayList<LocationValue>();
int lastPoint = 0;
int maxPoints = 10;
VoronoiPoint[] points = new VoronoiPoint[maxPoints];
PGraphics canvas;
String apiKey = "<your API key>";
```

```
void setup () {
  fullScreen();
  orientation(PORTRAIT);
  canvas = createGraphics(512, 512);
  imageMode(CENTER);
  requestPermission("android.permission.ACCESS_FINE_LOCATION",
  "initLocation");
}

void draw() {
  background(0);
  updatePositions();
  float h = max(width, height);
  image(canvas, width/2, height/2, h, h);
}

void updatePositions() {
  while (queue.available()) {
    LocationValue loc = queue.remove();
    if (0 < path.size()) {
      LocationValue last = path.get(path.size() - 1);
      if (last.distanceTo(loc) < 20) continue;
    }
    String url = "http://maps.googleapis.com/maps/api/streetview?location=" +
                 loc.latitude + "," + loc.longitude +
                 "&size=512x512&fov=90&pitch=-10&sensor=false&key=" +
                 apiKey;
    loc.setStreetView(requestImage(url));
    path.add(loc);
  }

  boolean newImage = false;
  for (int i = path.size() - 1; i >= 0; i--) {
    LocationValue loc = path.get(i);
    PImage img = loc.getStreetView();
    if (img.width == -1 || img.height == -1) {
      path.remove(i);
    } else if (img.width == 512 && img.height == 512) {
      float x = random(0, canvas.width);
      float y = random(0, canvas.height);
      points[lastPoint] = new VoronoiPoint(x, y, img);
      lastPoint = (lastPoint + 1) % maxPoints;
      newImage = true;
      path.remove(i);
    }
  }
}
```

```
  if (newImage) updateColors();
}

void updateColors() {
  int idx = 0;
  canvas.beginDraw();
  canvas.loadPixels();
  for (int y = 0; y < canvas.height; y++) {
    for (int x = 0; x < canvas.width; x++) {
      int closest = findClosestPoint(x, y);
      if (-1 < closest) canvas.pixels[idx] = points[closest].getColor(idx);
      idx++;
    }
  }
  canvas.updatePixels();
  canvas.endDraw();
}

void initLocation(boolean granted) {
  if (granted) {
    Context context = getContext();
    listener = new SimpleListener();
    manager = (LocationManager)
              context.getSystemService(Context.LOCATION_SERVICE);
    provider = LocationManager.NETWORK_PROVIDER;
    if (manager.isProviderEnabled(LocationManager.GPS_PROVIDER)) {
      provider = LocationManager.GPS_PROVIDER;
    }
    manager.requestLocationUpdates(provider, 30000, 20, listener);
  }
}

class SimpleListener implements LocationListener {
  public void onLocationChanged(Location loc) {
    queue.add(new LocationValue(loc.getLatitude(), loc.getLongitude()));
  }
  public void onProviderDisabled(String provider) { }
  public void onProviderEnabled(String provider) { }
  public void onStatusChanged(String provider, int status, Bundle extras) {
}
}

public void resume() {
  if (manager != null) {
    manager.requestLocationUpdates(provider, 30000, 20, listener);
  }
}
```

```
public void pause() {
  if (manager != null) {
    manager.removeUpdates(listener);
  }
}

class LocationValue {
  double latitude;
  double longitude;
  PImage streetView;

  LocationValue(double lat, double lon) {
    latitude = lat;
    longitude = lon;
  }

  void setStreetView(PImage img) {
    streetView = img;
  }

  PImage getStreetView() {
    return streetView;
  }

  double distanceTo(LocationValue dest) {
    double a1 = radians((float)latitude);
    double a2 = radians((float)longitude);
    double b1 = radians((float)dest.latitude);
    double b2 = radians((float)dest.longitude);

    double t1 = Math.cos(a1) * Math.cos(a2) * Math.cos(b1) * Math.cos(b2);
    double t2 = Math.cos(a1) * Math.sin(a2) * Math.cos(b1) * Math.sin(b2);
    double t3 = Math.sin(a1) * Math.sin(b1);
    double tt = Math.acos(t1 + t2 + t3);

    return 6366000 * tt;
  }
}

class LocationQueue {
  LocationValue[] values = new LocationValue[10];
  int offset, count;

  synchronized void add(LocationValue val) {
    if (count == values.length) {
      values = (LocationValue[]) expand(values);
    }
    values[count++] = val;
  }
```

207

```
  synchronized LocationValue remove() {
    if (offset == count) {
      return null;
    }
    LocationValue outgoing = values[offset++];
    if (offset == count) {
      offset = 0;
      count = 0;
    }
    return outgoing;
  }

  synchronized boolean available() {
    return 0 < count;
  }
}

class VoronoiPoint {
  float x, y;
  PImage img;

  VoronoiPoint(float x, float y, PImage img){
    this.x = x;
    this.y = y;
    this.img = img;
    img.loadPixels();
  }

  color getColor(int idx) {
    return img.pixels[idx];
  }
}

int findClosestPoint(float x, float y) {
  int minIdx = -1;
  float minDist = 1000;
  for (int i = 0; i < points.length; i++) {
    VoronoiPoint p = points[i];
    if (p == null) break;
    float d = dist(x, y, p.x, p.y);
    if (d < minDist) {
      minIdx = i;
      minDist = d;
    }
  }
  return minIdx;
}
```

Let's discuss the new code in this sketch, in particular the updatePositions() function. The first part is very similar to what we had before: removing new locations from the queue, skipping them if they are too close to the previous location (20 meters is the threshold here), and otherwise adding them to the path. We also generate the corresponding Street View request and store the PImage object inside the new LocationValue object. It then iterates backward through all the locations received so far and deletes those that either failed to receive a Street View image (by checking if the width or height of the requested image is -1) or did complete the image download. The latter locations are deleted because their image is assigned to a new Voronoi point, so they are no longer needed. In this way, we make sure that the memory usage of the app does not keep increasing until it runs of memory and is forced to quit; we only store up to a maximum of ten simultaneous images (with a resolution of 512 × 512), since this is the length of our array of Voronoi points.

A smaller detail, but one still important to ensure that the collage looks good, is ensuring that it covers the entire screen while keeping its original aspect ratio. If we look at the code in the draw() function, we see how to do it: we take the largest screen dimension with the line float h = max(width, height) and then draw the offscreen PGraphics canvas at this size h with the image() function, placing it at the screen's center. Since we set the image mode to CENTER in setup(), the canvas will appear properly centered on the screen.

We can run this sketch as a regular app or as a live wallpaper (in the second case, we may want to use the wallpaperPreview() function so the location permission is requested only after the wallpaper is selected). Some examples of the output are shown in Figure 9-8. If we plan to distribute it via the Play Store, we will also have to create a full set of icons, write down the full package and name of the app, as well as the version, in its manifest file, and export a release package, as we did for the final projects in chapters 3 and 6.

Figure 9-8. Different Street View collages generated with the final sketch, running as a live wallpaper

Summary

In this chapter, we explored in detail the possibilities offered by the Android location API and how we can use it in Processing for Android to create unconventional applications of geolocation in combination with other technologies such as Google Street View. As we just saw, Processing gives us a lot of freedom to access different data sources (GPS, images, etc.), but also provides a solid framework with which to successfully integrate these sources so we can take our ideas from concept sketches to finished apps.

PART IV

Wearables and Watch Faces

CHAPTER 10

■ ■ ■

Wearable Devices

In this chapter, we will use Processing to create watch faces for Android smartwatches. We will go through the specific features and constraints of wearable devices that we should take into consideration when writing smartwatch apps.

From Activity Trackers to Smartwatches

Even though we may think of phones and tablets first when considering mobile development, wearable devices have been present in many people's lives since the introduction of fitness trackers, such as the Fitbit, back in 2009, and more recently the list of such devices has expanded to include digital smartwatches from Apple and several Android manufacturers. With the rapid advance of sensor technology and the decrease in size of electronic components, these devices are capable of performing a wide array of functions well beyond counting steps and heartbeats. In fact, a 2017 smartwatch has many of the same capabilities as a smartphone (2D and 3D graphics, touchscreen, location and movement sensors, Wi-Fi connectivity).

The Android platform provides support for all these devices through the Wear version of the Android operating system. Devices running Android Wear 1.x need to be paired with an Android phone running Android 4.3 or higher to enable all the functionality in the wearable (for example, displaying email and message notifications from the phone), while watches running Wear 2.x can run standalone apps that don't require pairing the watch with a phone. Wear apps (https://developer.android.com/training/wearables/apps/index.html) on the Android platform have access to the watch's sensors and graphics. Watch faces are a special kind of Wear app that runs as the background of the watch, not unlike live wallpapers on phones and tablets. They are meant to display the time and other relevant information, such as physical activity.

Processing for Android currently allows us to run a sketch as a watch face on Android smartwatches, but not as a general Wear app. All the drawing, interaction, and sensing APIs discussed in previous chapters are applicable to watch faces, with a few additions needed to handle the unique features of smartwatches.

© Andrés Colubri 2017
A. Colubri, *Processing for Android*, https://doi.org/10.1007/978-1-4842-2719-0_10

■ **Note**   Version 4.0 of Android mode can be used to create watch faces for smartwatches running Android Wear 2.0 or higher. It does not support Wear 1.x devices.

Smartwatches

Several manufacturers offer Android smartwatches, and as result there is a wide range of models with different specifications and styles. Figure 10-1 shows a small selection of Android watches.

Figure 10-1. *A selection of Android smartwatches, from left to right: Sony Smartwatch 3, Moto 360, LG Watch Urbane, Polar M600*

Even though there is an ample variety of watches, all of them must conform to a minimum baseline of technical specifications. Watches released for version 1.x of Android Wear have (round or square) displays with densities between 200 and 300 dpi (so, falling in the hdpi range), Wi-Fi and Bluetooth connectivity, accelerometer, gyroscope, and typically heart-rate sensors, 4 GB of internal storage, and a battery life of up to two days of mixed use (fully active versus battery-saving "ambient" mode). As mentioned in the introduction of the chapter, Wear 2.0 will encourage watches packed with more sensors, higher display densities, and longer battery life given the increased autonomy of Wear 2.x devices.

■ **Note**   An important difference between Wear 1.x and 2.x is that with the former, watches always need to be paired with a smartphone to be fully functional (i.e., displaying messages, providing location), but with the latter, they can work entirely autonomously and run apps as powerful as those designed for phones.

Running Watch Face Sketches

Just as we can run Processing sketches for regular apps on an actual device or in the emulator, we can run our watch face sketches on a watch or in the emulator. The process of debugging on a physical device is generally more convenient, since the emulator is typically slower and not capable of simulating all the sensor data that we might need in order to debug our watch face, but the emulator allows us to test various display configurations and to run our watch face if we don't have an Android watch yet.

Using a Watch

To run a Processing sketch on an Android watch, we first need to enable "Developer Options" on the watch, as follows:

1. Open the Settings menu on the watch.

2. Scroll to the bottom of the menu and select "System | About."

3. Tap the build number seven times.

4. From the Settings menu, select "Developer Options."

5. Confirm that "ADB debugging" is enabled.

Once we have enabled the Developer Options, we must choose from between two alternatives to run and debug our watch face sketches on a Wear 2.x watch: Wi-Fi and Bluetooth. The developer guide from Google on debugging Wear apps goes through all the details (`https://developer.android.com/training/wearables/apps/debugging. html`), and we will now review the most important steps.

With Bluetooth, the watch must be paired with the phone. First, we need to enable Bluetooth debugging on both devices. On the watch, we do so by opening the "Settings|Developer Options" and enabling "Debug Over Bluetooth." On the phone, we open the Android Wear companion app, tap on its Settings icon, and then enable "Debug Over Bluetooth." Once we have done all of this, Processing should be able to connect to the watch via its Bluetooth pairing with the phone.

■ **Note** If the watch is paired with a phone over Bluetooth, and this phone is the only device plugged into the computer through USB, then Processing will be able to connect to the watch automatically. But if there is more than one phone, you need to connect the watch manually with the adb command ` ./adb -s ID forward tcp:4444 localabstract:/ adb-hub`, provide the ID of the phone the watch is paired to, and then use the command ` adb connect 127.0.0.1:4444`.

In the case of Wi-Fi, both the computer we are running Processing on and the watch must be connected to the same network. Then, we need to enable Wi-Fi debugging on the watch by going to "Settings|Developer Options" and enabling "Debug over Wi-Fi." After a moment, the watch will display its IP address (e.g., 192.168.1.100). Once we have obtained the IP address of the watch, we will open a terminal. From there, we will change to the platform-tools folder inside the Android SDK and run the command `adb connect 192.168.1.100`, as seen in Figure 10-2.

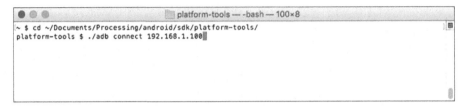

Figure 10-2. *Connecting to a watch over Wi-Fi from the command line*

Once we have connected the watch via either Wi-Fi or Bluetooth, we should see it in the list of devices under the Android menu. Also, we must make sure to select the "Watch Face" option, since Processing will not allow us to run other sketch types on a watch (Figure 10-3).

Figure 10-3. *Enabling running sketches as watch faces and listing a connected watch*

After connecting to our watch via either Bluetooth or Wi-Fi, we can follow Listing 10-1 to run an animated watch face.

Listing 10-1. Simple Animated Watch Face

```
void setup() {
  fullScreen();
  strokeCap(ROUND);
  stroke(255);
  noFill();
}

void draw() {
  background(0);
  if (wearAmbient()) strokeWeight(1);
  else strokeWeight(10);
  float angle = map(millis() % 60000, 0, 60000, 0, TWO_PI);
  arc(width/2, height/2, width/2, width/2, 0, angle);
}
```

After Processing installs the sketch on the device as a watch face, we have to select it as the active watch face. To do this, left swipe the screen to access the list of favorite watch faces. If ours does not show up in this list, tap on "Add more watch faces" at the rightmost end of the list, and you should find the sketch there, possibly among other available watch faces. Select it there first, and once it is added to the favorite list, you can tap on it to set is as the current background. The output would look like Figure 10-4.

Figure 10-4. *Output of the animated watch face example*

Please note that the watch face will not look like it does in this figure all the time. After a few seconds, the watch will enter ambient mode, where the display is updated only once every minute. The purpose of this mode is to save battery power when we are not looking at the watch. As soon as the watch detects (using its accelerometer) the typical gesture of turning the wrist to look at the time, it will return to interactive mode. The developer guides from Google recommend setting most of the screen to a black background when in ambient mode and drawing the remaining graphic elements with thin white lines. As we can see in the code, Processing gives us the wearAmbient() function to detect whether the watch is in ambient mode and update the graphics accordingly.

Using the Emulator

We saw in Chapter 1 that we should install a system image in order to run a phone Android Virtual Device (AVD) in the emulator. We also saw that we must decide whether we want to use ARM or x86 images. To use the emulator with watch faces, we need to install a separate watch AVD for the emulator to use. The first time we run a watch face sketch in the emulator, we would see a dialog asking us to download the watch system image (Figure 10-5), followed by the ARM/x86 selection. Once the image (and the HAXM software for x86 images, as we also discussed in Chapter 1) is downloaded and installed, Processing will copy the sketch into the emulator and inform us once the sketch has been installed successfully as a watch face.

Figure 10-5. *Downloading the watch system image*

Just as with actual devices, we need to select our watch face in order to set it as the current background, which we do by following the same series of steps we saw earlier, shown in Figure 10-6: add the watch face to the list of favorites and then select it from that list.

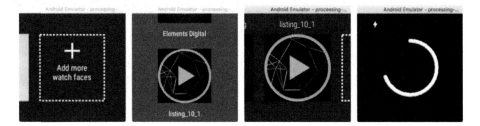

Figure 10-6. *Selecting a watch face in the emulator*

Processing by default creates a square watch AVD with a 280 × 280 resolution. However, in Chapter 3 we learned that we can create other AVDs with the avdmanager command-line tool. Processing will run our sketches on these AVDs as long as we launch them with the emulator tool on the right port. For instance, let's create a round watch AVD with the `"wear_round_360_300dpi"` device definition and launch it on port 5576 so we can use it from Processing. The commands to do this are shown in Figure 10-7 (after creating the AVD, remember to add the `skin` parameter to its `config.ini` file, as we saw in Chapter 3). The resulting emulator running our sketch in the round watch AVD is shown in Figure 10-8.

```
● ● ●                        tools — -bash — 100×6
~ $ cd ~/Documents/Processing/android/sdk/tools/
tools $ bin/avdmanager create avd -n round-watch -k "system-images;android-25;android-wear;x86" -d "
wear_round_360_300dpi" -p ~/Documents/Processing/android/avd/round-watch
Auto-selecting single ABI x86
tools $ ./emulator -avd round-watch -gpu auto -port 5576
```

Figure 10-7. *Creating and launching a custom watch AVD*

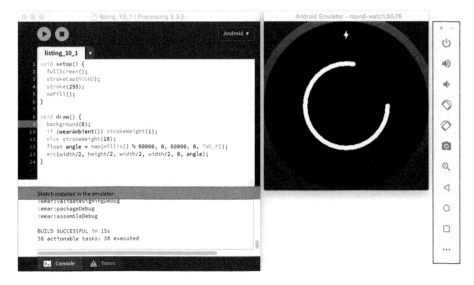

Figure 10-8. *Running our watch face sketch in the custom AVD*

Displaying Time

Displaying time is one of the basic functions of a watch, and with Processing we are able to create any visual representation of time we can imagine. Processing offers a number of functions to obtain the current time and date—year(), month(), day(), hour(), minute(), and second()—which will allow us to generate our own time visualizations. As a basic example, in Listing 10-2 we show the time using text.

Listing 10-2. Displaying the Time as Text

```
void setup() {
  fullScreen();
  frameRate(1);
  textFont(createFont("Serif-Bold", 48));
  textAlign(CENTER, CENTER);
  fill(255);
}

void draw() {
  background(0);
  if (wearInteractive()) {
    String str = hour() + ":" + nfs(minute(), 2) + ":" + nfs(second(), 2);
    text(str, width/2, height/2);
  }
}
```

Notice that we use frameRate(1). Since we are showing the time down to seconds, there is no need to run the sketch at a higher framerate, which also helps save battery. The nfs() function conveniently adds zeros to the right of the number so the resulting string always has two digits. Finally, wearInteractive() simply returns the opposite of the wearAmbient() function, which we used in our first watch face.

Counting Steps

We can access the sensors available in our watch with the same techniques we learned in the previous chapters, either through the Android API or with the Ketai library. We will investigate the possibilities of body sensing in Chapter 12, but here in Listing 10-3 we present a simple step-counter example that uses the Android sensor API.

Listing 10-3. Simple Step Counter

```
import android.content.Context;
import android.hardware.Sensor;
import android.hardware.SensorManager;
import android.hardware.SensorEvent;
import android.hardware.SensorEventListener;

Context context;
SensorManager manager;
Sensor sensor;
SensorListener listener;

int offset = -1;
int steps;

void setup() {
  fullScreen();
  frameRate(1);
  Context context = (Context) surface.getComponent();
  manager = (SensorManager)context.getSystemService(Context.SENSOR_SERVICE);
  sensor = manager.getDefaultSensor(Sensor.TYPE_STEP_COUNTER);
  listener = new SensorListener();
  manager.registerListener(listener, sensor, SensorManager.SENSOR_DELAY_
NORMAL);
  textFont(createFont("SansSerif", 40 * displayDensity));
  textAlign(CENTER, CENTER);
  fill(255);
}
```

```
void draw() {
  background(0);
  if (wearInteractive()) {
    String str = steps + " steps";
    float w = textWidth(str);
    text(str, width/2, height/2);
  }
}

void resume() {
  if (manager != null)
    manager.registerListener(listener, sensor,
                             SensorManager.SENSOR_DELAY_NORMAL);
}

void pause() {
  if (manager != null) manager.unregisterListener(listener);
}

class SensorListener implements SensorEventListener {
  public void onSensorChanged(SensorEvent event) {
    if (offset == -1) offset = (int)event.values[0];
    steps = (int)event.values[0] - offset;
  }
  public void onAccuracyChanged(Sensor sensor, int accuracy) { }
}
```

Since the values returned by the step-counter sensor (which is not an actual hardware sensor, but rather a "derived" sensor that uses information from the accelerometer to compute the steps) are cumulative from the time the watch booted up, we store the first value to start the counting from the moment that particular watch face is open.

Designing for Smartwatches

Using Processing's drawing API to create watch faces opens up innumerable directions for representation of time in combination with contextual and sensor data. The limited size of smartwatch displays poses challenges in terms of visual design and information density. We will look more deeply into these challenges in the next two chapters.

The official Google developer site includes a section specifically on watch face design (https://developer.android.com/design/wear/watchfaces.html), which provides some useful guidance on design concepts and language, as well as on how to handle aspects unique to smartwatches.

Screen Shape and Insets

A first important aspect to consider is adapting the graphics of the watch face to both round and square displays so that our visual design works effectively in both scenarios.

■ **Note** Even if the display is round, the width and height values refer to the largest extent of the display along the horizontal and vertical directions.

You can determine the shape of the screen by calling the wearRound() or the wearSquare() functions, which will return true for round/square screens, and false otherwise, as demonstrated in Listing 10-4.

Listing 10-4. Adjusting Graphics to the Screen Shape

```
void setup() {
  fullScreen();
  if (wearSquare()) rectMode(CENTER);
}

void draw() {
  background(0);
  if (wearAmbient()) {
    stroke(255);
    noFill();
  } else {
    noStroke();
    fill(255);
  }
  float scale = map(second(), 0, 59, 0, 1);
  if (wearRound()) {
    ellipse(width/2, height/2, scale * width, scale * width);
  } else {
    rect(width/2, height/2, scale * width, scale * height);
  }
}
```

However, if we run the sketch from Listing 10-4 on a device that has an inset (or "chin") at the bottom of the screen, such as the Moto 360, we will notice that the circle is off-center with respect to the bezels of the watch, even though it is centered with respect to the display itself (Figure 10-9).

Figure 10-9. *"Chin" in a Moto 360 smartwatch. Graphics centered at the screen center (left), and translated by half of the bottom inset to properly center them with respect to the bezels*

We can use the wearInsets() function to properly center the sketch graphics in these cases. This function returns an object containing the inset borders around the display: top, bottom, left, and right. In the case of devices with a lower chin, we only need to add the call translate(0, wearInsets().bottom/2) to center the graphics with respect to the bezel center, although at the cost of clipping the lower portion of the graphics (Listing 10-5).

Listing 10-5. Watch Face Insets

```
void setup() {
  fullScreen();
  if (wearSquare()) rectMode(CENTER);
}

void draw() {
  background(0);
  if (wearAmbient()) {
    stroke(255);
    noFill();
  } else {
    noStroke();
```

```
    fill(255);
  }
  translate(0, wearInsets().bottom/2);
  float scale = map(second(), 0, 59, 0, 1);
  if (wearRound()) {
    ellipse(width/2, height/2, scale * width, scale * width);
  } else {
    rect(width/2, height/2, scale * width, scale * height);
  }
}
```

Watch Face Preview Icons

In addition to the regular app icons we discussed in Chapter 3, Android requires a set of preview icons to show the watch face in the selection list. The regular icons will be used in other parts of the UI, such as the App Info and Uninstall menus.

Since the watch can be either round or square, we need to provide only two preview icons: one for the round case (with 320 × 320 resolution) and the other for the square case (with 280 × 280 resolution). Both icons need to be copied into the sketch's folder, and they must have the names preview_circular.png and preview_rectangular.png.

Figure 10-10 shows the preview icons, note that the red portion in the circular preview won't be visible. When exporting the sketch as a signed package, Processing will not let us complete the export until all eight icons—six regular for ldpi, mdpi, hdpi, xhdpi, xxhdpi, and xxxhdpi resolutions, and two preview—are included in the sketch folder.

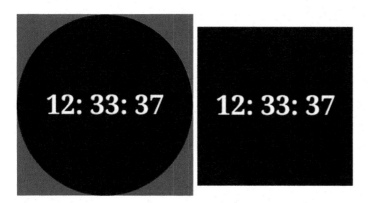

Figure 10-10. *Preview images for round (left) and square (right) devices. The red portion in the round preview will be ignored.*

Summary

In this first chapter about Android smartwatches, we have learned the basics about wearable devices and apps, as well as how to create watch faces for these novel devices. We also took a detailed look at the setup required to connect Processing to either actual watches or the emulator to test our watch face sketches across different display configurations.

CHAPTER 11

■ ■ ■

Visualizing Time

Displaying the time is one of the main functions of a watch, and in this chapter we will learn how to apply Processing's drawing API to experiment with different visual representations of time.

From Sundials to Smartwatches

The visual representation of time dates to the beginnings of civilization, when sundials were used to keep track of the time during the daylight hours. Mechanical pocket and then smaller wrist watches have been in use since the sixteenth century. In the digital era of the past few decades, electronic watches with multiple features became popular. The long history of the machines used for measuring and displaying time (Figure 11-1) gives us a rich technical and cultural background to draw inspiration from or to reinterpret via the nearly boundless possibilities offered by the smartwatch.

Figure 11-1. *From left to right: Sundial at the Imperial Palace in Beijing (eighth century BC); design for a ring watch, from Livre d'Aneaux d'Orfevrerie (1561); a late Victorian silver open-faced pocket watch (c.1890), Casio DBC 600 digital calculator watch (1985)*

© Andrés Colubri 2017
A. Colubri, *Processing for Android*, https://doi.org/10.1007/978-1-4842-2719-0_11

Although we can already find thousands of different watch faces on the Google Play Store, many of them translate analog concepts into very realistic digital representations. This is a valid approach, but the digital canvas also allows us to represent time in entirely original ways. Figure 11-2 shows a few examples of Android watch faces, all available on the Google Play Store, which demonstrate some interesting ideas, from eyes staring back at the user, abstract patterns, and whimsical animations representing the passage of time, to reinterpretations of an analog watch face through the use of digital zoom.

Figure 11-2. *From left to right: Gaze Effect (by Fathom Information Design); Waves (by ustwo); Space and Time (by Geng Gao); and Spotlight (by Maize)*

■ **Note** In order to take a screenshot of a watch face, we can use the adb tool in the Android SDK. First, save the screen grab to an image file on the watch: `adb -s 127.0.0.1:4444 shell screencap -p /sdcard/screenshot.png`. Then, download the resulting image to the computer: `adb -s 127.0.0.1:4444 pull -p /sdcard/ screenshot.png`. We can also use third-party graphics tools to make this process even easier, like the Android tool for Mac: https://github.com/mortenjust/androidtool-mac.

Using Time to Control Motion

Processing includes a time API that allows us to obtain the current time and date. Let's begin by using hour, minutes, and seconds to control a simple animation. If we were to work with a digital implementation of an analog concept, such as rotating hands, the transformation between time and angular values is fairly straightforward: we can map the values between their respective ranges; for instance, between 0 and 60 for minutes and seconds, and 0 to TWO_PI (2π) for angles. This mapping is demonstrated in Listing 11-1.

Listing 11-1. Concentric Circles for Seconds, Minutes, and Hours

```
void setup() {
  noStroke();
  strokeWeight(2);
}

void draw() {
  background(0);

  float hAngle = map(hour() % 12, 0, 12, 0, TWO_PI);
  float mAngle = map(minute(), 0, 60, 0, TWO_PI);
  float sAngle = map(second(), 0, 60, 0, TWO_PI);

  translate(width/2, height/2 + wearInsets().bottom/2);
  fill(ambientMode ? 0 : #F0DB3F);
  ellipse(0, 0, width, width);
  drawLine(hAngle, width/2);

  fill(ambientMode ? 0 : #FFB25F);
  ellipse(0, 0, 0.75 * width, 0.75 * width);
  drawLine(mAngle, 0.75 * width/2);

  fill(ambientMode ? 0 : #ED774D);
  ellipse(0, 0, 0.5 * width, 0.5 * width);
  drawLine(sAngle, 0.5 * width/2);

  fill(0);
  ellipse(0, 0, 0.25 * width, 0.25 * width);
}

void drawLine(float a, float r) {
  pushStyle();
  stroke(wearAmbient() ? 255 : 0);
  pushMatrix();
  rotate(a);
  line(0, 0, 0, -r);
  popMatrix();
  popStyle();
}
```

The output of this sketch (Figure 11-3) is three concentric circles, where the lines correspond to the hands for hour, minute, and second. Since the lines are drawn from the center of the screen pointing upward, which is the typical reference position in an analog watch, the rotation can be applied directly between 0 and TWO_PI.

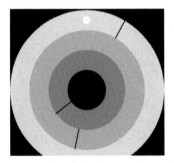

Figure 11-3. *Concentric circles watch face*

Once we run this watch face on the device or in the emulator, we can notice that the animation of the hands is not smooth. The innermost circle jumps from one second to the next because we are not interpolating the intermediate angles between two consecutive seconds. One solution to this problem is to use the millis() function, which returns the milliseconds elapsed since the sketch started running. We can calculate the difference between consecutive millis() calls to calculate the difference in milliseconds between two points in time, and then use that value to create a smoother animation.

More concretely, if we add two new variables to our previous sketch, say s0 and m0, we can keep track of the moment when the value of the second changes (either by incrementing by one or resetting to zero), store the milliseconds at that particular moment, and then use it to compute the fraction of the second we are at for each successive moment. This is, in fact, easier done than said, and Listing 11-2 shows the additions to our previous sketch that make this work.

Listing 11-2. Concentric Circles with Second Animation

```
void draw() {
  background(0);

  int h = hour() % 12;
  int m = minute();
  int s = second();

  if (s0 != s) {
    m0 = millis();
    s0 = s;
  }
  float f = (millis() - m0)/1000.0;
```

```
float sf = s + f;
float mf = m + sf/60.0;
float hf = h + mf/60.0;

float hAngle = map(hf, 0, 12, 0, TWO_PI);
float mAngle = map(mf, 0, 60, 0, TWO_PI);
float sAngle = map(sf, 0, 60, 0, TWO_PI);
...
}
```

The sf, mf, and hf variables are the decimal second, minute, and hour values, which we can map to the angular ranges as we did before and which now result in a continuous rotation.

Square Versus Round Watch Faces

Android smartwatches can have either a square or a round frame, and we need to ensure our watch face design can work with both, or if we prioritize one over the other, we should still provide a usable experience with the other one. The preference of round over square watches, or vice versa, is a contested topic in watch UI design: "In my experience, round-faced watches sell better than square-faced watches. I don't know exactly why that is. . . . It's most likely purely psychological; people's semantic notion of what a clock or a watch should look like" (https://www.wareable.com/smartwatches/round-v-square-smartwatches-which-is-best). On the opposite end: "I think that Round's days are numbered. We underestimate people's ability to get used to new things, to new paradigms. I think the experience of using a more squared watch will make more sense to people when they use both, and they will come around" (https://birchtree.me/blog/data-is-square/).

Regardless of which format becomes more popular in the end, Android supports both, and it is up to us to come up with designs that contemplate square and round watches. As an illustration of this problem, let's go ahead with a simple design for a square watch face: a rectangular grid with 24 squares, split into six rows and four columns. Each square corresponds to one hour, hours that already have passed are entirely grayed out, and the current hour is grayed up to the percentage given by the current minute. An implementation of this design is presented in Listing 11-3.

Listing 11-3. Rectangular Hour Grid

```
void setup() {
  textFont(createFont("Monospaced", 15 * displayDensity));
  textAlign(CENTER, CENTER);
  noStroke();
}

void draw() {
  background(0);
  int h = hour();
```

```
int m = minute();
float cellW = 0.9 * width/4.0;
float cellH = 0.9 * height/6.0;
translate(0.05 * cellW, 0.05 * cellH + wearInsets().bottom/2);
for (int n = 0; n < 24; n++) {
  int i = n % 4;
  int j = n / 4;
  float x = map(i, 0, 4, 0, width);
  float y = map(j, 0, 6, 0, height);
  float w = n == h ? map(m, 0, 60, 0, cellW) : cellW;

  if (!wearAmbient()) {
    fill(#578CB7);
    rect(x, y, cellW, cellH);
  }

  fill(255);
  text(str(n), x, y, cellW, cellH);

  if (n <= h) {
    fill(0, 170);
    rect(x, y, w, cellH);
  }
 }
}
```

Since in this watch face we are working with text, we create a monospaced font at a size that is scaled by the displayDensity system variable, as we did in previous chapters to ensure the consistent appearance of the text across devices with different DPIs. The screen resolution of an Android watch is typically between 300 and 400 pixels, but because of the small screen size, the DPI is usually in the xhdpi range (~320dpi).

This design will clearly not work on a round-faced watch. We could replace this rectangular grid with a polar one, but in that case each cell would have a different size, as shown in the left panel of Figure 11-4, and it would also be harder to implement the partially grayed-out cell that corresponds to the current hour. Another alternative could be to still use a rectangular grid, this time of 6 × 6, and remove the six corner cells that are either entirely or mostly outside of the circumscribed circle (right panel in Figure 11-4).

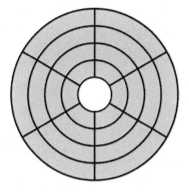 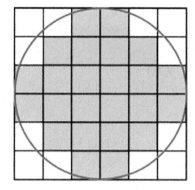

Figure 11-4. *Adapting a 6 × 4 rectangular grid to fit inside a round watch face, either as a polar grid (left) or as a larger 6 × 6 grid with some elements removed (right)*

The option here will depend on the desired visual result, and in certain cases the polar grid might be a better choice, while the trimmed rectangular grid might be in others. Since our priority is to keep all the elements the same size, we chose the latter option, shown in Listing 11-4.

Listing 11-4. Rectangular Grid for a Circular Watch

```
import java.util.Arrays;
import java.util.List;
List<Integer> corners = Arrays.asList(1, 2, 5, 6, 7, 12, 25,
                                      30, 31, 32, 35, 36);

void setup() {
  textFont(createFont("Monospaced", 15 * displayDensity));
  textAlign(CENTER, CENTER);
  noStroke();
}

void draw() {
  background(0);
  int h = hour();
  int m = minute();
  float cellW = 0.9 * width/6.0;
  float cellH = 0.9 * height/6.0;
  translate(0.05 * cellW, 0.05 * cellH + wearInsets().bottom/2);
  int n = 0;
  for (int n0 = 0; n0 < 36; n0++) {
    if (corners.contains(n0 + 1)) continue;

    int i = n0 % 6;
    int j = n0 / 6;
    float x = map(i, 0, 6, 0, width);
```

233

```
      float y = map(j, 0, 6, 0, height);
      float cw = n == h ? map(m, 0, 60, 0, cellW) : cellW;

      if (!wearAmbient()) {
        fill(#578CB7);
        rect(x, y, cellW, cellH);
      }

      fill(255);
      text(str(n), x, y, cellW, cellH);

      if (n <= h) {
        fill(0, 170);
        rect(x, y, cw, cellH);
      }
      n++;
    }
}
```

The output of these two watch faces sketches, from Listings 11-3 and 11-4, can be seen in Figure 11-5. The code of the two sketches can be combined into a single watch face sketch that selects the appropriate visualization depending on the value returned by the wearRound() or wearSquare() functions.

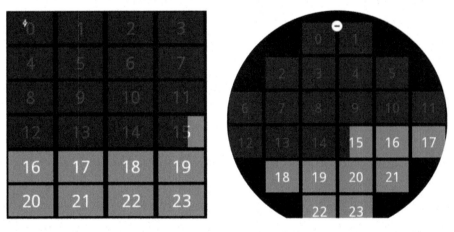

Figure 11-5. *Hour grid for square (left) and round (right) watches*

Working with a Watch Face Concept

Creating a watch face involves balancing several factors. As mentioned at the beginning of this chapter, there is an established visual language that people expect when communicating time. Smartwatches give us ample latitude to expand upon this existing language, and to come up with entirely new concepts. Also, watch faces can be interactive, configurable, and augmented with additional information (physical activity, calendar events, and so forth). Some of these considerations are covered in the design guide from Google (https://www.google.com/design/spec-wear/patterns/interactive-watch-faces.html), but experimentation can lead us to new ideas for displaying time.

As we saw with earlier projects in the book, a fundamental methodology in visual design is sketching and iteration, and this remains true for designing watch faces. A concept might be original and attractive, but it is unlikely that it will be successful in the first implementation. In the next sections, we will carry one concept through several iterations until reaching a definitive version.

Elapsed/Remaining Time

The concept for this watch face is not so much to serve as a functional timepiece, but rather to provide a reminder of the amount of time elapsed since the beginning of the day, and the remaining time until it ends. To accentuate this progression, we can measure time in total seconds since and from midnight, displaying it as it changes continuously from and toward zero.

As a visual representation of this progression, the waxing crescent of the moon could work as a metaphor for the diminishing day (Figure 11-6). Of course, this is not the only visual representation possible (and one could argue that it would mislead users into thinking the watch face is displaying the actual phases of the moon), but it will suffice as our first design.

Figure 11-6. *Crescent moon*

Bezier curves are handy for creating the shape of the waxing crescent by partially covering an ellipse with a shape containing the edge of the dark region, which is illustrated in Figure 11-7.

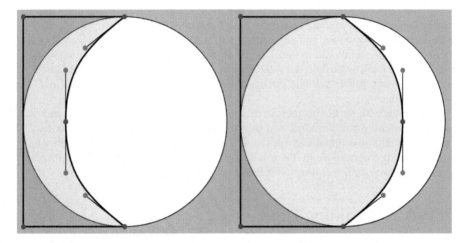

Figure 11-7. *Drawing a waxing crescent moon with Bezier curves*

As the elapsed seconds increase from 0 to 86,400 (24 × 60 × 60), the control vectors of the Bezier curve at the top and bottom of the shape start pointing toward the left side of the screen (left panel of Figure 11-7), and gradually rotate to point toward the opposite side (right panel). So, we could map the seconds to an angular value from PI to 0, and then use this value to rotate the control points.

The code in Listing 11-7 implements this idea and shows the remaining seconds as text, which is scaled according to the space left in the visible crescent.

Listing 11-5. Moon Watch Face

```
int totSec = 24 * 60 * 60;
PFont font;

void setup() {
  font = createFont("Serif", 62);
  textAlign(LEFT, CENTER);
}

void draw() {
  background(0);
  int sec = 60 * 60 * hour() + 60 * minute() + second();
  float a = map(sec, 0, totSec, PI, 0);
  float x = map(sec, 0, totSec, 0, width);
  float r = sec < totSec/2 ? map(sec, 0, totSec/2, 90, 50) :
                             map(sec, totSec/2, totSec, 50, 90);
```

```
    int t = totSec - sec;
    String strt = str(t);
    int n = strt.length();
    float d = (width - x) / n;
    textFont(font, 1.75 * d);

    float rad = 0.5 * width;
    float diam = width;
    if (wearAmbient()) {
      fill(255);
      text(strt, x, rad);
    } else {
      fill(255);
      ellipse(rad, rad, diam, diam);
      noStroke();
      fill(0);
      beginShape();
      vertex(0, 0);
      vertex(rad, 0);
      float cx = r * cos(a);
      float cy = r * sin(a);
      bezierVertex(rad + cx, cy, x, rad - r, x, rad);
      vertex(x, rad);
      bezierVertex(x, rad + r, rad + cx, diam - cy, rad, diam);
      vertex(0, diam);
      endShape(CLOSE);

      fill(0, 170);
      text(strt, x, rad);
    }
}
```

In this code, we create a large font for the numbers in the watch face. Since these numbers change size as the available space in the moon crescent grows and shrinks, we set the original font size to be the largest possible (in this case, 62 pixels) so that the text looks good after resizing it with textFont(font, 1.75 * d). Remember that text will look blurry when we create the font with a certain size but then set a larger size for drawing.

Adding Interaction

Watch faces can receive touch events via the touch screen just like regular apps do on phones and tablets. Likewise, we can handle these events in Processing using the mousePressed() and mouseReleased() functions. However, dragging events are not supported on watch faces, since these events are captured by the Android system to drive the swipes that give access to the different menus in the watch UI. Multi-touch events are not supported either.

Given the small size of the watch screen, touch events are typically meant to toggle between different views on the watch face and not to drive precise interaction using the x and y coordinates associated with the touch. In the case of our watch face, we can use a single touch to toggle between showing the elapsed and the remaining seconds. The entire code, including the new interaction handling, is shown in Listing 11-6.

Listing 11-6. Moon Watch Face with Interaction

```
int totSec = 24 * 60 * 60;
boolean showElapsed = false;
PFont font;

void setup() {
  font = createFont("Serif", 62);
  textAlign(LEFT, CENTER);
}

void draw() {
  background(0);
  int sec = 60 * 60 * hour() + 60 * minute() + second();
  float a = map(sec, 0, totSec, PI, 0);
  float x = map(sec, 0, totSec, 0, width);
  float r = sec < totSec/2 ? map(sec, 0, totSec/2, 90, 50) :
                             map(sec, totSec/2, totSec, 50, 90);

  int t = showElapsed ? sec : totSec - sec;
  String strt = str(t);
  int n = strt.length();
  float d = showElapsed ? x / n : (width - x) / n;
  textFont(font, 1.75 * d);

  float rad = 0.5 * width;
  float diam = width;
  if (wearAmbient()) {
    fill(255);
    text(strt, x, rad);
  } else {
    fill(255);
    ellipse(rad, rad, diam, diam);
    noStroke();
    fill(0);
    beginShape();
    vertex(0, 0);
    vertex(rad, 0);
    float cx = r * cos(a);
    float cy = r * sin(a);
    bezierVertex(rad + cx, cy, x, rad - r, x, rad);
    vertex(x, rad);
```

```
    bezierVertex(x, rad + r, rad + cx, diam - cy, rad, diam);
    vertex(0, diam);
    endShape(CLOSE);

    if (showElapsed) fill(255, 170);
    else fill(0, 170);
    text(strt, x, rad);
  }
}

void mousePressed() {
  showElapsed = !showElapsed;
  if (showElapsed) textAlign(RIGHT, CENTER);
  else textAlign(LEFT, CENTER);
}
```

Loading/Displaying Images

Images are supported in watch faces in exactly the same way as we discussed previously for regular and wallpaper apps. We can rely on loadImage() to load an image file into our sketch and the image() function to display the image on the screen. With the help of this functionality, we can complete our watch face in Listing 11-7 with an actual image of the moon as the background. Different outputs of the watch face, with and without the background image, are included in Figure 11-8.

Listing 11-7. Moon Watch Face with Background Image

```
int totSec = 24 * 60 * 60;
boolean showElapsed = false;
PFont font;
PImage moon;

void setup() {
  moon = loadImage("moon.png");
  font = createFont("Serif", 62);
  textAlign(LEFT, CENTER);
}

void draw() {
  background(0);
  int sec = 60 * 60 * hour() + 60 * minute() + second();
  float a = map(sec, 0, totSec, PI, 0);
  float x = map(sec, 0, totSec, 0, width);
  float r = sec < totSec/2 ? map(sec, 0, totSec/2, 90, 50) :
                             map(sec, totSec/2, totSec, 50, 90);
```

```
  int t = showElapsed ? sec : totSec - sec;
  String strt = str(t);
  int n = strt.length();
  float d = showElapsed ? x / n : (width - x) / n;
  textFont(font, 1.75 * d);

  float rad = 0.5 * width;
  float diam = width;
  if (wearAmbient()) {
    fill(255);
    text(strt, x, rad);
  } else {
    image(moon, 0, 0, 2*rad, 2*rad);
    noStroke();
    fill(0);
    beginShape();
    vertex(0, 0);
    vertex(rad, 0);
    float cx = r * cos(a);
    float cy = r * sin(a);
    bezierVertex(rad + cx, cy, x, rad - r, x, rad);
    vertex(x, rad);
    bezierVertex(x, rad + r, rad + cx, diam - cy, rad, diam);
    vertex(0, diam);
    endShape(CLOSE);

    if (showElapsed) fill(255, 170);
    else fill(200, 230);
    text(strt, x, rad);
  }
}

void mousePressed() {
  showElapsed = !showElapsed;
  if (showElapsed) textAlign(RIGHT, CENTER);
  else textAlign(LEFT, CENTER);
}
```

Figure 11-8. *Versions of the "moon" watch face showing remaining seconds in the day, elapsed, and moon texture*

One small change we made in this new version of our watch face was to use a different color for the text of the remaining seconds. In the version without a background image, we had a dark gray (0, 170) that offered good contrast with the white background. Now, the moon image is too dark to ensure that the text is readable, so we switched to a brighter gray with the color values (200, 230).

Summary

In this chapter, we looked at watch faces for time display. As part of this subject, we discussed some of the issues one needs to be aware of, starting with using time values to implement dynamic visualizations of time, moving on to how to create designs for round and square watches, and concluding with an example illustrating the importance of iteration in watch face design. These materials should provide guidance for a first foray into the topic, and many possibilities await those interested in delving deeper into the development of watch faces.

CHAPTER 12

■ ■ ■

Visualizing Physical Activity

In this chapter, we will go over some of the body sensors available on smartwatches and wearable devices in general, and the techniques we have at our disposal to read and use data from these sensors in real-time.

Body Sensors

There are body sensors in many different kinds of wearable devices, particularly fitness trackers designed for personal monitoring of physical activity. These devices are often linked to mobile apps that help users track their progress over time. Most Android smartwatches come with at least two kinds of body sensors, a pedometer, or step counter, and a heart-rate sensor. This shows that there is some overlap between activity trackers (which also include clock functions) and proper smartwatches. Some Android smartwatches (like the Polaris M600) are even meant to be used primarily as activity trackers.

In the previous two chapters, we learned how to use Processing to create animated watch faces, and, before that, we went through the details of accessing sensor data using the Android API and the Ketai library. We should now be able to combine these techniques to create watch faces that read the data from the body sensors on the watch and present this data to the user through dynamic visualization.

Step Counter

The step counter is the most common sensor for monitoring physical activity. It reads data from the accelerometer to infer the movement patterns of the wearer, specifically those associated with walking or running. Step count is a proxy for overall physical activity, although of limited accuracy, as it is not able to measure other forms of activity that do not involve walking or running or the intensity of the movement.

A daily step count of 10,000 is a typically accepted goal for an adequate level of physical activity, but there has been some controversy surrounding this number as a universal target for fitness (https://www.ncbi.nlm.nih.gov/pubmed/14715035).

© Andrés Colubri 2017

A. Colubri, *Processing for Android*, https://doi.org/10.1007/978-1-4842-2719-0_12

Heart Rate

Heart rate is a very precise indicator of physical exertion, and the heart-rate monitor on a smartwatch allows us to access this information in real-time. Optical heart-rate monitors, like those available in smartwatches, are generally less reliable than other types of monitors. Optical monitors measure heart rate in a process called photoplethysmography, where they shine light, typically from an LED, into the skin and detect the differences in light diffraction due to changes in blood flow. The watch processes this data to generate a pulse reading that can be displayed back to the user.

On the other hand, electrocardiogram (ECG) sensors measure the electrical signals from heart activity directly, but they require that electrodes be attached to different parts of the body, following the same principles as the first electrocardiographs in the early twentieth century (Figure 12-1). Medical ECG sensors can use up to 12 electrodes, but sport chest straps rely on a single ECG sensor placed near the heart. However, optical monitors in smartwatches and other wearables have evolved to monitor heart rate accurately enough and continuously throughout the day with minimal inconvenience.

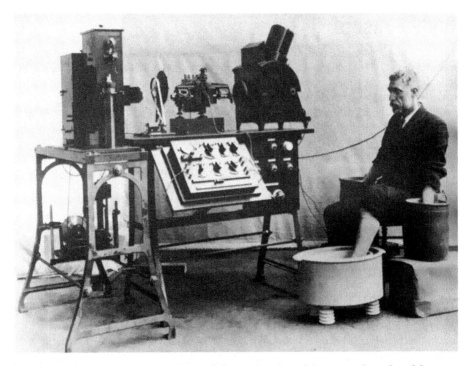

Figure 12-1. *An early electrocardiograph from 1911. Note the arms and one leg of the patient immersed in buckets, which contain a saline solution to conduct the body's current. Modern ECG sensors are still based on this three-point principle, but optical sensors rely on a completely different physical process to measure heart rate.*

Visualizing Physical Activity in Real-time

Using Processing to implement a watch face that displays step count or heart rate data is not difficult. We can retrieve the sensor data in the same way we did with other sensors earlier, like the accelerometer and the gyroscope. All we need to do is create a sensor manager, get the corresponding sensor object from it, and attach a listener that will return the actual values as they are measured by the hardware.

Simple Step Counter

Accessing the step-counter sensor does not require any special permission. This sensor runs continuously, even if our watch face does not access it. One peculiarity is that it returns the number of steps since the last startup of the watch, and it is reset to zero only on a system reboot. Because of this, if we want to show the number of steps since we launched the watch face, we have to store the first step count value we receive from the listener and subtract it from all subsequent values, as shown in Listing 12-1.

Listing 12-1. Displaying the Step Count

```
import android.content.Context;
import android.hardware.Sensor;
import android.hardware.SensorManager;
import android.hardware.SensorEvent;
import android.hardware.SensorEventListener;

Context context;
SensorManager manager;
Sensor sensor;
SensorListener listener;

int offset = -1;
int steps;

void setup() {
  fullScreen();
  frameRate(1);
  textFont(createFont("SansSerif", 28 * displayDensity));
  textAlign(CENTER, CENTER);
  initCounter();
}

void draw() {
  background(0);
  translate(0, wearInsets().bottom/2);
  text(steps + " steps", 0, 0, width, height);
}
```

```
void initCounter() {
  Context context = getContext();
  manager = (SensorManager)context.getSystemService(Context.SENSOR_SERVICE);
  sensor = manager.getDefaultSensor(Sensor.TYPE_STEP_COUNTER);
  listener = new SensorListener();
  manager.registerListener(listener, sensor,
                           SensorManager.SENSOR_DELAY_NORMAL);
}

class SensorListener implements SensorEventListener {
  public void onSensorChanged(SensorEvent event) {
    if (offset == -1) offset = (int)event.values[0];
    steps = (int)event.values[0] - offset;
  }
  public void onAccuracyChanged(Sensor sensor, int accuracy) { }
}
```

Here, we use the offset variable, initialized to -1, to store the initial step count. Also, if we are planning to create a watch face that keeps track of daily step counts, we should implement our own "overnight reset," since Android will not reset the step count automatically at the end of the day.

Accessing the Heart-rate Sensor

The heart rate requires the BODY_SENSORS permission, which is classified as a critical or dangerous permission because of the personal nature of the data. As with geolocation, it is not enough to select the permission through the Android Permission Selector in the PDE (Figure 12-2); we have to manually request the permission in the code with the requestPermission() function, providing the name of the function that will be called upon the result of the permission request. See Listing 12-2.

Listing 12-2. Displaying the Heart Rate

```
import android.content.Context;
import android.hardware.Sensor;
import android.hardware.SensorManager;
import android.hardware.SensorEvent;
import android.hardware.SensorEventListener;

Context context;
SensorManager manager;
Sensor sensor;
SensorListener listener;
```

```
int bpm;

void setup() {
  fullScreen();
  frameRate(1);
  textFont(createFont("SansSerif", 28 * displayDensity));
  textAlign(CENTER, CENTER);
  requestPermission("android.permission.BODY_SENSORS", "initMonitor");
}

void draw() {
  background(0);
  translate(0, wearInsets().bottom/2);
  text(bpm + " beats/min", 0, 0, width, height);
}

void initMonitor(boolean granted) {
  if (granted) {
    Context context = getContext();
    manager = (SensorManager)context.
              getSystemService(Context.SENSOR_SERVICE);
    sensor = manager.getDefaultSensor(Sensor.TYPE_HEART_RATE);
    listener = new SensorListener();
    manager.registerListener(listener, sensor,
                       SensorManager.SENSOR_DELAY_NORMAL);
  }
}

class SensorListener implements SensorEventListener {
  public void onSensorChanged(SensorEvent event) {
    bpm = int(event.values[0]);
  }
  public void onAccuracyChanged(Sensor sensor, int accuracy) { }
}
```

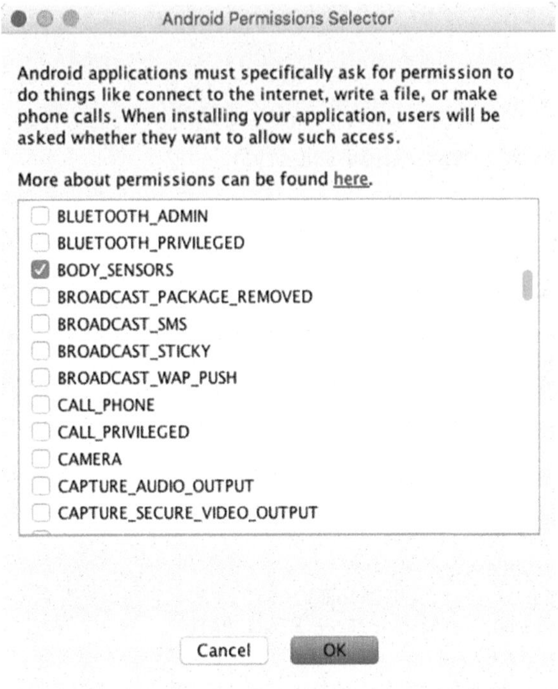

● ◎ ●   Android Permissions Selector

Android applications must specifically ask for permission to
do things like connect to the internet, write a file, or make
phone calls. When installing your application, users will be
asked whether they want to allow such access.

More about permissions can be found here.

- ☐ BLUETOOTH_ADMIN
- ☐ BLUETOOTH_PRIVILEGED
- ☑ BODY_SENSORS
- ☐ BROADCAST_PACKAGE_REMOVED
- ☐ BROADCAST_SMS
- ☐ BROADCAST_STICKY
- ☐ BROADCAST_WAP_PUSH
- ☐ CALL_PHONE
- ☐ CALL_PRIVILEGED
- ☐ CAMERA
- ☐ CAPTURE_AUDIO_OUTPUT
- ☐ CAPTURE_SECURE_VIDEO_OUTPUT

Cancel   OK

Figure 12-2. *The BODY_SENSORS permission in the selector*

When we open the watch face for the first time, we should see a dialog similar to the
one in Figure 12-3 asking to allow or deny access to body-sensor data.

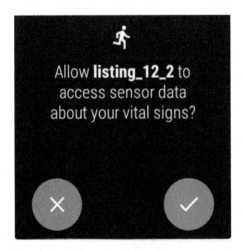

Figure 12-3. *Permission request when launching the watch face*

Visualizing Step-count Data

A simple way of visualizing activity data is by using a radial representation that depicts the progression toward a set goal. We already used the arc() function to display elapsed time, and we can adapt it easily to show progress toward a desired step-count value; for example, 100, as in Listing 12-3.

Listing 12-3. Radial Step-count Visualization

```
...
void setup() {
  frameRate(1);
  strokeCap(ROUND);
  stroke(255);
  noFill();
  textFont(createFont("SansSerif", 18 * displayDensity));
  textAlign(CENTER, CENTER);
  initCounter();
}

void draw() {
  background(0);
  translate(0, wearInsets().bottom/2);
  if (wearAmbient()) strokeWeight(1);
  else strokeWeight(10);
  float angle = map(min(steps, 100), 0, 100, 0, TWO_PI);
  arc(width/2, height/2, width/2, width/2,
      PI + HALF_PI, PI + HALF_PI + angle);
  if (steps == 0) text("0 steps", 0, 0, width, height);
}
...
```

The rest of the sketch is identical to Listing 12-1. Next, we can add a multiplier to show how many times the user has reached the goal already by simply dividing the number of steps by the target, in this case 100, and drawing that value as text in the center of the screen. The updated draw() function is shown in Listing 12-4, and the output of this new watch face can be seen in Figure 12-4.

Listing 12-4. Adding a Multiplier

```
void draw() {
  background(0);
  translate(0, wearInsets().bottom/2);
  if (wearAmbient()) strokeWeight(1);
  else strokeWeight(10);
  int mult = int(steps / 100);
  float angle = map(steps - mult * 100, 0, 100, 0, TWO_PI);
  noFill();
```

```
arc(width/2, height/2, width/2, width/2,
    PI + HALF_PI, PI + HALF_PI + angle);
fill(255);
if (0 < steps) {
  text("x" + (mult + 1), 0, 0, width, height);
} else {
  text("0 steps", 0, 0, width, height);
}
}
```

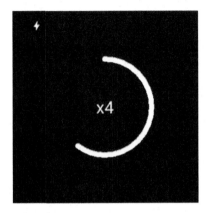

Figure 12-4. *Step-count watch face, with multiplier counter*

A Beating Heart

For a visual representation of the heart-rate data, we can rely on a very direct translation: a beating heart, or a beating circle for simplicity. We already know how to obtain the beats-per-minute value from the sensor; the problem is animating the circle based on this rate so it is accurate enough to convey the intensity and rhythm of the heartbeat. An actual ECG signal is reproduced in Figure 12-5, where we see that the electric signal of a single beat has several peaks and valleys. This signal depicts the so-called sinus rhythm (https://en.wikipedia.org/wiki/Sinus_rhythm), with the large peak corresponding to contraction of the heart ventricles (https://en.wikipedia.org/wiki/Heart#Blood_flow).

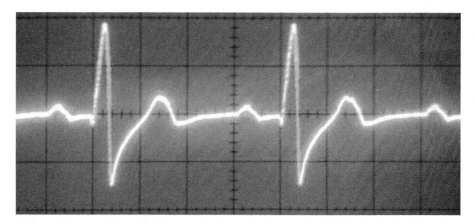

Figure 12-5. *An ECG signal*

We can approximate this pattern with an "impulse" curve that presents a rapid initial increase followed by a decay until the next beat (Figure 12-6). A simple mathematical function that generates this impulse curve is the following:

```
float impulse(float k, float t) {
  float h = k * t;
  return h * exp(1.0 - h);
}
```

In this formula, the constant *k* determines how quickly the impulse reaches its peak (the position of the peak is exactly t =1/k). From inspecting the ECG signal in Figure 12-5, we could conclude that the first peak in a heartbeat occurs at around 25 percent of the entire duration of the beat. As an example, if our heart is beating at 80 beats per minute (bpm), then a single beat would last 60,000/80 = 750 milliseconds, and its first peak should occur approximately 0.25 × 750 = 187.5 milliseconds. From this, we can calculate k, since t = 187.5 = 1/k, giving in this case k ~ 0.0053. In general, for any measured bpm value, the constant k will be equal to bpm/(0.25×60,000).

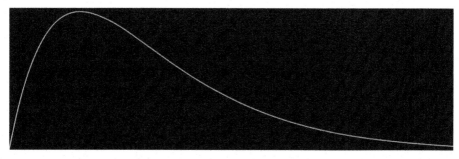

Figure 12-6. *An impulse function, generated with Graph Toy, by Inigo Quilez (http://www.iquilezles.org/apps/graphtoy/index.html)*

251

We can control the animation of any shape in Processing using this impulse formula. Of course, this formula is not exact, and its maximum does not necessarily coincide with the exact moment of ventricular contraction, but it should be enough as an approximation to convey the beating pace. Listing 12-5 extends our previous heart-rate watch face from Listing 12-2 by incorporating an ellipse whose radius follows the impulse function. As before, we must add the BODY_SENSORS permission through the PDE, granting this permission once the watch face launches on the device or in the emulator.

Listing 12-5. Creating a Heart-beat Animation

```
import android.content.Context;
import android.hardware.Sensor;
import android.hardware.SensorManager;
import android.hardware.SensorEvent;
import android.hardware.SensorEventListener;

Context context;
SensorManager manager;
Sensor sensor;
SensorListener listener;

int bpm;

void setup() {
  fullScreen();
  noStroke();
  textFont(createFont("SansSerif", 28 * displayDensity));
  textAlign(CENTER, CENTER);
  requestPermission("android.permission.BODY_SENSORS", "initMonitor");
}

void draw() {
  background(0);
  translate(0, wearInsets().bottom/2);
  if (wearAmbient()) {
    fill(255);
    text(bpm + " bpm", 0, 0, width, height);
  } else {
    int duration = 750;
    if (0 < bpm) duration = 60000 / bpm;
    float x = millis() % duration;
    float k = 1/(0.25 * duration);
    float a = impulse(k, x);
    float r = map(a, 0, 1, 0.75, 0.9) * width;
    translate(width/2, height/2);
    fill(247, 47, 47);
    ellipse(0, 0, r, r);
  }
}
```

```
float impulse(float k, float x) {
  float h = k * x;
  return h * exp(1.0 - h);
}

void initMonitor(boolean granted) {
  if (!granted) return;
  Context context = getContext();
  manager = (SensorManager)context.getSystemService(Context.SENSOR_SERVICE);
  sensor = manager.getDefaultSensor(Sensor.TYPE_HEART_RATE);
  listener = new SensorListener();
  manager.registerListener(listener, sensor,
                        SensorManager.SENSOR_DELAY_NORMAL);
}

class SensorListener implements SensorEventListener {
  public void onSensorChanged(SensorEvent event) {
    bpm = int(event.values[0]);
  }
  public void onAccuracyChanged(Sensor sensor, int accuracy) { }
}
```

The ellipse is drawn only when the watch is in interactive mode. We calculate the duration of a single beat at the current bpm and store it in the duration variable, which we use in all the other parameters needed to evaluate the impulse function. Since the impulse ranges between 0 and 1, we map it to the (0.75, 0.9) interval so that the size of the ellipse varies between contracted and expanded states that are neither too small nor too big. We can tweak these parameters until we arrive at a result that we find visually satisfactory.

Sensor Debugging

Testing a watch face that makes use of sensors can be difficult, since we may need to move around to get enough data from the step counter or heart-rate sensor to ensure that we evaluate the different instances in our code. Since Processing allows us to easily switch back and forth between modes, and the great majority of the Processing API remains the same between Java and Android modes, we could use Java mode to test the parts of the code that do not depend on the actual sensors, particularly the rendering code.

However, we often still have to inspect the actual sensor data to determine if something is wrong, either with our assumptions about this data or with the way we are processing it in our code. One way we could do this is by recording the values from the sensors into a text file and then pulling this file from the watch to look for any patterns of interest. Listing 12-6 exemplifies this approach to save the data from the heart-rate sensor. Since we write the data to a file in the external storage, we need to add the WRITE_ EXTERNAL_STORAGE permission to the sketch, and the corresponding request in the sketch code, since it is also a dangerous permission.

Listing 12-6. Saving Sensor Data to a File

```
import android.content.Context;
import android.hardware.Sensor;
import android.hardware.SensorManager;
import android.hardware.SensorEvent;
import android.hardware.SensorEventListener;
import android.os.Environment;

Context context;
SensorManager manager;
Sensor sensor;
SensorListener listener;

int bpm;
String[] data = { "time,rate" };

void setup() {
  fullScreen();
  frameRate(1);
  textFont(createFont("SansSerif", 28 * displayDensity));
  textAlign(CENTER, CENTER);
  requestPermission("android.permission.BODY_SENSORS", "initMonitor");

  requestPermission("android.permission.WRITE_EXTERNAL_STORAGE");
}

void draw() {
  background(0);
  translate(0, wearInsets().bottom/2);
  text(bpm + " beats/min", 0, 0, width, height);
}

void mousePressed() {
  background(200, 40, 40);
  File sd = Environment.getExternalStorageDirectory();
  String path = sd.getAbsolutePath();
  File directory = new File(path, "out");
  File file = new File(directory, "sensor-data.csv");
  saveStrings(file, data);
}

void initMonitor(boolean granted) {
  if (granted) {
    Context context = getContext();
    manager = (SensorManager)
            context.getSystemService(Context.SENSOR_SERVICE);
    sensor = manager.getDefaultSensor(Sensor.TYPE_HEART_RATE);
    listener = new SensorListener();
```

```
    manager.registerListener(listener, sensor,
                            SensorManager.SENSOR_DELAY_NORMAL);
  }
}

class SensorListener implements SensorEventListener {
  public void onSensorChanged(SensorEvent event) {
    bpm = int(event.values[0]);
    data = (String[]) append(data, millis() + "," + bpm);
  }
  public void onAccuracyChanged(Sensor sensor, int accuracy) { }
}
```

First, notice how the request for the WRITE_EXTERNAL_STORAGE permission does not include a function to call after the permission has been granted (or denied). This is because there is no additional initialization required to write to the external storage.

In this sketch, every time we receive a new sensor value, we append it to the string array data, together with the time in milliseconds. We save this array as a CSV (comma-separated values) file into the device's external storage only when touching the screen, with the saveStrings() function. The external storage in a watch is emulated in its internal storage, as smartwatches don't include SD cards. In order to download the file to the development computer, we can run the following command from the terminal:

```
adb -s 127.0.0.1:4444 pull /storage/emulated/0/out/sensor-data.csv
```

Once we have downloaded the data file, we can read it in a text editor or spreadsheet software. We could also use it as the input in a Processing sketch, like the one in Listing 12-7, where we read the CSV file with the loadTable() function (https://processing.org/reference/loadTable_.html). This function returns a Table object containing all the data organized in rows and columns. In this case, we simply draw a line plot with a LINE_STRIP shape, connecting the values in each consecutive row. A typical outcome of this sketch is depicted in Figure 12-7.

Listing 12-7. Plotting Sensor Data in Processing

```
size(700, 200, P2D);
Table table = loadTable("sensor-data.csv", "header");
background(90);
stroke(247, 47, 47);
strokeWeight(4);
beginShape(LINE_STRIP);
for (int i = 0; i < table.getRowCount(); i++) {
  TableRow row = table.getRow(i);
  int r = row.getInt("rate");
  float x = map(i, 0, table.getRowCount() - 1, 0, width);
  float y = map(r, 0, 100, height, 0);
  vertex(x, y);
}
endShape();
```

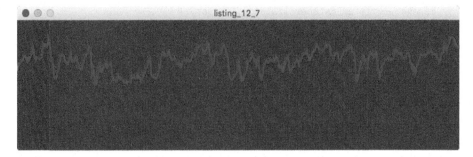

Figure 12-7. *Line plot of heart-rate data*

In these two examples, our goal was to record the sensor data in order to conduct a later analysis to identify any issues with the data. A different, but related, aim is to debug our data-processing code in a more controlled fashion. We could do this by generating "synthetic" data resembling what would come out from the sensors. For example, Listing 12-8 shows the heart-rate example from earlier, modified to print random bpm values generated in a continuously running thread.

Listing 12-8. Generating Synthetic Sensor Data

```
int bpm;

void setup() {
  fullScreen();
  frameRate(1);
  textFont(createFont("SansSerif", 28 * displayDensity));
  textAlign(CENTER, CENTER);
  thread("generateData");
}

void draw() {
  background(0);
  translate(0, wearInsets().bottom/2);
  text(bpm + " beats/min", 0, 0, width, height);
}

void generateData() {
  while (true) {
    bpm = int(random(60, 100));
    delay(2000);
  }
}
```

We discussed threads back in Chapter 6, including how we can use them to run calculations that would otherwise slow down the framerate of our app. Here, we launch the generateData() function in a new thread at the end of setup(). In this function, we keep generating random bpm values between 60 and 100, with a delay of two seconds between each consecutive value, which approximates the behavior of the real heart-rate sensor well enough for testing (the delay interval could also be random to add even more variability). Also in Chapter 6, we considered the use of synchronized methods to prevent different threads from accessing the same data concurrently. In this minimal example, concurrency is not an issue, but we will need to take care of it in the final project we are about to consider for the rest of this chapter.

Growing a Tree as You Exercise

So far, our physical activity watch faces have been relatively simple. Can we make an activity tracker more interesting (and maybe more rewarding) by offering a visual output that not only tracks the activity level, but also introduces some visual variation? If we think of the step count as a value that starts at 0 and grows until reaching a set goal, say 10,000 steps, would it be possible to use it to drive the "growth" of some organic element in our sketch—for example, a plant or a tree?

Generating a natural-looking tree with code is a problem that can take us to fascinating ideas in mathematics, like self-similarity and fractals (https://en.wikipedia.org/wiki/Self-similarity). We can find several techniques to simulate tree growth, some of them shown in Figure 12-8.

Figure 12-8. *Different algorithms for tree generation. Left: fractal recursion (by Daniel Shiffman, https://processing.org/examples/tree.html). Center: branching tree (by Ryan Chao, https://www.openprocessing.org/sketch/186129). Right: particle system tree (by Asher Salomon, https://www.openprocessing.org/sketch/144159)*

Most importantly, we need an algorithm that lets us grow our tree as the step count increases. Both the fractal-recursion and particle-system algorithms referred to in Figure 12-8 can be unfolded through time. Particularly the latter, as it gradually grows until it reaches its full size, and it gives a more organic look than the fractal recursion does. Furthermore, its code is available on OpenProcessing, so we can use it as the starting point for our project.

■ **Note**   OpenProcessing (https://www.openprocessing.org/) is an online library of Processing sketches, most of which can be run inside the browser, available for modification and sharing under a Creative Commons license.

Generating a Tree with a Particle System

We already made use of particle systems in Chapter 6 to generate an animation that follows the brightness patterns in an image. Particle systems can be used in many different scenarios to create organic movement, as is the case here. Making some changes to the OpenProcessing sketch by Asher Salomon, we arrive at the code seen in Listing 12-9, which gives us the output shown in Figure 12-9 when running it in Java mode.

Listing 12-9. Growing Tree

```
ArrayList<Branch> branches = new ArrayList<Branch>();

void setup() {
  size(500, 500);
  noStroke();
  branches.add(new Branch());
  background(155, 211, 247);
}

void draw() {
  for (int i = 0; i < branches.size(); i++) {
    Branch branch = branches.get(i);
    branch.update();
    branch.display();
  }
}

class Branch {
  PVector position;
  PVector velocity;
  float diameter;

  Branch() {
    position = new PVector(width/2, height);
    velocity = new PVector(0, -1);
    diameter = width/15.0;
  }
  Branch(Branch parent) {
    position = parent.position.copy();
    velocity = parent.velocity.copy();
```

```
    diameter = parent.diameter / 1.4142;
    parent.diameter = diameter;
  }
  void update() {
    if (1 < diameter) {
      position.add(velocity);
      float opening = map(diameter, 1, width/15.0, 1, 0);
      float angle = random(PI - opening * HALF_PI,
                           TWO_PI + opening * HALF_PI);
      PVector shake = PVector.fromAngle(angle);
      shake.mult(0.1);
      velocity.add(shake);
      velocity.normalize();
      if (random(0, 1) < 0.04) branches.add(new Branch(this));
    }
  }
  void display() {
    if (1 < diameter) {
      fill(175, 108, 44, 50);
      ellipse(position.x, position.y, diameter, diameter);
    }
  }
}
```

Figure 12-9. *Output of the tree-generation algorithm*

To understand this code, we should look at how the Branch class is used to represent a swarm of moving particles that, as they leave a trail on the screen, generate the branches of the tree. The basic idea is the following: each particle is a small ellipse with a position, velocity, and diameter. Initially, there is a single particle, placed at the bottom of the screen, with a diameter of width/15 (more about this choice later) and an upward velocity of 1. From time to time, a new particle branches out from an existing one, so we eventually get many branches coming out from a single trunk. For this to work properly, we must be careful to call background() only in setup() so the trails of the particles are not erased in the next frame.

Every time the update() method of a particle is called in draw(), its position is updated according to the current velocity, and the velocity is slightly jolted by the shake vector. This vector has a magnitude of 0.1 and a random direction determined by the angle variable. However, there is one important detail in the way this angle is calculated that makes it not completely random. The reason for this is that we want to avoid having the tree swing to the sides early on, so we map the branches' diameters, ranging from width/15 at the beginning to 1 at the end, to the opening variable between 0 and 1. If the diameter of a branch approaches 1, it means that the tree is already well grown, so the branch does not need to be straight, and the angle of the shake vector can be anywhere between PI - opening * HALF_PI and TWO_PI + opening * HALF_PI. If the opening is exactly 1, then the angle is chosen from the entire circle range. On the other hand, when the opening is close to 0 at the beginning, the angle can only range between PI and TWO_PI, which represents the upper half of the circle. In this way, the branches are forced to move upward when the tree is starting to grow.

The other key aspect of the algorithm is the branching mechanism: every time a particle is updated, it creates a new branch at the current position if a random draw between 0 and 1 is smaller than 0.04. The new branch is just another particle object, which is initialized from its parent by having the same position and velocity, but a diameter scaled down by a factor of $1/\sqrt{2}$. As a result of the branching, the parent particle also gets its diameter reduced by the same factor.

We just reviewed the main elements of the algorithm. As we see in the code, there are several numerical parameters we could modify to tweak the appearance of the tree. One such choice is the initial diameter of the branches, here set to width/15 because it gives reasonably sized trees. Also, as the result of this particular parameter selection, the algorithm will take a fairly well-defined number of iterations to reach a full-grown tree, which in this case is around 300 (we will come back to this number soon).

Incorporating Step-count Data

We have a working version of the tree-generation algorithm, but it is not tied to the step-count sensor yet. Inspecting the values returned by this sensor, we realize that steps are not detected one by one, but rather we get a number that increases by irregular amounts. So, we could compute the difference in the step count between the current and the last onSensorChanged() event and update our particles as many times as needed. Let's try this approach in Listing 12-10.

Listing 12-10. Driving the Growth of the Tree with the Step Count

```
import android.content.Context;
import android.hardware.Sensor;
import android.hardware.SensorManager;
import android.hardware.SensorEvent;
import android.hardware.SensorEventListener;
```

```
Context context;
SensorManager manager;
Sensor sensor;
SensorListener listener;

int offset = -1;
int psteps, steps;
int stepInc = 0;

ArrayList<Branch> branches = new ArrayList<Branch>();
PGraphics canvas;

void setup() {
  fullScreen();
  noStroke();
  branches.add(new Branch());
  initCanvas();
  initCounter();
}

void draw() {
  background(0);
  if (wearInteractive()) growTree();
  image(canvas, 0, 0);
}

synchronized void growTree() {
  canvas.beginDraw();
  for (int s = 0; s < stepInc; s++) {
    for (int i = 0; i < branches.size(); i++) {
      Branch branch = branches.get(i);
      branch.update();
      branch.display();
    }
  }
  canvas.endDraw();
  stepInc = 0;
}

synchronized void updateSteps(int value) {
  if (offset == -1) offset = value;
  steps = value - offset;
  stepInc += steps - psteps;
  psteps = steps;
}
```

```
void initCanvas() {
  canvas = createGraphics(width, height);
  canvas.beginDraw();
  canvas.background(155, 211, 247);
  canvas.noStroke();
  canvas.endDraw();
}

class Branch {
  PVector position;
  PVector velocity;
  float diameter;

  Branch() {
    position = new PVector(width/2, height);
    velocity = new PVector(0, -1);
    diameter = width/15.0;
  }
  Branch(Branch parent) {
    position = parent.position.copy();
    velocity = parent.velocity.copy();
    diameter = parent.diameter / 1.4142;
    parent.diameter = diameter;
  }
  void update() {
    if (1 < diameter) {
      position.add(velocity);
      float opening = map(diameter, 1, width/15.0, 1, 0);
      float angle = random(PI - opening * HALF_PI,
                           TWO_PI + opening * HALF_PI);
      PVector shake = PVector.fromAngle(angle);
      shake.mult(0.1);
      velocity.add(shake);
      velocity.normalize();
      if (random(0, 1) < 0.04) branches.add(new Branch(this));
    }
  }
  void display() {
    if (1 < diameter) {
      canvas.fill(175, 108, 44, 50);
      canvas.ellipse(position.x, position.y, diameter, diameter);
    }
  }
}
```

```
void initCounter() {
  Context context = getContext();
  manager = (SensorManager)context.getSystemService(Context.SENSOR_SERVICE);
  sensor = manager.getDefaultSensor(Sensor.TYPE_STEP_COUNTER);
  listener = new SensorListener();
  manager.registerListener(listener, sensor,
                            SensorManager.SENSOR_DELAY_NORMAL);
}

class SensorListener implements SensorEventListener {
  synchronized void onSensorChanged(SensorEvent event) {
    updateSteps(int(event.values[0]));
  }
  void onAccuracyChanged(Sensor sensor, int accuracy) { }
}
```

We reused most of the code from Listing 12-9 and added the standard Android event handlers. But there are several new things we should consider. First, we are drawing the branches into an offscreen PGraphics surface, which we used already in Chapter 9. The reason is the following: as a watch face, our sketch will have to present a different output for ambient mode. Since this would require erasing the entire screen, we would lose the particle trails making the tree. Drawing them into a separate surface, which we can display at any time, is one easy way to solve this problem.

We also have two synchronized functions, growTree() and updateSteps(). Both access and modify the stepInc variable, which contains the number of steps counted since the last onSensorChanged() event. Since growTree() is called from draw(), and hence from Processing's Animation thread, and updateSteps() from onSensorChanged(), which in turn is triggered from the app's main thread, we need synchronization to avert concurrent modifications to stepInc from these two threads.

Tweaking the Watch Face

We still have two issues with our first version of the tree watch face. One is that, since one step equates to one branch update cycle, the tree will grow too quickly, especially if we want it to reach full size only when the step count is high enough, say 10,000. The second problem results from the nature of the step-counter sensor: onSensorChanged() may be called at irregular intervals, with a large step increase at one moment and a small change at another. In particular, if the increase is very large, growTree() may take a long time to run, freezing the watch face, because it updates all particles as many times as steps were counted since the last sensor-changed event.

To solve the first problem, let's recall our earlier observation that the algorithm, with this current parameter selection, takes around 300 updates to completely grow the tree. This means that one step should represent only a fraction of an update iteration. More precisely, if our goal is to complete the tree at 10,000 steps, then the contribution of one single step toward one update iteration would be 300/10,000.

Secondly, a simple solution for the freezing issue could be to remove the first loop in the growTree() function and run just one update per particle, while decreasing the value of stepInc by exactly one. In this way, we do a single update per frame, so the watch face does not freeze, but rather will keep growing the tree until stepInc reaches zero. Listing 12-11 shows the changes needed in the code to implement these tweaks.

Listing 12-11. Controlling Growth Rate

```
...
int offset = -1;
int psteps, steps;
float stepInc = 0;
int stepGoal = 10000;
float stepScale = stepGoal / 300.0;
...
synchronized void growTree() {
  if (1 <= stepInc) {
    canvas.beginDraw();
    for (int i = 0; i < branches.size(); i++) {
      Branch branch = branches.get(i);
      branch.update();
      branch.display();
    }
    canvas.endDraw();
    stepInc--;
  }
}

synchronized void updateSteps(int value) {
  if (offset == -1) offset = value;
  steps = value - offset;
  stepInc += (steps - psteps) / stepScale;
  psteps = steps;
}
...
```

Blooming the Tree

We are very close to completing our watch face! We still need some improvements: an ambient mode, which could simply be a text drawing of the total step count and the time; an extra animation when approaching the desired step-count goal—the proverbial 10,000, for example; and a restart after reaching the goal. Listing 12-12 adds these improvements, which we will discuss right after the code.

Listing 12-12. Adding Flowers, Time, and Step Count

```
import android.content.Context;
import android.hardware.Sensor;
import android.hardware.SensorManager;
import android.hardware.SensorEvent;
import android.hardware.SensorEventListener;

Context context;
SensorManager manager;
Sensor sensor;
SensorListener listener;

int offset = -1;
int tsteps, psteps, steps, phour;
float stepInc = 0;
int stepGoal = 10000;
float stepScale = stepGoal / 300.0;

ArrayList<Branch> branches = new ArrayList<Branch>();
PGraphics canvas;
color bloomColor = color(230, 80, 120, 120);

void setup() {
  fullScreen();
  noStroke();
  textFont(createFont("SansSerif-Bold", 28 * displayDensity));
  branches.add(new Branch());
  initCanvas();
  initCounter();
}

void draw() {
  background(0);
  String str = hour() + ":" + nfs(minute(), 2) + ":" +
                           nfs(second(), 2) + "\n" +
               tsteps + " steps";
  if (wearInteractive()) {
    growTree();
    if (stepGoal <= steps) clearTree();
    image(canvas, 0, 0);
    textAlign(CENTER, BOTTOM);
    textSize(20 * displayDensity);
    fill(0, 80);
  } else {
```

```
    textAlign(CENTER, CENTER);
    textSize(28 * displayDensity);
    fill(200, 255);
    translate(0, wearInsets().bottom/2);
  }
  text(str, 0, 0, width, height);
}

synchronized void growTree() {
  if (1 <= stepInc) {
    canvas.beginDraw();
    for (int i = 0; i < branches.size(); i++) {
      Branch branch = branches.get(i);
      branch.update();
      branch.display();
      branch.bloom();
    }
    canvas.endDraw();
    stepInc--;
  }
}

synchronized void updateSteps(int value) {
  if (hour() < phour) tsteps = steps;
  if (offset == -1) offset = value;
  steps = value - offset;
  tsteps += steps - psteps;
  stepInc += (steps - psteps) / stepScale;
  psteps = steps;
  phour = hour();
}

synchronized void clearTree() {
  canvas.beginDraw();
  canvas.background(155, 211, 247);
  canvas.endDraw();
  branches.clear();
  branches.add(new Branch());
  offset = -1;
  steps = psteps = 0;
  bloomColor = color(random(255), random(255), random(255), 120);
}
```

```
void initCanvas() {
  canvas = createGraphics(width, height);
  canvas.beginDraw();
  canvas.background(155, 211, 247);
  canvas.noStroke();
  canvas.endDraw();
}

class Branch {
  PVector position;
  PVector velocity;
  float diameter;

  Branch() {
    position = new PVector(width/2, height);
    velocity = new PVector(0, -1);
    diameter = width/15.0;
  }
  Branch(Branch parent) {
    position = parent.position.copy();
    velocity = parent.velocity.copy();
    diameter = parent.diameter / 1.4142;
    parent.diameter = diameter;
  }
  void update() {
    if (1 < diameter) {
      position.add(velocity);
      float opening = map(diameter, 1, width/15.0, 1, 0);
      float angle = random(PI - opening * HALF_PI,
                           TWO_PI + opening * HALF_PI);
      PVector shake = PVector.fromAngle(angle);
      shake.mult(0.1);
      velocity.add(shake);
      velocity.normalize();
      if (random(0, 1) < 0.04) branches.add(new Branch(this));
    }
  }
  void display() {
    if (1 < diameter) {
      canvas.fill(175, 108, 44, 50);
      canvas.ellipse(position.x, position.y, diameter, diameter);
    }
  }
}
```

```
  void bloom() {
    if (0.85 * stepGoal < steps && random(0, 1) < 0.001) {
      float x = position.x + random(-10, +10);
      float y = position.y + random(-10, +10);
      float r = random(5, 20);
      canvas.fill(bloomColor);
      canvas.ellipse(x, y, r, r);
    }
  }
}

void initCounter() {
  Context context = getContext();
  manager = (SensorManager)context.getSystemService(Context.SENSOR_SERVICE);
  sensor = manager.getDefaultSensor(Sensor.TYPE_STEP_COUNTER);
  listener = new SensorListener();
  manager.registerListener(listener, sensor,
                           SensorManager.SENSOR_DELAY_NORMAL);
}

class SensorListener implements SensorEventListener {
  void onSensorChanged(SensorEvent event) {
    updateSteps(int(event.values[0]));
  }
  void onAccuracyChanged(Sensor sensor, int accuracy) { }
}
```

The implementation of ambient mode is fairly straightforward: drawing a screen-centered text message. The tree blooming is also relatively simple: once we reach 85 percent of the total step goal, we place an ellipse near the current position of each branch particle, with a probability of 0.001. One other function we need in the final watch face is a reset after reaching the goal, so the canvas is cleared and all particles are removed to start a new tree from scratch. This is done in the clearTree() function, synchronized since it modifies the offset, pstep, and step variables that are also altered in every sensor-changed event. Also, we added a "midnight reset" so that the total step count, tstep, is set to the current step value when the hour wraps around back to zero (situation which can only happen at midnight), with the line if (hour() < phour) tsteps = steps in updateSteps().

Figure 12-10 shows a sequence of three screen captures with a tree at different growth stages, from early in the step tracking until blooming when nearing the step-count goal. In Figure 12-11, we can see how the watch face looks like in ambient and interactive modes on an actual watch.

Figure 12-10. *Three stages in the growth of the tree*

Figure 12-11. *Final version of the tree watch face, in ambient (left) and interactive (right) modes*

Testing and debugging this watch face can be challenging, as we discussed previously, since we need to walk around long enough to observe changes in the growth of the tree. However, we can easily generate synthetic data that resembles the output of the step-count sensor. Listing 12-13 illustrates the changes needed in the code in order to use a step-count generator instead of the step-count listener. These changes are in fact fairly minimal, essentially launching a thread that runs the data-generation loop. We can adjust the values in the loop to increase or decrease the frequency of the updates, as well as the range of the values. This gives us enough flexibility to evaluate our code under different scenarios that would be hard to test with real step-count data.

Listing 12-13. Testing with Synthetic Data

```
...
void setup() {
  ...
  branches.add(new Branch());
  initCanvas();
  thread("generateData");
}
...
void generateData() {
  int total = 0;
  while (true) {
    total += int(random(10, 20));
    updateSteps(total);
    delay(500);
  }
}
```

The final step in the development process is to upload our watch face to the Google Play Store. Android devices running Wear 2.x can install standalone apps and watch faces without the need for a "companion" mobile app, as indicated in the online developer documentation on packaging and distributing Wear apps: https://developer.android. com/training/wearables/apps/packaging.html. To get the signed package for the watch face from the PDE, we can follow the same steps for regular apps described in Chapter 3.

First, we must write a package name in the manifest file inside the sketch's folder. A label for the service and the application are optional, but highly recommended, as it will be used throughout the watch UI to identify the watch face. A complete manifest file for the tree watch face is provided below:

```
<?xml version="1.0" encoding="UTF-8"?>
<manifest xmlns:android="http://schemas.android.com/apk/res/android"
          android:versionCode="1" android:versionName="1.0"
          package="com.example.running_tree">
    <uses-sdk android:minSdkVersion="25" android:targetSdkVersion="25"/>
    <uses-feature android:name="android.hardware.type.watch"/>
    <application android:icon="@drawable/icon"
                 android:label="Running Tree" android:supportsRtl="true">
        <uses-library android:name="com.google.android.wearable"
                      android:required="false"/>
        <meta-data android:name="com.google.android.wearable.standalone"
                   android:value="true"/>
        <service android:label="Running Tree" android:name=".MainService"

                 android:permission="android.permission.BIND_WALLPAPER">
            <meta-data android:name="android.service.wallpaper"
                       android:resource="@xml/watch_face"/>
            <meta-data android:name=
```

```
                    "com.google.android.wearable.watchface.preview"

                    android:resource="@drawable/preview_rectangular"/>
            <meta-data android:name=

                    "com.google.android.wearable.watchface.preview_
                    circular"

                    android:resource="@drawable/preview_circular"/>
            <meta-data android:name=
        "com.google.android.wearable.watchface.companionConfigurationAction"
                    android:value=
                        "com.catinean.simpleandroidwatchface.CONFIG_DIGITAL"/>
            <intent-filter>
                <action android:name=
                        "android.service.wallpaper.WallpaperService"/>
                <category android:name=
                "com.google.android.wearable.watchface.category.WATCH_FACE"/>
            </intent-filter>
        </service>
        <activity android:name="processing.android.PermissionRequestor"/>
    </application>
    <uses-permission android:name="android.permission.WAKE_LOCK"/>
</manifest>
```

Finally, we need to create a full icon set, including the six app icons for all DPI levels (xxxhdpi through ldpi) and the circular and rectangular preview icons (Figure 12-12). Although most current watches offer xhdpi resolution, this will probably change in the near future as devices sporting screens with even higher resolutions become available.

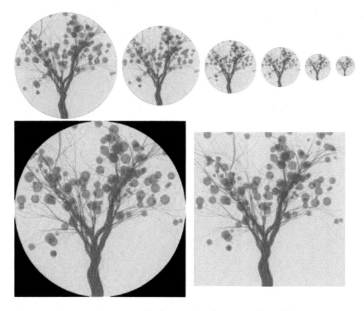

Figure 12-12. Icon set needed to export the signed package

Summary

This chapter concludes the section on wearable devices and watch faces. Although wearable development is an entire field in its own right, we were able to apply most of the techniques we learned in previous chapters to create interactive graphics and dynamic visualizations of sensor data, all while taking into account some of the unique aspects of wearable devices in terms of screen size, resolution, and battery life.

■ ■ ■

PART V

3D and VR

CHAPTER 13

3D in Processing

Our journey through Virtual Reality (VR) starts with this introduction to the basic concepts of 3D programming with Processing: coordinate systems, 3D transformations, lighting, texturing, and the creation of 3D shapes, which we can apply not only in VR apps, but in any situation where we may need interactive 3D graphics.

The P3D Renderer

The development of VR apps has an important pre-requisite: learning how to create interactive 3D graphics. Up to this point, we have only made two-dimensional drawings, using either the default or the P2D renderer. Even though 2D rendering is a special case of 3D, there are many aspects of motion and interaction that are specific to 3D graphics with which we need to become familiar.

Processing includes a renderer for drawing 3D scenes, appropriately called P3D. It supports basic 3D features, such as lighting and texturing objects, but also more advanced functionality, such as shaders. We can use P3D by setting the renderer parameter in the size() or fullScreen() functions during setup(); e.g., size(width, height, P3D) or fullScreen(P3D). After doing that, we can not only use all the 3D rendering functions available in Processing, but also continue to make 2D drawings as we did before.

A 3D Hello World

Let's start by writing a simple sketch that demonstrates the basics of 3D in Processing: a rotating cube. Listing 12-1 includes translation and rotation transformations, as well as default lighting.

© Andrés Colubri 2017
A. Colubri, *Processing for Android*, https://doi.org/10.1007/978-1-4842-2719-0_13

Listing 13-1. Basic 3D Sketch

```
float angle = 0;

void setup() {
  fullScreen(P3D);
  fill(#AD71B7);
}

void draw() {
  background(#81B771);
  lights();
  translate(width/2, height/2);
  rotateY(angle);
  rotateX(angle*2);
  box(300);
  angle += 0.01;
}
```

We will look at these functions more closely in subsequent sections, but as an overview of what happens in draw(), we first "turn on" a set of default lights with lights(), then translate the entire scene to the center of the screen with translate(width/2, height/2), and apply two rotations, one along the y-axis with rotateY(angle), and a second along the x-axis with rotateX(angle*2). As in 2D drawing, these transformations affect all shapes we draw afterward, in this case the cube drawn with box(300). We end by increasing the rotation angle so we have continuous animation. Figure 13-1 shows the output of this sketch.

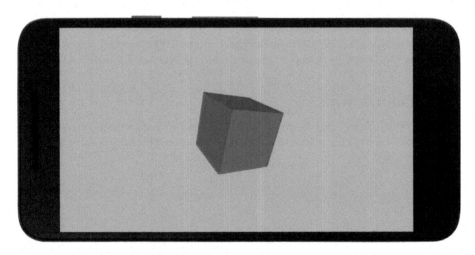

Figure 13-1. *Simple 3D rendering in Processing*

The Camera

When we draw any 3D scene, there is a "camera" looking into the virtual space, and we can think of the device's screen as the viewport of that camera. Processing includes some functions to manipulate the position and "virtual" lenses of the camera. In a VR sketch, on the other hand, the Processing camera will be controlled automatically by the movement of the phone in space. In either case, Processing's camera is defined by three vectors: the eye position, the center of the scene, and the "up" vector, illustrated in Figure 13-2.

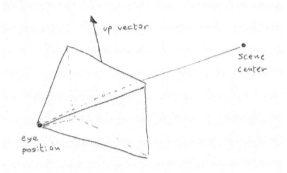

Figure 13-2. *Vectors defining position and orientation of the camera*

These vectors can be set using the camera() function: camera(eyeX, eyeY, eyeZ, centerX, centerY, centerZ, upX, upY, upZ). Calling camera() without any argument will set the default camera's position and orientation, in which the center is the (0, 0, 0) point, the eye is placed along the z-axis, and the up direction is the positive y vector. By continuously changing the eye's position, we can look at the scene from any vantage point. Listing 13-2 illustrates how to set these parameters.

Listing 13-2. Camera Parameters

```
void setup() {
  fullScreen(P3D);
  fill(#AD71B7);
}

void draw() {
  background(#81B771);
  float t = millis()/1000.0;
  float ex = width/2 + 500 * cos(t);
  float ey = height/2 + 500 * sin(t);
  float ez = 1000 + 100 * cos(millis()/1000.0);
  camera(ex, ey, ez, width/2, height/2, 0, 0, 1, 0);
  lights();
  translate(width/2, height/2);
  box(300);
}
```

We can not only set the camera's position and orientation, but also choose how the scene is projected onto the camera's viewport (which can be thought as of choosing the camera "lenses"). There are two types of projections: perspective and orthographic. They are illustrated in Figure 13-3. Perspective projection, the default setting in P3D, is the one that corresponds to how images are formed in the physical world. In it, objects are projected onto the viewport plane following lines of view that converge into the "eye" position behind the viewport. This simulates the effect of perspective, where distant objects look smaller. In fact, Processing uses default perspective parameters so that a rectangle of dimensions (0, 0, width, height) at z=0 exactly covers the entire output window. Thanks to these settings, we can draw 2D shapes in P3D in the same way we did before.

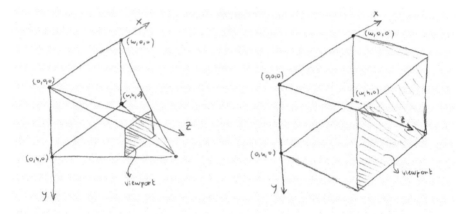

Figure 13-3. *Perspective (left) and orthographic (right) projections in Processing*

In orthographic projection, on the other hand, the objects are projected onto the viewport following lines perpendicular to it, so there is no decrease or increase in size as objects move away from or toward the camera eye. The default settings of the orthographic projection in Processing are such that the points of 3D coordinates (0, 0, z) and (width, height, z) fall exactly on the upper right and lower left corners of the output window, regardless of the value of z.

We can easily switch back and forth between these two projection modes with the perspective() and ortho() functions. These functions have default settings as just described, but we can also use them with additional arguments to adjust the field of vision, the position of the camera eye, and other parameters: perspective(fovy, aspect, zNear, zFar) and ortho(left, right, bottom, top, near, far). In Listing 13-3, we tie the field of vision to time through a cosine function so it oscillates back and forth between an angle of 10° (very narrow field of vision, object blows up to occupy almost the entire screen) to 80° (very wide, object looks smaller than normal).

Listing 13-3. Perspective Parameters

```
float angle = 0;

void setup() {
  fullScreen(P3D);
  fill(#AD71B7);
}

void draw() {
  background(#81B771);
  float fov = radians(map(cos(millis()/1000.0), -1, +1, 10, 80));
  float ratio = float(width)/height;
  perspective(fov, ratio, 1, 2000);
  lights();
  translate(width/2, height/2);
  rotateY(angle);
  rotateX(angle*2);
  box(300);
  angle += 0.01;
}
```

A couple of additional things to note here include the setting of the width-to-height aspect ratio, which in most situations should simply be the width/height, and the clipping planes. These planes determine the visible volume along the z direction by having a near and a far value: anything closer than the former or farther than the latter is clipped out.

■ **Note** The camera() and perspective() functions are not particularly intuitive to use, especially if one would like to think of camera movements and adjustments in physical space (like zooming, panning, and rolling), but there are libraries that simplify camera handling, among them PeasyCam, Obsessive Camera Direction, and proscene. Appendix B includes a list of libraries that we can use from Android mode.

Immediate Versus Retained Rendering

One important aspect about how we were handling 3D scenes in previous examples is that we were creating a new box from scratch in every frame and discarding it right afterward. This way of drawing 3D (and also 2D) graphics, known as *immediate rendering*, is fine if we have relatively few objects in our scene, but might slow down rendering if we have a more complex scene with many shapes. This is particularly relevant with our goal of writing VR apps, as we will discuss further in the following chapters, because the rendering animation should be as smooth as possible to ensure that the viewer does not experience motion sickness resulting from low or uneven framerates.

Processing provides another way of drawing geometry, called *retained rendering*, to improve performance. With retained rendering, we create our shapes once, and then redraw them as many times as needed. We already used this technique in Chapter 4, and it can be much faster when drawing complex scenes. Retained rendering will become very handy later when working with VR.

Using retained rendering is easy, we only need to store our shapes in a PShape object. Processing provides a few pre-defined 3D shapes, like boxes and spheres, which can be created with a single call, as shown in Listing 13-4.

Listing 13-4. Using Retained Rendering

```
float angle = 0;
PShape cube;

void setup() {
  fullScreen(P3D);
  perspective(radians(80), float(width)/height, 1, 1000);
  PImage tex = loadImage("mosaic.jpg");
  cube = createShape(BOX, 400);
  cube.setTexture(tex);
}

void draw() {
  background(#81B771);
  lights();
  translate(width/2, height/2);
  rotateY(angle);
  rotateX(angle*2);
  shape(cube);
  angle += 0.01;
}
```

In this code, once we obtain our cube object from the createShape() function, we can make changes to it. For example, we can apply a texture to it so its faces are "wrapped" with the image for a more interesting look. The final output is depicted in Figure 13-4.

In these first four examples, we have applied most of the basic 3D rendering techniques (creating shapes, applying transformations, defining lighting, and texturing), and we will go through each one of these topics in more detail in the remaining sections of this chapter.

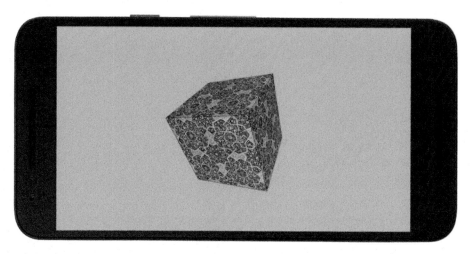

Figure 13-4. Drawing a textured PShape

3D Transformations

We have three types of 3D transformations: translations (moving from point A to B), rotations (turning around an axis), and scaling (contracting or expanding uniformly or along one direction). Listings 13-5 through 13-7 exemplify each one separately.

Listing 13-5. Applying a Translation

```
void setup() {
  fullScreen(P3D);
  fill(120);
}

void draw() {
  background(157);
  float x = map(cos(millis()/1000.0), -1, +1, 0, width);
  translate(x, height/2);
  box(200);
}
```

For the rotation, we need to do a translation to the center of the screen first, since the box() function places the cube at (0, 0, 0).

Listing 13-6. Applying a Rotation

```
void setup() {
  fullScreen(P3D);
  fill(120);
}

void draw() {
  background(157);
  translate(width/2, height/2);
  rotateY(millis()/1000.0);
  box(200);
}
```

For scaling, a similar observation applies—we apply the translation (width/2, height/2) first so the box appears in the center of the screen.

Listing 13-7. Applying Scaling

```
void setup() {
  fullScreen(P3D);
  fill(120);
}

void draw() {
  background(157);
  translate(width/2, height/2);
  float f = map(cos(millis()/1000.0), -1, +1, 0.1, 5);
  scale(f);
  box(200);
}
```

■ **Note** The relative size of the shapes in all these examples will be different depending on the device's DPI. We can use the `densityDisplay` system constant to scale them up or down so they look consistent across screens with different resolutions and sizes.

Combining Transformations

The previous examples showed how to use 3D transformations separately (although in the case of the rotation and scaling, there was the initial translation to the center of the screen). But in most situations we need to combine translations, rotations, and scalings, typically by defining a chain of transformations that put an object in the desired spot in 3D space and with the intended proportions. In fact, transformations can be composed to create very complex movements, with a couple of "rules" to keep in mind: (1) the order of transformations cannot be exchanged (for example, applying a rotation and then a translation is not equivalent to translating first and rotating later, as we discussed in the context of 2D drawing in Chapter 4); and (2) a chain of transformations can be manipulated with pushMatrix() and popMatrix(), with pushMatrix() preserving the current transformation composition, thus isolating the effect of additional transformations that happen between it and the matching popMatrix(). We saw some examples of this in Chapter 2.

Listing 13-8 shows an application of transformation composition, where the idea is to create and animate an articulated "arm" with multiple segments, which we can see in Figure 13-5.

Listing 13-8. Composing 3D Transformations

```
float[] r1, r2;

void setup() {
  fullScreen(P3D);
  noStroke();
  r1 = new float[100];
  r2 = new float[100];
  for (int i = 0; i < 100; i++) {
    r1[i] = random(0, 1);
    r2[i] = random(0, 1);
  }
}

void draw() {
  background(157);
  lights();
  translate(width/2, height/2);
  scale(4);
  for (int i = 0; i < 100; i++) {
    float tx = 0, ty = 0, tz = 0;
    float sx = 1, sy = 1, sz = 1;
    if (r1[i] < 1.0/3.0) {
      rotateX(millis()/1000.0);
      tz = sz = 10;
    } else if (1.0/3.0 < r1[i] && r1[i] < 2.0/3.0) {
      rotateY(millis()/1000.0);
      tz = sz = 10;
    } else {
      rotateZ(millis()/1000.0);
      if (r2[i] < 0.5) {
        tx = sx = 10;
      } else {
        ty = sy = 10;
      }
    }
```

```
    translate(tx/2, ty/2, tz/2);
    pushMatrix();
    scale(sx, sy, sz);
    box(1);
    popMatrix();
    translate(tx/2, ty/2, tz/2);
  }
}
```

The important points in this example are: first, we use random numbers (r1 and r2) to decide at each joint which axis we rotate the next segment around, and also which axis we extend the segment along; and second, the use of scale() in two different places— right after centering the scene, to increase the size of the entire arm, and before drawing each arm and only along the displacement axis, so the segments are properly connected with each other. Also, notice that the random numbers are pre-calculated in setup() and stored in float arrays; otherwise, the geometry would change entirely from frame to frame.

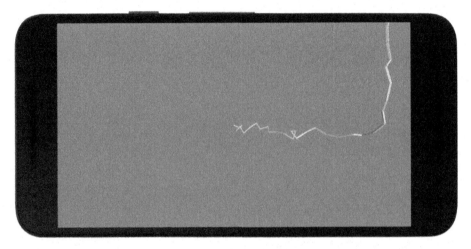

Figure 13-5. *Animated arm with combined 3D transformations*

3D Shapes

As we did in 2D, we can generate primitive shapes using Processing's functions. All the 2D primitives (triangle, ellipse, rect, and quads) can be used in 3D, with the addition of two new 3D primitives (box and sphere). Listing 13-9 draws all these primitives in a single sketch, and the output is shown in Figure 13-6.

Listing 13-9. 2D and 3D Primitives

```
float[] r1, r2;
void setup() {
  fullScreen(P3D);
}

void draw() {
  background(157);

  translate(width/2, height/2);

  pushMatrix();
  translate(-width/3, -height/4);
  rotateY(millis()/2000.0);
  ellipse(0, 0, 200, 200);
  popMatrix();

  pushMatrix();
  translate(0, -height/4);
  rotateY(millis()/2000.0);
  triangle(0, +150, -150, -150, +150, -150);
  popMatrix();

  pushMatrix();
  translate(+width/3, -height/4);
  rotateY(millis()/2000.0);
  rect(-100, -100, 200, 200, 20);
  popMatrix();

  pushMatrix();
  translate(-width/3, +height/4);
  rotateY(millis()/2000.0);
  quad(-40, -100, 120, -80, 120, 150, -80, 150);
  popMatrix();

  pushMatrix();
  translate(0, +height/4);
  rotateY(millis()/2000.0);
  box(200);
  popMatrix();

  pushMatrix();
  translate(+width/3, +height/4);
  rotateY(millis()/2000.0);
  sphere(150);
  popMatrix();
}
```

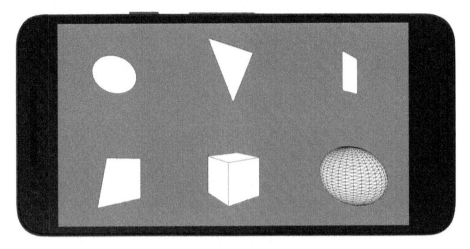

Figure 13-6. *2D and 3D primitives rendered with P3D*

Custom Shapes

We saw in Chapter 4 that it is possible to create custom shapes using the beginShape ()/vertex()/endShape() functions, with the appropriate shape type (POINTS, LINES, TRIANGLES, etc.). As with the earlier primitives, all the code we learned for 2D rendering can be reused in P3D without any changes, but now there is the possibility of adding a z coordinate. For instance, let's create in Listing 13-10 a terrain with QUADS and some randomness in the height from the noise() function.

Listing 13-10. Creating a Custom Shape with QUADS

```
void setup() {
  fullScreen(P3D);
}

void draw() {
  background(150);
  lights();
  translate(width/2, height/2);
  rotateX(QUARTER_PI);
  beginShape(QUADS);
  float t = 0.0001 * millis();
  for (int i = 0; i < 50; i++) {
    for (int j = 0; j < 50; j++) {
      float x0 = map(i, 0, 50, -width/2, width/2);
      float y0 = map(j, 0, 50, -height/2, height/2);
      float x1 = x0 + width/50.0;
      float y1 = y0 + height/50.0;
      float z1 = 200 * noise(0.1 * i, 0.1 * j, t);
```

```
      float z2 = 200 * noise(0.1 * (i + 1), 0.1 * j, t);
      float z3 = 200 * noise(0.1 * (i + 1), 0.1 * (j + 1), t);
      float z4 = 200 * noise(0.1 * i, 0.1 * (j + 1), t);
      vertex(x0, y0, z1);
      vertex(x1, y0, z2);
      vertex(x1, y1, z3);
      vertex(x0, y1, z4);
    }
  }
  endShape();
}
```

The noise is generated using the (i, j) indices of the vertices defining the mesh, so it ensures that the height displacement is consistent at the vertices shared between contiguous quads. We can see the result in Figure 13-7.

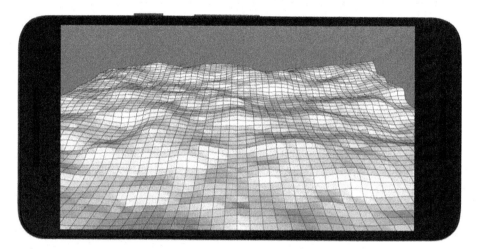

Figure 13-7. *Terrain generated with a QUADS shape*

PShape Objects

Creating a large shape as we just did could lead to reduced performance, especially on basic smartphones. If the geometry is static the whole time the sketch is running, we can store it in a PShape object for faster retained rendering, as shown in Listing 13-11.

Listing 13-11. Storing a Custom Shape Inside a PShape

```
PShape terrain;

void setup() {
  fullScreen(P3D);
  terrain = createShape();
  terrain.beginShape(QUADS);
  for (int i = 0; i < 50; i++) {
    for (int j = 0; j < 50; j++) {
      float x0 = map(i, 0, 50, -width/2, width/2);
      float y0 = map(j, 0, 50, -height/2, height/2);
      float x1 = x0 + width/50.0;
      float y1 = y0 + height/50.0;
      float z1 = 200 * noise(0.1 * i, 0.1 * j, 0);
      float z2 = 200 * noise(0.1 * (i + 1), 0.1 * j, 0);
      float z3 = 200 * noise(0.1 * (i + 1), 0.1 * (j + 1), 0);
      float z4 = 200 * noise(0.1 * i, 0.1 * (j + 1), 0);
      terrain.vertex(x0, y0, z1);
      terrain.vertex(x1, y0, z2);
      terrain.vertex(x1, y1, z3);
      terrain.vertex(x0, y1, z4);
    }
  }
  terrain.endShape();
}

void draw() {
  background(150);
  lights();
  translate(width/2, height/2);
  rotateX(QUARTER_PI);
  shape(terrain);
}
```

We can still modify a PShape object after we have created it. For example, Listing 13-12 adds some random displacement to the vertices in each frame with the setVertex() function (the setup is identical to Listing 13-11), so the entire surface is now animated.

Listing 13-12. Modifying a PShape After Creating It

```
...
void draw() {
  background(150);
  lights();
  translate(width/2, height/2);
  rotateX(QUARTER_PI);
  updateShape();
  shape(terrain);
  println(frameRate);
}

void updateShape() {
  float t = 0.0001 * millis();
  int vidx = 0;
  for (int i = 0; i < 50; i++) {
    for (int j = 0; j < 50; j++) {
      float x0 = map(i, 0, 50, -width/2, width/2);
      float y0 = map(j, 0, 50, -height/2, height/2);
      float x1 = x0 + width/50.0;
      float y1 = y0 + height/50.0;
      float z1 = 200 * noise(0.1 * i, 0.1 * j, t);
      float z2 = 200 * noise(0.1 * (i + 1), 0.1 * j, t);
      float z3 = 200 * noise(0.1 * (i + 1), 0.1 * (j + 1), t);
      float z4 = 200 * noise(0.1 * i, 0.1 * (j + 1), t);
      terrain.setVertex(vidx++, x0, y0, z1);
      terrain.setVertex(vidx++, x1, y0, z2);
      terrain.setVertex(vidx++, x1, y1, z3);
      terrain.setVertex(vidx++, x0, y1, z4);
    }
  }
}
```

However, by modifying all the vertices of the PShape object, we will likely see the performance of the sketch return to the levels of immediate rendering. If we modify only some vertices, then performance would still be better than in immediate rendering.

We can group PShape objects of different types as child objects into a single containing PShape. Processing will render them all together as a single entity, which will also result in higher framerates than if they were drawn either with immediate rendering or as separate PShape objects. In Listing 13-13, we read the 3D coordinates of 1,000 points from a text file using loadStrings() and then draw them as boxes or spheres.

Listing 13-13. Creating a Group Shape

```
PVector[] coords;
PShape group;

void setup() {
  fullScreen(P3D);
  textFont(createFont("SansSerif", 20 * displayDensity));
  sphereDetail(10);
  group = createShape(GROUP);
  String[] lines = loadStrings("points.txt");
  coords = new PVector[lines.length];
  for (int i = 0; i < lines.length; i++) {
    String line = lines[i];
    String[] valores = line.split(" ");
    float x = float(valores[0]);
    float y = float(valores[1]);
    float z = float(valores[2]);
    coords[i] = new PVector(x, y, z);
    PShape sh;
    if (random(1) < 0.5) {
      sh = createShape(SPHERE, 20);
      sh.setFill(#E8A92A);
    } else {
      sh = createShape(BOX, 20);
      sh.setFill(#4876B2);
    }
    sh.translate(x, y, z);
    sh.setStroke(false);
    group.addChild(sh);
  }
  noStroke();
}

void draw() {
  background(255);
  fill(0);
  text(frameRate, 50, 50);
  fill(255, 0, 0);
  lights();
  translate(width/2, height/2, 0);
  rotateY(map(mouseX, 0, width, 0, TWO_PI));
  shape(group);
}
```

We applied a few optimization tricks to this code to reduce the complexity of the scene: we set the sphere detail to 10 (the default is 30) and disabled the stroke. Stroke lines in particular can add a lot of extra geometry to a shape, and thus slow down rendering. The final result should look something like Figure 13-8, with a reasonable performance even on low-end phones (fps > 40).

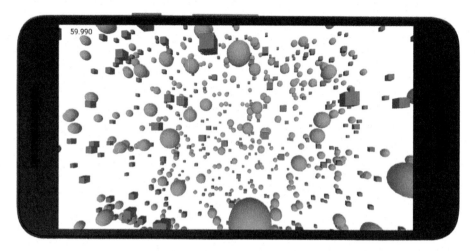

Figure 13-8. *Group shape containing shapes of different kinds*

▪ **Note** Performance in 3D is controlled by several factors, but one of the most important is the total vertex count in the scene. It is important that we do not add unnecessary vertices to a scene, keeping in mind that users will look at our sketches on a (relatively) small screen. Other optimizations, such as using PShapes to store static geometry, could be also useful to keep a high framerate.

Loading OBJ Shapes

The OBJ file format (http://paulbourke.net/dataformats/obj/) is a simple text-based format used to store 3D geometry and material definitions. It was created back in the 1980s by Wavefront Technologies, a company that developed animation software used in movies and other industries. Although it is fairly basic, it is supported by most 3D modeling tools, and there are many online repositories that include free 3D models in this format. Processing's API includes the loadShape() function, which we have already used to load SVG shapes in 2D, and which would read OBJ shapes in P3D, as demonstrated in Listing 13-14.

Listing 13-14. Loading an OBJ File

```
PShape model;
PVector center;

void setup() {
  fullScreen(P3D);
  model = loadShape("Deer.obj");
  center = getShapeCenter(model);
  float dim = max(model.getWidth(), model.getHeight(), model.getDepth());
  float factor = width/(3 * dim);
  model.rotateX(PI);
  model.scale(factor);
  center.mult(factor);
  center.y *= -1;
}

void draw() {
  background(157);
  lights();
  translate(width/2, height/2);
  translate(-center.x, -center.y, -center.z);
  rotateY(millis()/1000.0);
  shape(model);
}

PVector getShapeCenter(PShape sh) {
  PVector bot = new PVector(+10000, +10000, +10000);
  PVector top = new PVector(-10000, -10000, -10000);
  PVector v = new PVector();
  for (int i = 0; i < sh.getChildCount(); i++) {
    PShape child = sh.getChild(i);
    for (int j = 0; j < child.getVertexCount(); j++) {
      child.getVertex(j, v);
      bot.x = min(bot.x, v.x);
      bot.y = min(bot.y, v.y);
      bot.z = min(bot.z, v.z);
      top.x = max(top.x, v.x);
      top.y = max(top.y, v.y);
      top.z = max(top.z, v.z);
    }
  }
  return PVector.add(top, bot).mult(0.5);
}
```

In this code, we start by loading the shape, and then we calculate some parameters so it is placed it correctly in the scene. First, we compute the center position of the shape with the getShapeCenter() function, where we go over all the vertices in the shape and

292

get the maximum and minimum values across each axis. The two vectors holding the minimum and maximum values, bot and top, are the opposite corners of the bounding box enclosing the entire shape. The middle point of the bounding box is the center of the shape, which we want to coincide with the center of the screen, as seen in Figure 13-9.

Figure 13-9. *3D shape loaded from an OBJ file*

Also, the coordinates in an OBJ model might have a very different range of values from what we use in Processing (typically 0 – width and 0 – height), so by getting the dimensions of the model along each axis (using getWidth(), getHeight(), and getDepth()), we can calculate a factor by which to scale the shape up or down to fit the screen. The shape also needs to be rotated 180° around x, since it is upside down. This is often the case when loading OBJ files, since a common convention in 3D graphics is to have the y-axis pointing upward, while Processing uses an y-axis pointing down, a more common setting in graphic design tools. Note that we need to scale and invert the center vector separately, since it is computed from the input coordinates of the shape, which are not affected by the shape transformations.

We retrieve the shape's coordinates with a getVertex() call, where we reuse the same PVector object v. This is because if we were to create a new temporary PVector for each vertex, all these objects would need to be discarded from memory at the end. This memory-release operation, although very fast, could add up to a noticeable delay when freeing thousands of PVector objects, potentially causing a hiccup in the animation.

Lighting and Texturing

Lights and textures are two key aspects to consider when we create a 3D scene. Without them, most objects will look like flat shapes without any sense of depth or surface complexity. Lighting and texturing algorithms simulate how lights and materials interact with each other in the physical world so that 3D graphics are realistic enough to convey a credible space. We do not need photo-realism, but a combination of lights and materials that approximates reality to some extent is necessary to engage our users. Lights and textures become even more critical when working with VR, where users are entirely surrounded by a synthetic 3D scene.

Processing has several functions we can apply to create light sources and set the material properties of 3D shapes, including textures. The lighting model that underlies these functions in the P3D renderer is a first approximation of more complex models. As such, it is not capable of generating shadows or rendering rugged or bumpy surfaces, but it can handle phenomena such as brightness and emissivity of a material, light falloffs, directional light sources, and spotlights. However, we can implement our own, more realistic lighting models through custom shaders (https://processing.org/tutorials/pshader/).

Light Sources and Material Properties

The final color of a shape in a 3D scene in Processing is determined by the interplay between its material properties and the characteristics of the light sources. Very briefly, the color of a light source will affect a shape depending on whether the corresponding material property of the shape has been set to a color that matches to some degree the light-source color. The most important property is the fill color. For instance, if a light source has an RGB color of (200, 150, 150), and the fill color of the shape is (255, 255, 20), the shape will reflect the entirety of the red and green components of the light, but only a small fraction of its blue component.

There are four types of light sources in Processing:

1) Ambient: represents a light that doesn't come from a specific direction; the rays of light have bounced around so much that objects are evenly lit from all sides. The function that sets the ambient light is

```
ambientLight(c1, c2, c3);
```

The color of the ambient light is (c2, c2, c3), which is interpreted according to the current color mode.

2) Point light: a light that has a specific location in space and emits in all directions from that location, which is the center. Its function is

```
pointLight(c1, c2, c3, x, y, z);
```

The position of the point light is given by (x, y, z), while its color is given by (c1, c2, c3).

3) Directional light: represents a light source that is far enough from the objects that all its rays follow the same direction (the sun being an example of a directional light source). We configure it with:

```
directionalLight(c1, c2, c3, nx, ny, nz);
```

The direction of the directional light is given by (nx, ny, nz), while its color is given by (c1, c2, c3).

4) Spotlight: a source that illuminates all objects within a cone centered at the light position. A spotlight has several parameters:

```
spotLight(c1, c2, c3, x, y, z, nx, ny, nz, angle,
concentration)
```

As before, the position of the spotlight is given by (x, y, z), and its color by (c1, c2, c3). The additional parameters are (nx, ny, nz), the direction of the cone (not of the rays though, which are cast away from the origin as in a point light), the aperture angle of the cone, and the concentration toward the center of the cone.

Let's now consider Listing 13-15 to see how this works with a few shapes and a couple of objects.

Listing 13-15. Lighting a 3D Scene

```
void setup() {
  fullScreen(P3D);
  noStroke();
}

void draw() {
  background(20);
  translate(width/2, height/2);

  float pointX = map(mouseX, 0, width, -width/2, +width/2);
  float dirZ = map(mouseY, 0, height, 0, -1);
  pointLight(200, 200, 200, pointX, 0, 600);
  directionalLight(100, 220, 100, 0, 1, dirZ);

  rotateY(QUARTER_PI);

  fill(255, 250, 200);
  box(320);
```

```
translate(-400, 0);
fill(200, 200, 250);
sphere(160);

translate(0, +110, 360);
fill(255, 200, 200);
box(100);
}
```

In this example, we have two light sources: a bright gray point light and a green directional light. We can control the x coordinate of the point light by swiping horizontally and the z coordinate of the directional light by swiping vertically. Since each object has a different fill color that "reflects" each of the incoming lights to a different extent, the final appearance of the scene can change quite significantly depending on the position and direction of the lights, as we can see in Figure 13-10. For example, the larger the coordinate of the directional light along z, the more directly it impacts the shapes with faces that are perpendicular to z, and so we see an increase of the overall green hue.

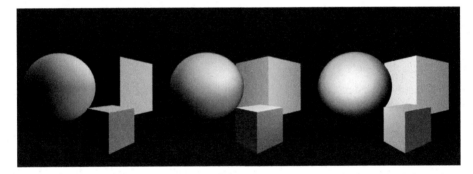

Figure 13-10. *Color of shapes in a scene change as light sources move around*

■ **Note** We should set the lights in every call of the draw() function; otherwise, they won't be active. We can set a default lighting configuration, sometimes enough for quick tests, by calling the lights() function.

The fill color, which determines how the surface reflects the incoming light color, is not the only material property we can adjust. We have the following additional properties:

1) Emissiveness: the capacity of emitting light on its own. It is controlled by the following function:

```
emissive(c1, c2, c2)
```

where (c1, c2, c3) the emissive color of the material.

2) Shininess: the amount of gloss on the surface of shapes. We
    only need to set a single parameter with

```
shininess(s)
```

with s being the level of gloss, going from 0 (no shininess) to 1
(maximum shininess).

3) Specularity: the capacity to create specular reflections. The
    way it works is by calling the following function:

```
specular(c1, c2, c2)
```

with the color (c1, c2, c3) of the highlights.

By adjusting these three material properties, we can generate a wide range of
material surfaces, even if the fill color is the same across the materials, as demonstrated
in Listing 13-16, whose output is depicted in Figure 13-11.

Listing 13-16. Material Properties

```
void setup() {
  fullScreen(P3D);
  noStroke();
}

void draw() {
  background(0);
  translate(width/2, height/2);

  directionalLight(255, 255, 255, 0, 0, -1);

  pushMatrix();
  translate(-width/3, 0);
  fill(250, 100, 50);
  specular(200, 250, 200);
  emissive(0, 0, 0);
  shininess(10.0);
  sphere(200);
  popMatrix();

  pushMatrix();
  fill(250, 100, 50);
  specular(255);
  shininess(1.0);
  emissive(0, 20, 0);
  sphere(200);
  popMatrix();
```

297

```
  pushMatrix();
  translate(+width/3, 0);
  fill(250, 100, 50);
  specular(255);
  shininess(2.0);
  emissive(50, 10, 100);
  sphere(200);
  popMatrix();
}
```

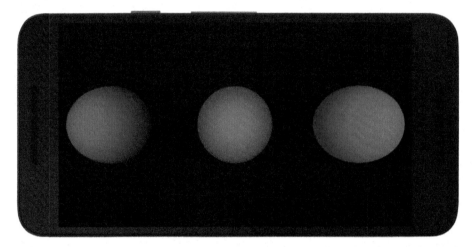

Figure 13-11. *Spheres with different material properties*

As with other properties in Processing, the emissive(), specular(), and shininess() functions set the corresponding properties for all shapes drawn afterward. Calling pushStyle() and popStyle() also act on the material properties, including the fill, emissiveness, and specular colors, and the shininess factor.

Texture Mapping

The use of fill color and other material properties gives us significant latitude to define how a specific shape will look under different lighting scenarios, ranging from no lights (in which case the fill color is used to paint shapes uniformly) to more complex situations with multiple light sources. However, shapes are still relatively "flat" in the sense that they look like they are made of a single material. Texture mapping allows us to address that uniformity and to create more-complex-looking surfaces with ease by simply "wrapping" the 3D shapes with a texture image, illustrated with a sphere in Figure 13-12.

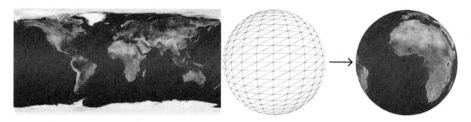

Figure 13-12. *Texture mapping a sphere with an image of Earth*

Primitive shapes, such as boxes and spheres, can be textured right away by providing a suitable image, which is done in Listing 13-17.

Listing 13-17. Texturing a Sphere

```
PShape earth;
PImage texmap;

void setup() {
  fullScreen(P3D);
  texmap = loadImage("earthmap1k.jpg");
  earth = createShape(SPHERE, 300);
  earth.setStroke(false);
  earth.setTexture(texmap);
}

void draw() {
  background(255);
  translate(width/2, height/2);
  rotateY(0.01 * frameCount);
  shape(earth);
}
```

When we create custom shapes, we need to provide some extra information to apply a texture successfully: texture coordinates. These coordinates indicate which pixel (u, v) in the image goes to which vertex (i, j) in the shape, and using those specifications, P3D is able to apply all the pixels in the image onto the entire shape.

The simplest texture mapping would be that of a rectangle, illustrated by Listing 13-18, where we only need to match the corners of the image with the four vertices of the QUAD.

Listing 13-18. Texturing a QUAD Shape

```
PImage texmap;

void setup() {
  fullScreen(P3D);
  texmap = loadImage("woodstock.png");
  noStroke();
}

void draw() {
  background(255);
  translate(width/2, height/2);
  rotateY(0.01 * frameCount);
  scale(displayDensity);
  beginShape(QUAD);
  texture(texmap);
  vertex(-150, -150, 0, 0);
  vertex(-150, 150, 0, texmap.height);
  vertex(150, 150, texmap.width, texmap.height);
  vertex(150, -150, texmap.width, 0);
  endShape();
}
```

Sometimes, we might find it more convenient to specify the image pixels using normalized coordinates, which allow us to texture a shape without referring to the image's width and height. For instance, we can use the normalized value (0.5, 0.5) to indicate the center pixel of an image, instead of (img.width/2, img.height/2). We switch between default (IMAGE) and normalized (NORMAL) modes using the textureMode() function. Once we select the normal mode, the (u, v) values should range between 0 and 1, as in Listing 13-19.

Listing 13-19. Using Normalized Texture Coordinates

```
PImage texmap;

void setup() {
  fullScreen(P3D);
  texmap = loadImage("woodstock.png");
  textureMode(NORMAL);
  noStroke();
}

void draw() {
  background(255);
  translate(width/2, height/2);
  rotateY(0.01 * frameCount);
  beginShape(QUAD);
```

```
  texture(texmap);
  vertex(-150, -150, 0, 0);
  vertex(-150, 150, 0, 1);
  vertex(150, 150, 1, 1);
  vertex(150, -150, 1, 0);
  endShape();
}
```

With more complex shapes, we need to make sure that the texture coordinates are calculated correctly so the final textured object looks as we intended. For example, if we go back to the terrain example from Listing 13-11, we have the (i, j) indices of the grid, which we can use to obtain the corresponding normalized texture coordinates with the map() function. Listing 13-20 shows how to do this, and the corresponding output is shown in Figure 13-13.

Listing 13-20. Texturing a Complex Shape

```
PShape terrain;

void setup() {
  fullScreen(P3D);
  PImage dirt = loadImage("dirt.jpg");
  textureMode(NORMAL);
  terrain = createShape();
  terrain.beginShape(QUADS);
  terrain.noStroke();
  terrain.texture(dirt);
  for (int i = 0; i < 50; i++) {
    for (int j = 0; j < 50; j++) {
      float x0 = map(i, 0, 50, -width/2, width/2);
      float y0 = map(j, 0, 50, -width/2, width/2);
      float u0 = map(i, 0, 50, 0, 1);
      float v0 = map(j, 0, 50, 0, 1);
      float u1 = map(i + 1, 0, 50, 0, 1);
      float v1 = map(j + 1, 0, 50, 0, 1);
      float x1 = x0 + width/50.0;
      float y1 = y0 + width/50.0;
      float z1 = 200 * noise(0.1 * i, 0.1 * j, 0);
      float z2 = 200 * noise(0.1 * (i + 1), 0.1 * j, 0);
      float z3 = 200 * noise(0.1 * (i + 1), 0.1 * (j + 1), 0);
      float z4 = 200 * noise(0.1 * i, 0.1 * (j + 1), 0);
      terrain.vertex(x0, y0, z1, u0 ,v0);
      terrain.vertex(x1, y0, z2, u1 ,v0);
      terrain.vertex(x1, y1, z3, u1 ,v1);
      terrain.vertex(x0, y1, z4, u0 ,v1);
    }
  }
  terrain.endShape();
}
```

301

```
void draw() {
  background(150);
  lights();
  translate(width/2, height/2);
  rotateX(QUARTER_PI);
  shape(terrain);
}
```

Figure 13-13. *Terrain shape with a dirt texture applied to it*

It is worth noting that (u, v) texture coordinates, in the same way as (x, y, z) coordinates, don't have to be static. Even in a PShape object, we can modify the texture coordinates dynamically using the setTextureUV() function.

Summary

With the help of the techniques we learned in this chapter, we will be able to create interactive 3D graphics in Android apps using Processing, including lighting, texturing, objects created on the fly and also those loaded from OBJ models, as well as performance tricks. Irrespective of whether we are interested in VR or not, these techniques provide a useful toolkit for any 3D development we may want to do for games, visualizations, and other types of applications.

CHAPTER 14

VR Basics

In this chapter, we will learn some of the basic techniques to create VR apps with Processing. These techniques cover object selection, interaction, and movement in VR space, as well as using eye coordinates to create static frames of reference to facilitate the user experience.

Google VR

We may think of virtual reality as a recent invention, but it has a long history dating back at least to the 1950s (https://en.wikipedia.org/wiki/Virtual_reality#History), and even earlier if we consider stereoscopic photo viewers from the nineteenth century as predecessors to modern VR. After entering the popular consciousness a few decades ago thanks to movies and early VR headsets for gaming consoles, rapid advances in computer technology have made it possible to experience VR with highly immersive graphics and interaction. Part of the wider appeal of VR in recent years was spearheaded by the Oculus Rift headset, which began as a Kickstarter project in 2012 and sparked a growing industry that now includes the HTC Vive, the PlayStation VR, and Google VR.

Google VR, in contrast to systems like the Vive or the Oculus, which require a dedicated desktop computer to drive the graphics, can be experienced just with a smartphone attached to an inexpensive cardboard headset. This has advantages and disadvantages: on one hand, it makes VR very accessible and easy to try out, while on the other hand the experience may not be as rich as the one you could have with more sophisticated VR systems.

Cardboard and Daydream

The VR platform from Google supports two kinds of hardware: the original Cardboard and the newer Daydream. With Cardboard, the headset can be as simple as a folded cardboard cutout to support the phone, paired with plastic lenses for viewing. A Cardboard headset is not meant to be worn for extended periods of time, as we must hold it as if it were binoculars. Most recent Android phones could be used with a Cardboard headset (the next section goes over the hardware requirements). With Daydream, Google introduced a more elaborate headset made of fabric to ensure its light weight when wearing it for a long time. Daydream also uses standalone smartphones to drive the VR experience; however, Daydream-compatible hardware is more limited, as it must be of higher capacity than that used with Cardboard. All VR content designed for Cardboard should work on Daydream, but the reverse is not necessarily true.

© Andrés Colubri 2017
A. Colubri, *Processing for Android*, https://doi.org/10.1007/978-1-4842-2719-0_14

Hardware Requirements

Cardboard requires a smartphone with at least a gyroscope so head motion can be properly tracked. This is a fairly minimal requirement, since most Android phones on the market in the last couple of years have included a gyro. Daydream is supported by high-end devices, like the Google Pixel and Asus ZenFone AR (https://vr.google. com/daydream/smartphonevr/phones/). In general, both for Cardboard and Daydream, a smartphone with a fast processor is recommended, or the animation might not be smooth enough, dramatically affecting the quality of the VR experience.

VR in Processing

Processing for Android includes a VR library, which acts as a simplified interface to Google VR and automatically configures Processing's 3D view based on the head-tracking data from the phone's sensors. Using VR in Processing requires two steps. First, select the VR option in the Android menu in the PDE, as seen in Figure 14-1.

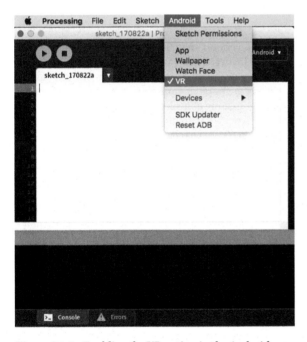

Figure 14-1. *Enabling the VR option in the Android menu*

The second step is to import the VR library into our code and set the STEREO renderer in the fullScreen() function. This renderer draws the 3D scene in our sketch with the camera transformations required to follow the head movement in VR space and to account for the differences between each eye's point of view. Listing 14-1 shows a minimal VR sketch in Processing.

Listing 14-1. Basic VR Sketch

```
import processing.vr.*;

void setup() {
  fullScreen(STEREO);
  fill(#AD71B7);
}

void draw() {
  background(#81B771);
  translate(width/2, height/2);
  lights();
  rotateY(millis()/1000.0);
  box(500);
}
```

We can see the result in Figure 14-2—a rotating cube in VR! If we placed the phone in a Cardboard or Daydream headset, we would be able to see the cube from different angles as we rotate our head around it. However, walking in physical space will not have any effect on the VR viewing, as Google VR headsets do not (at the time of this writing) support positional tracking.

Figure 14-2. *Output of a simple VR sketch*

■ **Note**   In order to run our sketch on a Daydream headset, we need to manually edit the manifest file in the sketch's folder and replace the category com.google.intent.category. CARDBOARD in the intent-filter section to com.google.intent.category.DAYDREAM.

Stereo Rendering

As we noticed in our first example, a VR sketch generates two copies of the scene, one for the left eye and the other for the right. They are slightly different since they correspond to how the scene is viewed from each eye. A consequence of this is that the draw() function is called twice in each frame (we will discuss this aspect further).

All the techniques we saw in the previous chapter on 3D drawing using the P3D renderer translate over to VR with almost no modifications. We can use shapes, textures, and lights in the same way as before. By default, the orientation of the XYZ axes is the same as in the P3D renderer, meaning that the origin is located at the upper-left corner of the screen and the y-axis points down. Listing 14-2 implements a simple scene to visualize those settings (Figure 14-3).

Listing 14-2. Axes in VR

```
import processing.vr.*;

void setup() {
  fullScreen(STEREO);
  strokeWeight(2);
}

void draw() {
  background(0);
  translate(width/2, height/2);
  lights();
  drawAxis();
  drawGrid();
}

void drawAxis() {
  line(0, 0, 0, 200, 0, 0);
  drawBox(200, 0, 0, 50, #E33E3E);
  line(0, 0, 0, 0, -200, 0);
  drawBox(0, -200, 0, 50, #3E76E3);
  line(0, 0, 0, 0, 0, 200);
  drawBox(0, 0, 200, 50, #3EE379);
}

void drawGrid() {
  beginShape(LINES);
  stroke(255);
  for (int x = -10000; x < +10000; x += 500) {
    vertex(x, +500, +10000);
    vertex(x, +500, -10000);
  }
```

```
  for (int z = -10000; z < +10000; z += 500) {
    vertex(+10000, +500, z);
    vertex(-10000, +500, z);
  }
  endShape();
}

void drawBox(float x, float y, float z, float s, color c) {
  pushStyle();
  pushMatrix();
  translate(x, y, z);
  noStroke();
  fill(c);
  box(s);
  popMatrix();
  popStyle();
}
```

Since the origin is at the upper-left corner of the screen, we need the translate(width/2, height/2) call to center the scene at the middle of the screen. Also, we can see that the blue box, placed at (0, -200, 0), is above the line of sight, consistent with the downward orientation the y-axis.

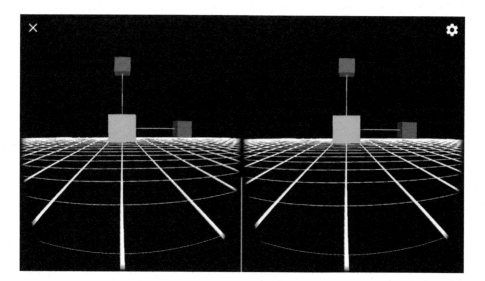

Figure 14-3. *Default coordinate axes in VR*

■ **Note**   Most frameworks for developing VR apps use a coordinate system where the origin is located at the center of the screen and the y-axis points up. In Processing for Android, we can switch to this system by calling `cameraUp()` in `setup()`.

Monoscopic Rendering

The Processing VR library includes another renderer that we can use to draw 3D scenes that respond to the phone's movement, but not in stereo mode. This can be useful if we simply want to peek into a 3D space without a VR headset. The only change we need in our code is to use the MONO renderer instead of STEREO, like we do in Listing 14-3. The result is shown in Figure 14-4.

Listing 14-3. Using the MONO Renderer

```
import processing.vr.*;

float angle = 0;
PShape cube;

void setup() {
  fullScreen(MONO);
  PImage tex = loadImage("mosaic.jpg");
  cube = createShape(BOX, 400);
  cube.setTexture(tex);
}

void draw() {
  background(#81B771);
  translate(width/2, height/2);
  lights();
  rotateY(angle);
  rotateX(angle*2);
  shape(cube);
  angle += 0.01;
}
```

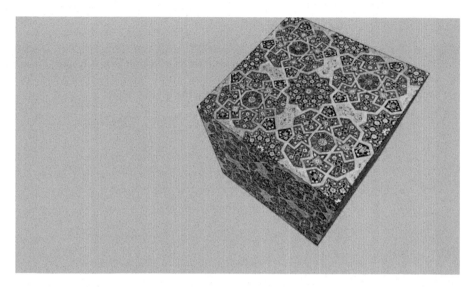

Figure 14-4. *Monoscopic rendering*

VR Interaction

The code examples so far have shown us that creating a VR scene in Processing is fairly simple: all we need is to select the VR mode in the PDE, import the VR library into our sketch, and use the STEREO renderer. With these steps, we can apply all the 3D rendering techniques we learned earlier. But as soon as we start thinking about user interaction in VR, we will find new challenges. First of all, Cardboard headsets do not include any controller, like more expensive headsets do. Manual input is limited to a button that triggers a touch on the screen, and some basic headsets don't even have this button. We must ask ourselves a few fundamental questions about interaction in VR: how do we select 3D objects/UI elements, and how do we move around in VR space?

Developers have been experimenting with various solutions to these problems, and an overview of VR apps on the Google Play Store can give us some hints. A common technique for interaction is gaze selection: the app detects which object we are looking at, and a touch press (or staring at it long enough) triggers the desired action. All VR apps use this technique in one way or another, in combination with other interesting ideas: head gestures (tilting, etc.), use of special areas in VR space to place UI elements (i.e., looking up or down), and automation of certain actions (walking, shooting).

■ **Note**   A successful VR experience needs to pay special attention to interaction so that users feel they are indeed inside of this space. Given the constraints of VR headsets in terms of graphic realism and controls, we need to craft the interaction very carefully so it makes sense in terms of the specific experience we are trying to convey.

Eye and World Coordinates

Before we start looking at interaction techniques for VR, we need to familiarize ourselves with the coordinate systems we will be dealing with when developing our VR apps. There are two systems that are important to keep in mind: the world coordinate system and the eye coordinate system, which are illustrated in Figure 14-5.

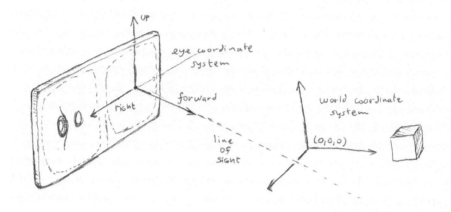

Figure 14-5. *Eye coordinate system with forward, right, and up vectors at the eye position, and world coordinate system*

We have been using world coordinates all along, since Processing relies on these coordinates to characterize the position and movement of shapes, in both 2D and 3D. Eye coordinates are new though, and are very specific to the way the VR view is constructed automatically for us from the head-tracking information. The eye coordinate system is defined by three vectors: forward, right, and up (Figure 14-5). The forward vector represents the direction of our line of sight, and the right and up vectors complete the system. These vectors get updated automatically in each frame to reflect the movement of the head.

Eye coordinates are the natural choice to represent shapes and other graphic elements that need to be aligned with our view, such as a text message in front of our eyes or a piece of geometry that provides a static frame of reference; for example, a helmet or the interior of a spaceship. The use of eye coordinates makes it very easy to draw those elements correctly; for example, a box right in front of our eyes would have coordinates (0, 0, 200).

Processing lets us switch from world to eye coordinates simply by calling the eye() function, as demonstrated in Listing 14-4. The quad, box, and text are always in front of our view, as we see in Figure 14-6.

Listing 14-4. Drawing in Eye Coordinates

```
import processing.vr.*;

public void setup() {
  fullScreen(STEREO);
  textFont(createFont("SansSerif", 30));
  textAlign(CENTER, CENTER);
}

public void draw() {
  background(255);
  translate(width/2, height/2);
  lights();
  fill(#EAB240);
  noStroke();
  rotateY(millis()/1000.0);
  box(300);
  drawEye();
}

void drawEye() {
  eye();

  float s = 50;
  float d = 200;
  float h = 100;

  noFill();
  stroke(0);
  strokeWeight(10);
  beginShape(QUADS);
  vertex(-s, -s, d);
  vertex(+s, -s, d);
  vertex(+s, +s, d);
  vertex(-s, +s, d);
  endShape();

  pushMatrix();
  translate(0, 0, d);
  rotateX(millis()/1000.0);
  rotateY(millis()/2000.0);
  fill(#6AA4FF);
  noStroke();
  box(50);
  popMatrix();

  fill(0);
  text("Welcome to VR!", 0, -h * 0.75, d);
}
```

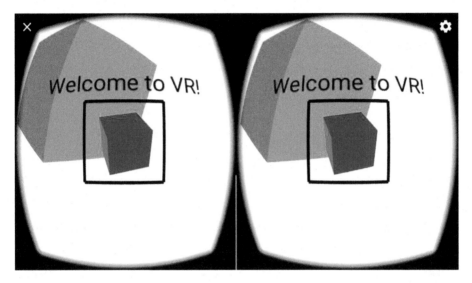

Figure 14-6. *Geometry defined in eye coordinates*

The Line of Sight

The most immediate way of interacting in VR space is by looking around! In order to implement gaze selection, we can refer to Figure 14-5, which shows the actual line of sight extending from the eye (or camera) position along the forward vector. If a 3D object is in the path of this line, we can conclude it is being looked at by the user (unless there is another object blocking the view). So, how can we draw the line of sight? As we saw in the previous section, eye coordinates should be the answer, since this line starts at (0, 0, 0) and extends to (0, 0, L), where L is how far we want to go along the line.

In Listing 14-5, we draw the line of sight with an offset at the origin along x and y so we can see where it intersects a box placed at the center of the world system (otherwise, it would be perfectly perpendicular to our view and thus be hard to see).

Listing 14-5. Drawing the Line of Sight

```
import processing.vr.*;

PMatrix3D mat = new PMatrix3D();

void setup() {
  fullScreen(STEREO);
  hint(ENABLE_STROKE_PERSPECTIVE);
}

void draw() {
  background(120);
  translate(width/2, height/2);
  lights();
```

```
noStroke();
pushMatrix();
rotateY(millis()/1000.0);
fill(#E3993E);
box(150);
popMatrix();

eye();
stroke(#2FB1EA);
strokeWeight(50);
line(100, -100, 0, 0, 0, 10000);
}
```

In this code, we also use the ENABLE_STROKE_PERSPECTIVE hint so the line becomes thinner as it moves away from the eye (Figure 14-7).

■ **Note**   Hints are special settings for the renderer that are enabled by passing an ENABLE_name constant to the hint() function and disabled by passing the corresponding DISABLE_name constant.

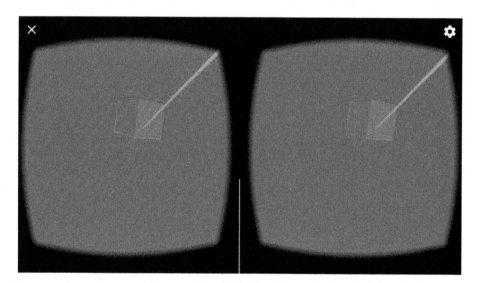

Figure 14-7. *Line of sight intersecting a box placed at the origin of coordinates*

We can also use a point stroke to show the exact location of the screen center by drawing it at the eye coordinates (0, 0), like we do in Listing 14-6. Any 3D shape crossing the screen center is intersected by the line of sight, so this gives us another way of indicating what object the user might be looking at.

313

Listing 14-6. Drawing a Circular Aim

```
import processing.vr.*;

void setup() {
  fullScreen(STEREO);
}

void draw() {
  background(120);
  translate(width/2, height/2);

  lights();

  noStroke();
  fill(#E3993E);
  beginShape(QUAD);
  vertex(-75, -75);
  vertex(+75, -75);
  vertex(+75, +75);
  vertex(-75, +75);
  endShape(QUAD);

  eye();
  stroke(47, 177, 234, 150);
  strokeWeight(50);
  point(0, 0, 100);
}
```

The point stroke we draw with the function point() can be made as large as we need by setting the weight with strokeWeight(). It serves the purpose of a "view aim" with which to point to objects in VR. Figure 14-8 shows the aim with a weight of 50. In the next section, we will learn how to determine if a 3D point falls inside the aim.

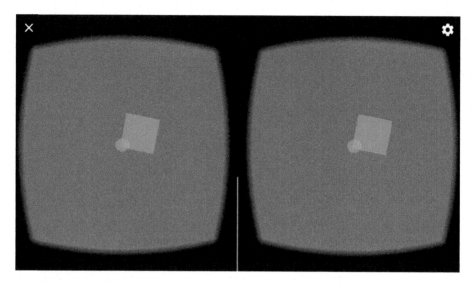

Figure 14-8. *View aim drawn with a point stroke*

Selecting a Shape with Screen Coordinates

As we just saw, a seemingly easy way to determine if a vertex in 3D space falls within our line of sight would be to determine if its "screen coordinates" are close enough to the center of the screen. This condition is simple to check visually by drawing a view aim at the exact center of the screen, like we did in Listing 14-6. However, we need a way to check the condition with code. Processing has the functions screenX() and screenY(), which allow us to do exactly that. These functions take as arguments the coordinates (x, y, z) of a point in 3D space and return the screen coordinates (sx, sy) of that point when projected onto the screen. If these screen coordinates are close enough to (width/2, height/2), then we can conclude that the shape is being selected by the user. Let's use this technique in Listing 14-7.

Listing 14-7. Gaze Selection with Button Press

```
import processing.vr.*;

void setup() {
  fullScreen(STEREO);
}

void draw() {
  background(120);
  translate(width/2, height/2);
  lights();
  drawGrid();
  drawAim();
}
```

```
void drawGrid() {
  for (int i = 0; i < 4; i++) {
    for (int j = 0; j < 4; j++) {
      beginShape(QUAD);
      float x = map(i, 0, 3, -315, +315);
      float y = map(j, 0, 3, -315, +315);
      float sx = screenX(x, y, 0);
      float sy = screenY(x, y, 0);
      if (abs(sx - 0.5 * width) < 50 && abs(sy - 0.5 * height) < 50) {
        strokeWeight(5);
        stroke(#2FB1EA);
        if (mousePressed) {
          fill(#2FB1EA);
        } else {
          fill(#E3993E);
        }
      } else {
        noStroke();
        fill(#E3993E);
      }
      vertex(x - 100, y - 100);
      vertex(x + 100, y - 100);
      vertex(x + 100, y + 100);
      vertex(x - 100, y + 100);
      endShape(QUAD);
    }
  }
}

void drawAim() {
  eye();
  stroke(47, 177, 234, 150);
  strokeWeight(50);
  point(0, 0, 100);
}
```

The mousePressed variable is set to true if we push the button in the headset, allowing us to confirm the selection of the shape we are looking at and to get the entire rectangle highlighted, like in Figure 14-9. However, if the headset lacks a button, we need a different strategy. We can confirm the selection by looking at the shape for a specific duration of time, which we do in Listing 14-8 (only the code different from that in the previous listing is shown).

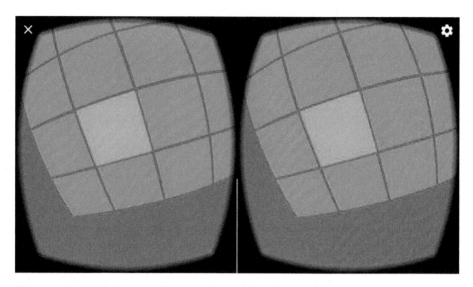

Figure 14-9. *Selecting a quad using screen coordinates*

Listing 14-8. Gaze Selection with Staring Time

```
import processing.vr.*;

int seli = -1;
int selj = -1;
int startSel, selTime;
...
void drawGrid() {
  boolean sel = false;
  for (int i = 0; i < 4; i++) {
    for (int j = 0; j < 4; j++) {
      ...
      if (abs(sx - 0.5 * width) < 50 && abs(sy - 0.5 * height) < 50) {
        strokeWeight(5);
        stroke(#2FB1EA);
        if (seli == i && selj == j) {
          selTime = millis() - startSel;
        } else {
          startSel = millis();
          selTime = 0;
        }
        seli = i;
        selj = j;
        sel = true;
        if (2000 < selTime) {
          fill(#2FB1EA);
```

```
      } else {
        fill(#E3993E);
      }
    } else {
      ...
  }
  if (!sel) {
    seli = -1;
    selj = -1;
    selTime = 0;
  }
}
```

The idea here is to keep track of the indexes of the currently selected rectangle and to only confirm the selection when the `selTime` variable is greater than a desired threshold, which in this case is set to 2,000 milliseconds.

Bounding Box Selection

The technique of selecting a 3D object by calculating its screen coordinates works well for simple shapes and can be useful when creating a UI. However, it may not be well suited for more complex objects that have irregular silhouettes when projected onto the screen plane.

A common approach to determining object selection in 3D is bounding box intersection. A bounding box is a cube that completely encloses a given 3D object. If the line of sight does not intersect the bounding box of an object, we can be certain that the object is not being selected, and if it does, we could just select it or perform a more detailed test. An axis-aligned bounding box (AABB) is a particular type of bounding box where the edges are aligned to the coordinate axes. This property makes computations simpler and faster, which is very important in the context of VR apps where we may have to test for hundreds or even thousands of bounding box intersections. The AABB of a 3D object can be calculated easily by taking the minimum and maximum of the xyz coordinates of the vertices in the object and storing them in a pair of vectors, which completely determine the AABB.

There are many algorithms with which to test the intersection of a line with an AABB (http://www.realtimerendering.com/intersections.html). One that is efficient and simple to implement was proposed by Amy Williams and collaborators in 2005 (http://dl.acm.org/citation.cfm?id=1198748). In this algorithm, we need to provide the minimum and maximum vectors defining the AABB, as well as a point along the line and its direction vector (in the case of the intersection with the line of sight, these are the eye position and the forward vector). The problem is that if we apply transformations to the object, its bounding box may no longer be aligned to the axes. We can remediate this by applying the inverse transformation to the line so that the relative orientation of the line and the AABB is the same as if we had applied the transformations on the bounding box. This inverse transformation is encoded in the so-called object matrix, which we can obtain with the getObjectMatrix() function.

As we already pointed out, this algorithm requires the eye position and the forward vector. These are part of the "eye matrix" that we have used before when switching to eye coordinates using the eye() function. In order to get a copy of this matrix, we also have the getEyeMatrix() in the Processing API. Listing 14-9 puts all of this together by applying Williams' algorithm to a grid of boxes (see the result in Figure 14-10).

Listing 14-9. AABB-Line of Sight Intersection

```
import processing.vr.*;

PMatrix3D eyeMat = new PMatrix3D();
PMatrix3D objMat = new PMatrix3D();
PVector cam = new PVector();
PVector dir = new PVector();
PVector front = new PVector();
PVector objCam = new PVector();
PVector objFront = new PVector();
PVector objDir = new PVector();
float boxSize = 140;
PVector boxMin = new PVector(-boxSize/2, -boxSize/2, -boxSize/2);
PVector boxMax = new PVector(+boxSize/2, +boxSize/2, +boxSize/2);
PVector hit = new PVector();

void setup() {
  fullScreen(PVR.STEREO);
}

void draw() {
  getEyeMatrix(eyeMat);
  cam.set(eyeMat.m03, eyeMat.m13, eyeMat.m23);
  dir.set(eyeMat.m02, eyeMat.m12, eyeMat.m22);
  PVector.add(cam, dir, front);
  background(120);
  translate(width/2, height/2);
  lights();
  drawGrid();
  drawAim();
}

void drawGrid() {
  for (int i = 0; i < 4; i++) {
    for (int j = 0; j < 4; j++) {
      float x = map(i, 0, 3, -350, +350);
      float y = map(j, 0, 3, -350, +350);
      pushMatrix();
      translate(x, y);
      rotateY(millis()/1000.0);
      getObjectMatrix(objMat);
```

319

```
      objMat.mult(cam, objCam);
      objMat.mult(front, objFront);
      PVector.sub(objFront, objCam, objDir);
      boolean res = intersectsLine(objCam, objDir, boxMin, boxMax,
                                   0, 1000, hit);
    if (res) {
      strokeWeight(5);
      stroke(#2FB1EA);
      if (mousePressed) {
        fill(#2FB1EA);
      } else {
        fill(#E3993E);
      }
    } else {
      noStroke();
      fill(#E3993E);
    }
    box(boxSize);
    popMatrix();
    }
  }
}

void drawAim() {
  eye();
  stroke(47, 177, 234, 150);
  strokeWeight(50);
  point(0, 0, 100);
}

boolean intersectsLine(PVector orig, PVector dir,
  PVector minPos, PVector maxPos, float minDist, float maxDist, PVector hit)
{
  PVector bbox;
  PVector invDir = new PVector(1/dir.x, 1/dir.y, 1/dir.z);

  boolean signDirX = invDir.x < 0;
  boolean signDirY = invDir.y < 0;
  boolean signDirZ = invDir.z < 0;

  bbox = signDirX ? maxPos : minPos;
  float txmin = (bbox.x - orig.x) * invDir.x;
  bbox = signDirX ? minPos : maxPos;
  float txmax = (bbox.x - orig.x) * invDir.x;
  bbox = signDirY ? maxPos : minPos;
  float tymin = (bbox.y - orig.y) * invDir.y;
  bbox = signDirY ? minPos : maxPos;
  float tymax = (bbox.y - orig.y) * invDir.y;
```

```
  if ((txmin > tymax) || (tymin > txmax)) {
    return false;
  }
  if (tymin > txmin) {
    txmin = tymin;
  }
  if (tymax < txmax) {
    txmax = tymax;
  }

  bbox = signDirZ ? maxPos : minPos;
  float tzmin = (bbox.z - orig.z) * invDir.z;
  bbox = signDirZ ? minPos : maxPos;
  float tzmax = (bbox.z - orig.z) * invDir.z;

  if ((txmin > tzmax) || (tzmin > txmax)) {
    return false;
  }
  if (tzmin > txmin) {
    txmin = tzmin;
  }
  if (tzmax < txmax) {
    txmax = tzmax;
  }
  if ((txmin < maxDist) && (txmax > minDist)) {
    hit.x = orig.x + txmin * dir.x;
    hit.y = orig.y + txmin * dir.y;
    hit.z = orig.z + txmin * dir.z;
    return true;
  }
  return false;
}
```

Each box in the grid has a different object matrix, since the transformations are different (same rotation, but different translation). Once we obtain the object matrix, we have to apply it to the eye position and forward vector, since they define the line we want to intersect with the AABB of the object. We apply the transformation by matrix-vector multiplication. The eye position is stored in the cam variable, and is transformed into object space directly with objMat.mult(cam, objCam). However, the forward vector is a direction, not a position, so it cannot be transformed like that. Instead, first we need to transform the front vector, which stores the position of the point one unit ahead from the eye along the line of sight, with objMat.mult(front, objFront), and only then we can calculate the direction vector in object coordinates by calculating the difference between the transformed front and eye positions with PVector.sub(objFront, objCam, objDir).

The eye position and forward vector are encoded in the eye matrix as its third and fourth columns so we can get the individual components of the matrix, (m02, m12, m22) and (m03, m13, m23), and then copy them into the dir and cam vectors, respectively.

Figure 14-10. *Selecting a box with Williams' algorithm*

The intersectsLine() function holds the implementation of Williams' algorithm. It is completely self-contained, so we can reuse it in other sketches. Note that, besides returning true or false depending on whether the line intersects the AABB or not, the algorithm also returns the coordinates of the intersection point in the hit vector, which could be used to determine the closest intersection to the camera in case several are detected.

Movement in VR

Movement is a critical aspect of any VR experience that we need to consider carefully, as it is subject to some constraints and requirements. On one hand, we aim to convince the user to suspend their disbelief and immerse themselves in the virtual environment. Having some degree of freedom in this environment is important. On the other hand, this virtual movement will not completely match our senses, which could cause motion sickness, something to avoid at all costs in VR apps. Conversely, if we did move around in physical space while wearing a Google VR headset, we would experience another disconnect between our vision and physical senses.

Despite these constraints, we can still create convincing movement in VR space. One trick is to place some sort of reference object that remains fixed within the field of vision, matching our stationary condition in physical space. For example, in Listing 14-10 we load an OBJ shape for this purpose, placing it at the camera position in eye coordinates. The shape is a dodecahedron (Figure 14-11) that acts as a "helmet" of sorts during our navigation through VR.

Listing 14-10. Drawing a Stationary Reference Object

```
import processing.vr.*;

PShape frame;

void setup() {
  fullScreen(STEREO);
  frame = loadShape("dodecahedron.obj");
  prepare(frame, 500);
}

void draw() {
  background(180);
  lights();
  translate(width/2, height/2);
  eye();
  shape(frame);
}

void prepare(PShape sh, float s) {
  PVector min = new PVector(+10000, +10000, +10000);
  PVector max = new PVector(-10000, -10000, -10000);
  PVector v = new PVector();
  for (int i = 0; i < sh.getChildCount(); i++) {
    PShape child = sh.getChild(i);
    for (int j = 0; j < child.getVertexCount(); j++) {
      child.getVertex(j, v);
      min.x = min(min.x, v.x);
      min.y = min(min.y, v.y);
      min.z = min(min.z, v.z);
      max.x = max(max.x, v.x);
      max.y = max(max.y, v.y);
      max.z = max(max.z, v.z);
    }
  }
  PVector center = PVector.add(max, min).mult(0.5f);
  sh.translate(-center.x, -center.y, -center.z);
  float maxSize = max(sh.getWidth(), sh.getHeight(), sh.getDepth());
  float factor = s/maxSize;
  sh.scale(factor);
}
```

The prepare() function centers the shape at the origin and also scales it to have a size comparable to the dimensions of our scene. This step is important when loading OBJ files, since they may be defined using a different range of coordinate values, and so they could look either very small or very large. In this case, we place the dodecahedron shape so it is centered at (cameraX, cameraY, cameraZ), thus providing a reference to our vision in VR. We will see next how to move around with this reference in place.

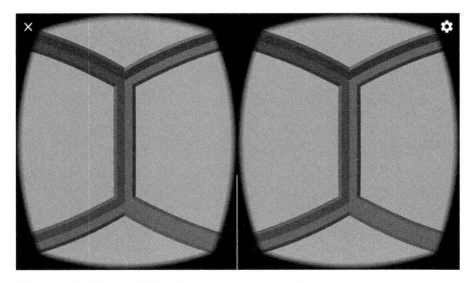

Figure 14-11. *Using an OBJ shape as a reference in our field of vision*

Automatic Movement

In some instances, we can create movement that is not controlled by the user, thus removing complexity from the interface. For example, this could be a good solution if the goal is to take the user through a predetermined path, or to transition between two checkpoints.

Once we have constructed the scene geometry, we can apply any transformations to it in order to create the movement, enclosing them between pushMatrix() and popMatrix() to keep the transformations from affecting any shapes that are fixed relative to the viewer. Listing 14-11 shows how to simulate a rotation around a circular track.

Listing 14-11. Moving Along a Predefined Path

```
import processing.vr.*;

PShape frame;
PShape track;

public void setup() {
  fullScreen(STEREO);

  frame = loadShape("dodecahedron.obj");
  prepare(frame, 500);
```

```
  track = createShape();
  track.beginShape(QUAD_STRIP);
  track.fill(#2D8B47);
  for (int i = 0; i <= 40; i++) {
    float a = map(i, 0, 40, 0, TWO_PI);
    float x0 = 1000 * cos(a);
    float z0 = 1000 * sin(a);
    float x1 = 1400 * cos(a);
    float z1 = 1400 * sin(a);
    track.vertex(x0, 0, z0);
    track.vertex(x1, 0, z1);
  }
  track.endShape();
}

public void draw() {
  background(255);
  translate(width/2, height/2);

  directionalLight(200, 200, 200, 0, +1, -1);

  translate(1200, +300, 500);
  rotateY(millis()/10000.0);
  shape(track);

  eye();
  shape(frame);
}

void prepare(PShape sh, float s) {
...
```

In this code, we store the circular track in a PShape object, apply a translation to the right of the camera so the user starts on top of the track, and then apply a rotation to create the desired movement around the track's center. The result of this sketch is shown in Figure 14-12.

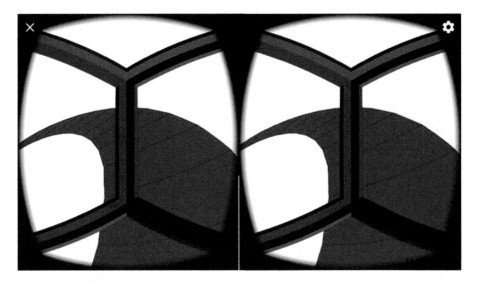

Figure 14-12. Using an OBJ shape as a reference in our field of vision

Free-range Movement

In contrast with the previous example, where movement is predefined and the user can only look around, we will now let the user roam freely in the VR space. This is not difficult to implement; all we need is to translate the objects in the scene along the forward vector, as is done in Listing 14-12. However, here we make use of the calculate() function for the first time, an important function in VR sketches that let us run calculations that should be performed only once per frame.

Listing 14-12. Moving Freely in VR Space

```
import processing.vr.*;

PShape frame;
PShape cubes;
PMatrix3D eyeMat = new PMatrix3D();
float tx, ty, tz;
float step = 5;

public void setup() {
  fullScreen(STEREO);

  frame = loadShape("dodecahedron.obj");
  prepare(frame, 500);

  cubes = createShape(GROUP);
  float v = 5 * width;
```

```
  for (int i = 0; i < 50; i++) {
    float x = random(-v, +v);
    float y = random(-v, +v);
    float z = random(-v, +v);
    float s = random(100, 200);
    PShape sh = createShape(BOX, s);
    sh.setFill(color(#74E0FF));
    sh.translate(x, y, z);
    cubes.addChild(sh);
  }
}

void calculate() {
  getEyeMatrix(eyeMat);
  if (mousePressed) {
    tx -= step * eyeMat.m02;
    ty -= step * eyeMat.m12;
    tz -= step * eyeMat.m22;
  }
}

public void draw() {
  background(255);
  translate(width/2, height/2);

  directionalLight(200, 200, 200, 0, +1, -1);

  translate(tx, ty, tz);
  shape(cubes);

  eye();
  shape(frame);
}

void prepare(PShape sh, float s) {
...
```

The calculate() function is called just once in each frame, right before draw() gets called twice, once for each eye. This is useful in this example because if we were to put the translation code inside draw(), we would be increasing the translation by double the intended amount, resulting in an incorrect translation. It is important that we think about what operations should be done inside draw()—typically anything drawing-related—and which ones inside calculate(), such as code that affects the left and right views in the same way.

A problem with fully unbounded movement in VR space is that it could become disorienting for many people. A more manageable situation would involve restricting the motion to the XZ plane. This can be accomplished with the forward vector as before, but you would only use its x and z components to update the translation, as is illustrated in Listing 14-13.

Listing 14-13. Moving in a 2D Plane

```
import processing.vr.*;

PShape cubes;
PShape grid;
PMatrix3D eyeMat = new PMatrix3D();
float tx, tz;
float step = 10;
PVector planeDir = new PVector();

public void setup() {
  fullScreen(STEREO);

  grid = createShape();
  grid.beginShape(LINES);
  grid.stroke(255);
  for (int x = -10000; x < +10000; x += 500) {
    grid.vertex(x, +200, +10000);
    grid.vertex(x, +200, -10000);
  }
  for (int z = -10000; z < +10000; z += 500) {
    grid.vertex(+10000, +200, z);
    grid.vertex(-10000, +200, z);
  }
  grid.endShape();

  cubes = createShape(GROUP);
  float v = 5 * width;
  for (int i = 0; i < 50; i++) {
    float x = random(-v, +v);
    float z = random(-v, +v);
    float s = random(100, 300);
    float y = +200 - s/2;
    PShape sh = createShape(BOX, s);
    sh.setFill(color(#FFBC6A));
    sh.translate(x, y, z);
    cubes.addChild(sh);
  }
}

void calculate() {
  getEyeMatrix(eyeMat);
  if (mousePressed) {
    planeDir.set(eyeMat.m02, 0, eyeMat.m22);
    float d = planeDir.mag();
    if (0 < d) {
      planeDir.mult(1/d);
```

```
      tx -= step * planeDir.x;
      tz -= step * planeDir.z;
    }
  }
}

public void draw() {
  background(0);
  translate(width/2, height/2);
  pointLight(50, 50, 200, 0, 1000, 0);
  directionalLight(200, 200, 200, 0, +1, -1);
  translate(tx, 0, tz);
  shape(grid);
  shape(cubes);
}
```

In the calculate() function, we construct a plane-direction vector from the m02 and m22 components of the eye matrix. We need to normalize this vector to ensure we keep making uniform strides as we move around, even if we are looking up and the forward vector has very small coordinates along the x and z axes. A view from this sketch is shown in Figure 14-13.

Figure 14-13. *Movement constrained to a 2D plane*

Summary

VR brings about exciting new possibilities as well as interesting challenges. In this chapter, we learned a few techniques in Processing to address some of these challenges and to explore where the possibilities of VR can take us. In particular, we discussed how intuitive interaction and movement are key to creating engaging VR experiences.

CHAPTER 15

■ ■ ■

Drawing in VR

In this final chapter, we will go step-by-step through the development of a fully-featured VR drawing app using Processing for Android. We will apply all the techniques we have learned so far, including gaze-controlled movement and user interface (UI).

Creating a Successful VR Experience

In the previous chapters, we learned the basics of the 3D API in Processing, as well as some techniques that we can apply to create interactive graphics in VR. Creating a successful VR experience is an exciting challenge. In contrast with "traditional" computer graphics, where we can rely on representations (e.g., perspective vs. isometric views) and interaction conventions (e.g., mouse- or touch-based gestures) that users are familiar with, VR is a new medium that presents many possibilities but also comes with unique constraints and limitations.

Arguably, a central goal in VR is for the user to suspend disbelief and immerse themselves in the virtual space, at least for a short while, even if the graphics are not photo-realistic or the interaction is limited. VR creates the unusual experience of being inside a synthetic 3D space without a body. Recent input hardware demoed at tech and gaming shows (for example, bicycle stands for biking in VR, air pressure to create the illusion of touch, even low electric discharges) illustrates the ongoing efforts to embody the VR experience.

We also need to be aware of the specific characteristics of the Cardboard and Daydream platforms supported by Processing for Android. Since we are generating the graphics with a smartphone, they are more limited than those generated by VR rigs driven by PCs. First, it is important to make sure that phones can handle the complexity of our scene and can keep a smooth framerate. Otherwise, choppy animation can cause dizziness and nausea for the users. Second, Cardboard headsets have limited interaction input, typically only a single button. Also, since we need to use both hands to hold them (see Figure 15-1), we cannot rely on external input devices. The interaction in our VR app should take all of these aspects of the experience into account.

© Andrés Colubri 2017
A. Colubri, *Processing for Android*, https://doi.org/10.1007/978-1-4842-2719-0_15

Figure 15-1. *Students using Google Cardboard during class activities*

Drawing in VR

Creating 3D objects in VR can be a very engaging activity, one where we are able to not only sculpt figures unbounded from the screen or laws of physics, but also be in the same space with our virtual creations. Google Tilt Brush (Figure 15-2) is an good example of how a well-designed VR experience can be extremely immersive and fun. Inspired by these thoughts, wouldn't it be a good exercise to implement our own drawing VR app for Cardboard/Daydream?

Figure 15-2. *Google Tilt Brush VR drawing app*

As we just discussed, we will have to deal with more-limited graphics and interaction capabilities. If we assume that no input device is available, and we only have one button with which to make single presses, we are essentially constrained to using gaze as our pencil. For this reason, some of the techniques in the previous chapter for selecting 3D elements in a VR space using line of sight will come in handy.

Initial Sketches

A good analogy for VR drawing is sculpting. Following this analogy, we could start off with a base or podium on top of which we will create our VR drawing/sculpture, with some UI controls to rotate it when we need to change the angle we are working on. We have to remember that Google VR does not track changes in position, only head rotations, which are not enough to make a 3D drawing from all possible angles. Figure 15-3 sketches out a pen-and-paper concept for the app.

The point where our line of sight reaches the space above the podium could be the tip of our pencil. The key detail is connecting this pencil to the movements of our head without interfering with the UI. We could use the button press as the mechanism to enable/disable drawing, so when we are not pressing the button, we are free to move our head around and to interact with the UI.

Figure 15-3. Pen-and-paper concept sketch for our VR drawing app

So, the app could work as follows: while we are in the drawing mode, we stay at the static vantage point from which we draw on top of the podium. We can add an additional element of immersion by letting the user move freely around after the drawing is completed, and by doing so be able to look at it from unusual angles. We saw how to implement free movement in VR in the previous chapter, so we could use this technique in our app as well.

A Simple VR UI

Let's start by creating an initial version of our app with only the base for our drawing and some initial UI elements, but with no actual drawing capability yet. As a temporary placeholder for Listing 15-1, we display a dummy shape that we can rotate using the UI.

Listing 15-1. Starting Point of Our Drawing App

```
import processing.vr.*;

PShape base;

void setup() {
  fullScreen(STEREO);
  createBase(300, 70, 20);
}

void draw() {
  background(0);
  translate(width/2, height/2);
  directionalLight(200, 200, 200, 0, +1, -1);
  drawBase();
  drawBox();
}

void drawBase() {
  pushMatrix();
  translate(0, +300, 0);
  shape(base);
  popMatrix();
}

void drawBox() {
  pushMatrix();
  translate(0, +100, 0);
  noStroke();
  box(200);
  popMatrix();
}
```

```
void createBase(float r, float h, int ndiv) {
  base = createShape(GROUP);
  PShape side = createShape();
  side.beginShape(QUAD_STRIP);
  side.noStroke();
  side.fill(#59C5F5);
  for (int i = 0; i <= ndiv; i++) {
    float a = map(i, 0, ndiv, 0, TWO_PI);
    float x = r * cos(a);
    float z = r * sin(a);
    side.vertex(x, +h/2, z);
    side.vertex(x, -h/2, z);
  }
  side.endShape();
  PShape top = createShape();
  top.beginShape(TRIANGLE_FAN);
  top.noStroke();
  top.fill(#59C5F5);
  top.vertex(0, 0, 0);
  for (int i = 0; i <= ndiv; i++) {
    float a = map(i, 0, ndiv, 0, TWO_PI);
    float x = r * cos(a);
    float z = r * sin(a);
    top.vertex(x, -h/2, z);
  }
  top.endShape();
  base.addChild(side);
  base.addChild(top);
}
```

The base is just a cylinder stored in a PShape, plus an ellipse to use as a top surface. As we saw previously, we can store different Processing shapes inside a group, and the resulting PShape group is all we need in order to draw this base shape. Figure 15-4 shows this first version of the app.

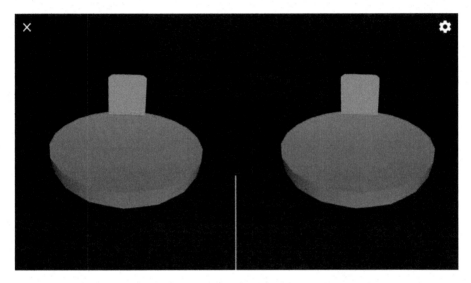

Figure 15-4. *First step in our VR drawing app: a base shape and a dummy object*

As a first iteration of the UI, we will add three buttons: two to rotate the base and box along the y-axis, and another button to reset the rotation. Listing 15-2 implements this initial UI (the createBase(), drawBase(), and drawBox() functions are omitted since they are identical to the previous code).

Listing 15-2. Adding a Basic UI

```
import processing.vr.*;

PShape base;
float angle;
Button leftButton, rightButton, resetButton;

void setup() {
  fullScreen(STEREO);
  textureMode(NORMAL);
  createBase(300, 70, 20);
  createButtons(300, 100, 380, 130);
}

void calculate () {
  if (mousePressed) {
    if (leftButton.selected) angle -= 0.01;
    if (rightButton.selected) angle += 0.01;
    if (resetButton.selected) angle = 0;
  }
}
```

```
void draw() {
  background(0);
  translate(width/2, height/2);
  directionalLight(200, 200, 200, 0, +1, -1);
  drawBase();
  drawBox();
  drawUI();
}
...
void createButtons(float dx, float hlr, float ht, float s) {
  PImage left = loadImage("left-icon.png");
  leftButton = new Button(-dx, hlr, 0, s, left);
  PImage right = loadImage("right-icon.png");
  rightButton = new Button(+dx, hlr, 0, s, right);
  PImage cross = loadImage("cross-icon.png");
  resetButton = new Button(0, +1.0 * ht, +1.1 * dx, s, cross);
}

void drawUI() {
  leftButton.display();
  rightButton.display();
  resetButton.display();
  drawAim();
}

void drawAim() {
  eye();
  pushStyle();
  stroke(220, 180);
  strokeWeight(20);
  point(0, 0, 100);
  popStyle();
}

boolean centerSelected(float d) {
  float sx = screenX(0, 0, 0);
  float sy = screenY(0, 0, 0);
  return abs(sx - 0.5 * width) < d && abs(sy - 0.5 * height) < d;
}

class Button {
  float x, y, z, s;
  boolean selected;
  PImage img;

  Button(float x, float y, float z, float s, PImage img) {
    this.x = x;
    this.y = y;
```

337

```
    this.z = z;
    this.s = s;
    this.img = img;
  }

  void display() {
    float l = 0.5 * s;
    pushStyle();
    pushMatrix();
    translate(x, y, z);
    selected = centerSelected(l);
    beginShape(QUAD);
    if (selected) {
      stroke(220, 180);
      strokeWeight(5);
    } else {
      noStroke();
    }
    tint(#59C5F5);
    texture(img);
    vertex(-1, +1, 0, 1);
    vertex(-1, -1, 0, 0);
    vertex(+1, -1, 1, 0);
    vertex(+1, +1, 1, 1);
    endShape();
    popMatrix();
    popStyle();
  }
}
```

The Button class encapsulating the selection functionality is the central element of this code. Its constructor takes five parameters: the (x, y, z) coordinates of the center of the button, the size, and an image to use as the button texture. In the implementation of the display() method, we determine if the button is selected by using the screen-coordinates technique from the previous chapter: if (screenX, screenY) is close enough to the screen center, then it is considered to be selected, in which case the button gets a stroke line. The UI events are triggered in the calculate() method to avoid applying them again when the "mouse" pressed (corresponding to the physical trigger available in the VR headset) event is detected.

The placement of the buttons is determined in the createButtons() function, with the left and right rotation buttons placed to the sides of the base, and the reset button slightly underneath. We also draw a stroke point at (0, 0, 100) in eye coordinates to use as an aim to help with drawing and selection.

At this moment, it is important to review the display() function in the Button class again, where, in addition to drawing the button, we also test if it is selected. This may look like the wrong place to put that logic, since a display function should take care of only drawing tasks. As it turns out, the screenX() and screenY() calls require that the 3D transformations affecting the button are current, or else they will return incorrect results. Since the transformations are applied when drawing the geometry, we perform the interaction detection in that stage as well. The result of this sketch should look like Figure 15-5.

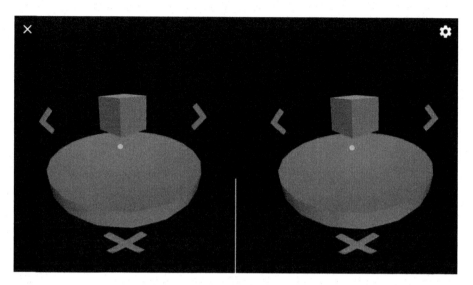

Figure 15-5. *Adding buttons to the UI*

Drawing in 3D

When we implemented the drawing app in Chapter 2, we only had to worry about making strokes in 2D. This was easy, thanks to the pmouseX/Y and mouseX/Y variables in Processing, which allowed us to draw a line between the previous and current mouse positions. In three dimensions, the idea is in fact the same: a stroke is a sequence of lines between successive positions, no longer constrained to be within the screen plane. But if we don't have an actual 3D pointer in VR space, we need to infer directionality in 3D space from gaze information alone.

We know that the direction of our gaze is contained in the forward vector, which is automatically updated to reflect any head movement. If at each frame we project the forward vector a fixed amount toward the center of the scene, we would have a sliding point that could generate the strokes in our drawing. In fact, this is not too different from what we did for 2D drawings, where the strokes were defined by the sequence of (mouseX, mouseY) positions. We can also compute the difference between the current and previous forward vectors, analogous to the vector (mouseX - pmouseX, mouseY - pmouseY) in 2D, to determine if we need to add new points to the drawing. Figure 15-6 shows the relationship between the difference vector and the corresponding displacement in the drawing.

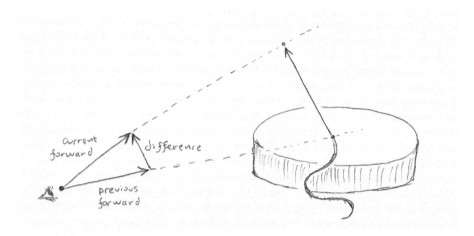

Figure 15-6. *Calculating displacement using previous and current forward vectors*

An important difference between the 3D and 2D cases is that in the latter we don't need to keep track of all the past positions, only the previous one. This is because if we don't clear the screen with background(), we can simply add the last line on top of the ones that are already drawn. But in 3D we have to refresh the screen in every frame, since the position of the camera is not static, and so the scene needs to be updated continuously. This means that all past lines since the first position recorded in our drawing have to be redrawn in each frame. In order to do so, we need to store all positions in an array.

However, if we want to break the stroke when the user stops pressing the trigger in the headset, then storing all positions along our drawing in a single array is not enough. We need to also save where breaks occur. One possibility is to store each continuous stroke in a separate array and have an array of arrays containing all past strokes.

With all these ideas in mind, we can go ahead and start working on the drawing functionality. Since the sketch is becoming fairly complex, it is a good idea to split it into separate tabs with related code in each one. For example, we could have the tab structure shown in Figure 15-7.

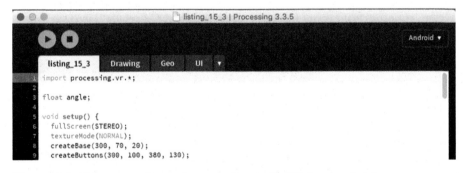

Figure 15-7. *Tabs to organize our increasingly complex VR drawing sketch*

Let's examine each tab separately. The main tab shown in Listing 15-3A contains the standard setup(), calculate(), draw(), and mouseReleased() functions. The rest of the functions we call from the main tab are implemented in the other tabs.

Listing 15-3A. Main Tab

```
import processing.vr.*;

float angle;

void setup() {
  fullScreen(STEREO);
  textureMode(NORMAL);
  createBase(300, 70, 20);
  createButtons(300, 100, 380, 130);
}

void calculate() {
  if (mousePressed) {
    if (leftButton.selected) angle -= 0.01;
    if (rightButton.selected) angle += 0.01;
  }
  if (mousePressed && !selectingUI()) {
    updateStrokes();
  }
}

void draw() {
  background(0);
  translate(width/2, height/2);
  directionalLight(200, 200, 200, 0, +1, -1);
  drawBase();
  drawStrokes();
  drawUI();
}

void mouseReleased() {
  if (resetButton.selected) {
    clearDrawing();
    angle = 0;
  } else {
    startNewStroke();
  }
}
```

A few important observations about mouse-event handlers. The updates of the rotation angle remain in calculate(), because this allows us to rotate the scene continuously by increasing/decreasing the angle in 0.01 steps as long as we keep pressing the trigger button on the headset. In contrast, the mousePressed()/mouseReleased() handlers are called only when a press event starts or ends, so they cannot be used for carrying out some task as long as the button is in pressed state. However, this behavior is useful to implement tasks that should be executed only upon button press or release. Clearing the drawing is an example of such tasks, and that's why clearDrawing() is placed inside mouseReleased().

■ **Note** The tab structure in a Processing sketch is entirely optional and does not affect how the sketch is run. It allows us to organize the code and make it more readable.

Moving on to the Drawing tab in Listing 15-3B, we can inspect the code that adds new positions to the current stroke in updateStrokes() and draws current and previous strokes by connecting all consecutive positions with lines in drawStrokes().

Listing 15-3B. Drawing Tab

```
ArrayList<PVector> currentStroke = new ArrayList<PVector>();
ArrayList[] previousStrokes = new ArrayList[0];

PMatrix3D eyeMat = new PMatrix3D();
PMatrix3D objMat = new PMatrix3D();
PVector pos = new PVector();
PVector pforward = new PVector();
PVector cforward = new PVector();

void updateStrokes() {
  translate(width/2, height/2);
  rotateY(angle);
  getEyeMatrix(eyeMat);
  float cameraX = eyeMat.m03;
  float cameraY = eyeMat.m13;
  float cameraZ = eyeMat.m23;
  float forwardX = eyeMat.m02;
  float forwardY = eyeMat.m12;
  float forwardZ = eyeMat.m22;
  float depth = dist(cameraX, cameraY, cameraZ, width/2, height/2, 0);
  cforward.x = forwardX;
  cforward.y = forwardY;
  cforward.z = forwardZ;
  if (currentStroke.size() == 0 || 0 < cforward.dist(pforward)) {
    getObjectMatrix(objMat);
    float x = cameraX + depth * forwardX;
    float y = cameraY + depth * forwardY;
```

```
    float z = cameraZ + depth * forwardZ;
    pos.set(x, y, z);
    PVector tpos = new PVector();
    objMat.mult(pos, tpos);
    currentStroke.add(tpos);
  }
  pforward.x = forwardX;
  pforward.y = forwardY;
  pforward.z = forwardZ;
}

void drawStrokes() {
  pushMatrix();
  rotateY(angle);
  strokeWeight(5);
  stroke(255);
  drawStroke(currentStroke);
  for (ArrayList p: previousStrokes) drawStroke(p);
  popMatrix();
}

void drawStroke(ArrayList<PVector> positions) {
  for (int i = 0; i < positions.size() - 1; i++) {
    PVector p = positions.get(i);
    PVector p1 = positions.get(i + 1);
    line(p.x, p.y, p.z, p1.x, p1.y, p1.z);
  }
}

void startNewStroke() {
  previousStrokes = (ArrayList[]) append(previousStrokes, currentStroke);
  currentStroke = new ArrayList<PVector>();
}

void clearDrawing() {
  previousStrokes = new ArrayList[0];
  currentStroke.clear();
}
```

We have a number of variables in this tab, starting with an array list of PVector objects holding the positions of the current stroke, as well as an array of array lists, where each list is a completed stroke. Once a mouse-released event is detected (in the mouseReleased() function defined in the main tab), the startNewStroke() function is called to append the current stroke to the array of previous strokes and initialize an empty array list for the next stroke.

The rest of the variables are used to compute the new positions of the current stroke. The code is based on our previous discussion about extending the forward vector by a predefined amount depth (Figure 15-6). This puts the "pencil's tip" right above the drawing base, since depth is the distance between the camera and the scene center. The use of the object matrix, objMat, in updateStrokes() should not be overlooked. It is necessary to ensure that the strokes are drawn correctly even if there are transformations applied to the scene (like a translation and a rotation around y, in this case). Notice how we apply these transformations at the beginning of updateStrokes(). Even though updateStrokes() is called from calculate(), which does not do any drawing, we still need to apply the same transformations we later use in draw() to make sure that the matrix we retrieve with getObjectMatrix() will apply all the transformations on the stroke vertices.

In the UI tab seen in Listing 15-3C, we have all the definitions of our Button class and all the button objects we are using so far in our interface.

Listing 15-3C. UI Tab

```
Button leftButton, rightButton, resetButton;

void createButtons(float dx, float hlr, float ht, float s) {
  PImage left = loadImage("left-icon.png");
  leftButton = new Button(-dx, hlr, 0, s, left);
  PImage right = loadImage("right-icon.png");
  rightButton = new Button(+dx, hlr, 0, s, right);
  PImage cross = loadImage("cross-icon.png");
  resetButton = new Button(0, +1.0 * ht, +1.1 * dx, s, cross);
}

void drawUI() {
  leftButton.display();
  rightButton.display();
  resetButton.display();
  drawAim();
}

void drawAim() {
  eye();
  pushStyle();
  stroke(220, 180);
  strokeWeight(20);
  point(0, 0, 100);
  popStyle();
}

boolean selectingUI() {
  return leftButton.selected || rightButton.selected ||
         resetButton.selected;
}
```

```
boolean centerSelected(float d) {
  float sx = screenX(0, 0, 0);
  float sy = screenY(0, 0, 0);
  return abs(sx - 0.5 * width) < d && abs(sy - 0.5 * height) < d;
}

class Button {
  float x, y, z, s;
  boolean selected;
  PImage img;

  Button(float x, float y, float z, float s, PImage img) {
    this.x = x;
    this.y = y;
    this.z = z;
    this.s = s;
    this.img = img;
  }

  void display() {
    float l = 0.5 * s;
    pushStyle();
    pushMatrix();
    translate(x, y, z);
    selected = centerSelected(l);
    beginShape(QUAD);
    if (selected) {
      stroke(220, 180);
      strokeWeight(5);
    } else {
      noStroke();
    }
    tint(#59C5F5);
    texture(img);
    vertex(-l, +l, 0, 1);
    vertex(-l, -l, 0, 0);
    vertex(+l, -l, 1, 0);
    vertex(+l, +l, 1, 1);
    endShape();
    popMatrix();
    popStyle();
  }
}
```

The Geo tab, shown in Listing 15-3D, just contains, for the time being, the code that creates and draws the base, which is the same from before.

Listing 15-3D. Geo Tab

```
PShape base;

void drawBase() {
  pushMatrix();
  translate(0, +300, 0);
  rotateY(angle);
  shape(base);
  popMatrix();
}

void createBase(float r, float h, int ndiv) {
  base = createShape(GROUP);
  PShape side = createShape();
  side.beginShape(QUAD_STRIP);
  side.noStroke();
  side.fill(#59C5F5);
  for (int i = 0; i <= ndiv; i++) {
    float a = map(i, 0, ndiv, 0, TWO_PI);
    float x = r * cos(a);
    float z = r * sin(a);
    side.vertex(x, +h/2, z);
    side.vertex(x, -h/2, z);
  }
  side.endShape();
  PShape top = createShape();
  top.beginShape(TRIANGLE_FAN);
  top.noStroke();
  top.fill(#59C5F5);
  top.vertex(0, 0, 0);
  for (int i = 0; i <= ndiv; i++) {
    float a = map(i, 0, ndiv, 0, TWO_PI);
    float x = r * cos(a);
    float z = r * sin(a);
    top.vertex(x, -h/2, z);
  }
  top.endShape();
  base.addChild(side);
  base.addChild(top);
}
```

After all this work, we should have a working drawing app for VR! We can try it out in a Cardboard or Daydream headset, and if everything goes well, we would be able to use it to create line drawings like the one shown in Figure 15-8.

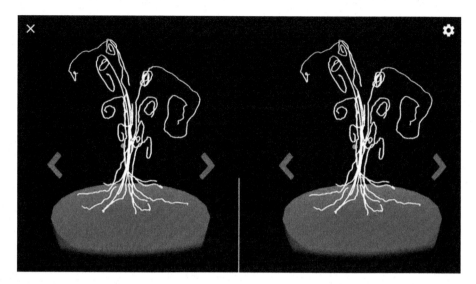

Figure 15-8. *Our VR drawing app in action!*

Flying Around

With the VR drawing app in its current form, we can direct strokes with our gaze and rotate the drawing around the horizontal direction to add new strokes from different angles. Even though this should give our users a lot to play with, we could still improve the app in many different ways.

One limitation so far is that we remain at a fixed position in front of the drawing podium. Although we can change our viewpoint by moving our head and rotating the drawing around the horizontal axis, we are not able to get any closer to it, for example. We saw in the previous chapter how to implement free-range movement in VR, so we could apply that code to implement this functionality in our app.

Since we want to create a fly-by through the drawing, we could add a pair of animated wings in the front of our view while we move around. These wings, fixed with respect to our position, would provide a visual reference to help users not feel disoriented.

We will go over all the changes we should introduce to the tabs of the previous version of the sketch. Let's start with the main tab in Listing 15-4A.

Listing 15-4A. Main Tab with Fly Mode Modifications

```
import processing.vr.*;

float angle;
boolean flyMode = false;
PVector flyStep = new PVector();

void setup() {
  fullScreen(STEREO);
  textureMode(NORMAL);
```

```
    createBase(300, 70, 20);
    createButtons(300, 100, 380, 130);
}

void calculate() {
    if (mousePressed) {
        if (leftButton.selected) angle -= 0.01;
        if (rightButton.selected) angle += 0.01;
        if (flyMode) {
            getEyeMatrix(eyeMat);
            flyStep.add(2 * eyeMat.m02, 2 * eyeMat.m12, 2 * eyeMat.m22);
        }
    }
    if (mousePressed && !selectingUI() && !flyMode) {
        updateStrokes();
    }
}

void draw() {
    background(0);
    translate(width/2, height/2);
    ambientLight(40, 40, 40);
    directionalLight(200, 200, 200, 0, +1, -1);
    translate(-flyStep.x, -flyStep.y, -flyStep.z);
    drawBase();
    drawStrokes();
    if (flyMode) drawWings();
    drawUI();
}

void mouseReleased() {
    if (resetButton.selected) {
        clearDrawing();
        angle = 0;
    } else if (flyToggle.selected) {
        flyToggle.toggle();
        if (flyToggle.state == 0) {
            flyMode = false;
            flyStep.set(0, 0, 0);
        } else {
            flyMode = true;
        }
    } else {
        startNewStroke();
    }
}
```

We introduced a few additional variables: a flyMode Boolean variable to keep track of whether we are in fly mode or not, as well as the actual displacement vector, flyStep, that we update by advancing along the forward vector when the headset button is pressed. Also, we added an ambient light so the wings are visible even when they don't receive direct light from the directional sources.

We also had to add some extra interaction handling in mouseReleased(). The problem is that now we need another UI element to switch between the normal draw mode and the new fly mode. We do this by implementing a specialized toggle button with two alternative images indicating which mode we can switch to. The placement of this toggle button is not obvious; it could just be in front of our view as we start the app, but then it would be not visible if we are in fly mode and we end up lost somewhere in VR. It would be better if this button were always visible when we do some specific gesture; for example, looking up. We can achieve this if the toggle button is not affected by the fly movement and is always placed exactly above the camera position. The code in Listing 15-4B does this.

Listing 15-4B. UI Tab with Fly Mode Modifications

```
Button leftButton, rightButton, resetButton;
Toggle flyToggle;

void createButtons(float dx, float hlr, float ht, float s) {
  ...
  PImage fly = loadImage("fly-icon.png");
  PImage home = loadImage("home-icon.png");
  flyToggle = new Toggle(-ht, s, fly, home);
}

void drawUI() {
  leftButton.display();
  rightButton.display();
  resetButton.display();
  noLights();
  flyToggle.display();
  if (!flyMode) drawAim();
}
...
boolean selectingUI() {
  return leftButton.selected || rightButton.selected ||
        resetButton.selected || flyToggle.selected;
}
...
class Toggle {
  float h, s;
  boolean selected;
  int state;
  PImage[] imgs;
  color[] colors;
```

```
Toggle(float h, float s, PImage img0, PImage img1) {
  this.h = h;
  this.s = s;
  imgs = new PImage[2];
  imgs[0] = img0;
  imgs[1] = img1;
  colors = new color[2];
  colors[0] = #F2674E;
  colors[1] = #59C5F5;
}

void display() {
  float l = 0.5 * s;
  pushStyle();
  pushMatrix();
  getEyeMatrix(eyeMat);
  translate(eyeMat.m03 + flyStep.x - width/2,
            eyeMat.m13 + h + flyStep.y - height/2,
            eyeMat.m23 + flyStep.z);
  selected = centerSelected(l);
  beginShape(QUAD);
  if (selected) {
    stroke(220, 180);
    strokeWeight(5);
  } else {
    noStroke();
  }
  tint(colors[state]);
  texture(imgs[state]);
  vertex(-l, 0, +l, 0, 0);
  vertex(+l, 0, +l, 1, 0);
  vertex(+l, 0, -l, 1, 1);
  vertex(-l, 0, -l, 0, 1);
  endShape();
  popMatrix();
  popStyle();
}

void toggle() {
  state = (state + 1) % 2;
}
}
```

The Toggle class is similar to Button, but it is textured with two images, one for each toggle state. We can make the toggle button to be always on top of the user by translating it to (eyeMat.m03 + flyStep.x - width/2, eyeMat.m13 + h + flyStep.y - height/2, eyeMat.m23 + flyStep.z), which cancels the translations we apply in draw(), so it is placed at exactly (eyeMat.m03, eyeMat.m13 + h, eyeMat.m23), the camera coordinates plus a displacement of h along the vertical direction.

Finally, Listing 15-4C shows the code for the animated wings we draw while in fly mode. The geometry is very simple: two larger, rotating quads for the wings and a smaller rectangle between them to create a body.

Listing 15-4C. Drawing Tab with Fly Mode Modifications

```
...
void drawWings() {
  pushMatrix();
  eye();

  translate(0, +50, 100);
  noStroke();
  fill(#F2674E);

  beginShape(QUAD);
  vertex(-5, 0, -50);
  vertex(+5, 0, -50);
  vertex(+5, 0, +50);
  vertex(-5, 0, +50);
  endShape();

  pushMatrix();
  translate(-5, 0, 0);
  rotateZ(map(cos(millis()/1000.0), -1, +1, -QUARTER_PI, +QUARTER_PI));
  beginShape(QUAD);
  vertex(-100, 0, -50);
  vertex(   0, 0, -50);
  vertex(   0, 0, +50);
  vertex(-100, 0, +50);
  endShape();
  popMatrix();

  pushMatrix();
  translate(+5, 0, 0);
  rotateZ(map(cos(millis()/1000.0), -1, +1, +QUARTER_PI, -QUARTER_PI));
  beginShape(QUAD);
  vertex(+100, 0, -50);
  vertex(   0, 0, -50);
  vertex(   0, 0, +50);
  vertex(+100, 0, +50);
  endShape();
  popMatrix();

  popMatrix();
}
```

With these additions, we can switch into fly mode to fly through our drawing and switch back to the default draw mode to continue the drawing or start a new one, a sequence of steps we can appreciate in Figure 15-9.

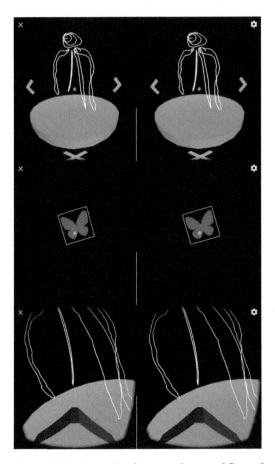

Figure 15-9. *Transition between draw and fly modes*

Final Tweaks and Packaging

We have arrived at a simple but fully functional drawing app for VR! During this process, we encountered challenges that are unique to VR development: constructing an immersive 3D environment, adding UI elements that can be accessed using gaze alone, and moving freely in VR. Our app makes use of some techniques to solve these challenges, which we should explore further in future VR projects. For the time being, we only need to make a few final tweaks to get the drawing app ready for release on the Play Store.

Intro Text

When users open our app for the first time, we cannot expect them to know what to do, so a good idea is to provide an introduction to explain the mechanics of the experience. We should keep this introduction as brief as possible, since most users don't want to go through very lengthy or complicated instructions, and a successful VR experience should be as self-explanatory as possible.

We could draw the intro page in eye coordinates so it is facing the user irrespective of their head position, and it should disappear as soon as the user presses the headset button to continue. Listing 15-5 shows the additions to the code to implement a simple intro, and the result is shown in Figure 15-10.

Listing 15-5. Adding an Intro Screen

```
import processing.vr.*;

float angle;
boolean flyMode = false;
PVector flyStep = new PVector();
boolean showingIntro = true;

void setup() {
  fullScreen(STEREO);
  textureMode(NORMAL);
  textFont(createFont("SansSerif", 30));
  textAlign(CENTER, CENTER);
  ...
}
...
void mouseReleased() {
  if (showingIntro) {
    showingIntro = false;
  } else if (resetButton.selected) {
  ...
}
...
void drawUI() {
  leftButton.display();
  rightButton.display();
  resetButton.display();
  noLights();
  flyToggle.display();
  if (showingIntro) drawIntro();
  else if (!flyMode) drawAim();
}
```

```
void drawIntro() {
  noLights();
  eye();
  fill(220);
  text("Welcome to VR Draw!\nLook around while clicking to draw.\n" +
       "Click on the side buttons\nto rotate the podium,\n" +
       "and on the X slightly below\nto reset.\n\n" +
       "Search for the wings to fly", 0, 0, 300);
}
...
```

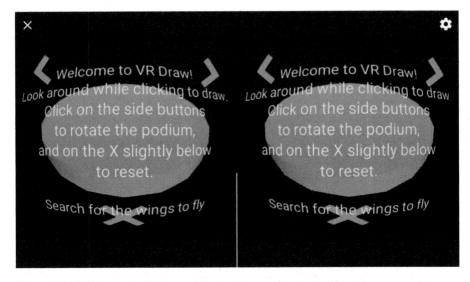

Figure 15-10. *Intro screen with some instructions on how to use the app*

The logic for the intro screen is as follows: we use the showingIntro variable to indicate whether we should be drawing the intro, and set it to true by default. As soon as the user releases the first button press, the intro will go away.

Icons and Package Export

The final steps in the creation of the app are designing the icons, setting the final package name, labels, and versions in the manifest file, and then exporting the signed package that is ready to upload to the Play Store, all of which we covered in Chapter 3.

As for the icons, we need a full set, including 192 × 192 (xxxhdpi), 144 × 144 (xxhdpi), 96 × 96 (xhdpi), 72 × 72 (hdpi), 48 × 48 (mdpi), and 32 × 32 (ldpi) versions, such as the one shown in Figure 15-11.

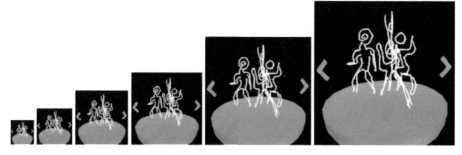

Figure 15-11. *App icons in all required resolutions*

The manifest file for the exported package should include a unique full package name, the version code and name, and the Android label that is used in the UI to identify the app. The following is an example with all these values filled in:

```
import processing.vr.*;
<?xml version="1.0" encoding="UTF-8"?>
<manifest xmlns:android="http://schemas.android.com/apk/res/android"
          android:versionCode="1" android:versionName="1.0"
          package="com.example.vr_draw">
    <uses-sdk android:minSdkVersion="19" android:targetSdkVersion="25"/>
    <uses-permission android:name="android.permission.VIBRATE"/>
    <uses-permission android:name=
                    "android.permission.READ_EXTERNAL_STORAGE"/>
    <uses-feature android:name=
                    "android.hardware.sensor.accelerometer"
                    android:required="true"/>
    <uses-feature android:name="android.hardware.sensor.gyroscope"
                    android:required="true"/>
    <uses-feature android:name="android.software.vr.mode"
                    android:required="false"/>
    <uses-feature android:name="android.hardware.vr.high_performance"
                    android:required="false"/>
    <uses-feature android:glEsVersion="0x00020000" android:required="true"/>
    <application android:icon="@drawable/icon"
                android:label="VR Draw"
                android:theme="@style/VrActivityTheme">
        <activity android:configChanges=
                    "orientation|keyboardHidden|screenSize"
                    android:name=".MainActivity"
                    android:resizeableActivity="false"
                    android:screenOrientation="landscape">
          <intent-filter>
              <action android:name="android.intent.action.MAIN"/>
              <category android:name="android.intent.category.LAUNCHER"/>
              <category android:name=
```

```
                        "com.google.intent.category.CARDBOARD"/>
            </intent-filter>
        </activity>
    </application>
</manifest>
```

Summary

We just completed our last project in the book! This was the most complex of all, but hopefully it helped recognizing the challenges involved in creating VR apps, and learning how to allow users to interact with their VR surroundings in intuitive ways. By addressing the challenges involved in such apps, we have discovered how to apply Processing's 3D API to implement immersive graphics and interactions. Now you have the tools to create new and original Android apps, not only for VR, but also for watches, phones, and tablets. Have fun sketching your ideas into reality!

APPENDIX A

Gradle and Android Studio Integration

In this appendix, we will learn to export Processing sketches as Gradle projects that can be compiled from the command line or imported into Android Studio.

Google's Tools for Android Development

Android Studio is the official integrated development environment (IDE) for Android. It is available for free from Google (https://developer.android.com/studio/index.html). Android Studio offers a rich interface to write and debug Android apps that includes not only an editor for source code (Figure A-1), but also a visual UI designer.

© Andrés Colubri 2017
A. Colubri, *Processing for Android*, https://doi.org/10.1007/978-1-4842-2719-0

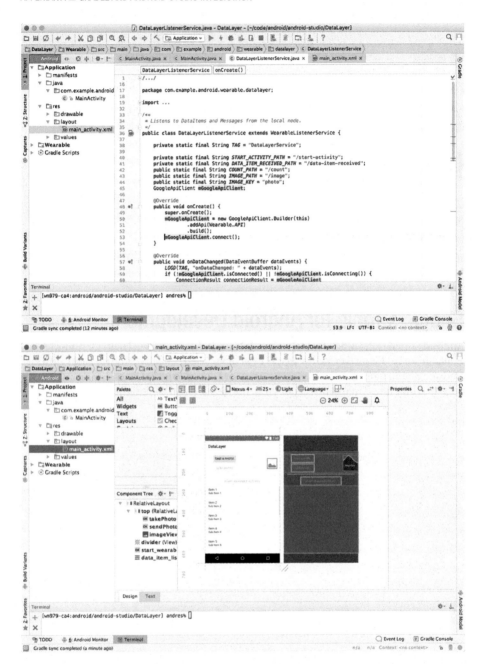

Figure A-1. *Android Studio interface for code editing (top) and visual app design (bottom)*

Android Studio uses software called Gradle (https://gradle.org/) to build its projects. Gradle is a "build automation system" in which we can specify all the information needed to compile the source code, resolve dependencies, and package the final app. This is accomplished with a set of build files written in a Groovy-based language, specifically customized for software-building tasks. This provides great flexibility for handling the complexity of Android projects, which often involve several files, including source code, libraries, and resources. Processing uses Gradle to build the sketches into apps, but keeps this complexity hidden away from the user.

Although Processing for Android aims at a group of users (artists, designers, students) and uses (sketching, prototyping, teaching) that is often not the focus of more advanced IDEs do, integration with Android Studio can be very convenient in many cases. For example, we may want to incorporate some interactive graphics we created with Processing into a larger Android app. Also, being able to access the underlying Gradle build files for our sketch allows us to tweak things in ways that are not possible from the PDE.

There are two main ways to combine Processing for Android with Gradle and Android Studio:

1. Exporting a Processing sketch as a Gradle project from the PDE. This project can be compiled from the command line using the Gradle Wrapper tool (https://docs.gradle.org/current/userguide/gradle_wrapper.html) that is included with the exported project. This project can also be imported into Android Studio.

2. Importing the processing-core package into an existing or new Android Studio project and using it to access all the core Processing's API for drawing and interaction. This makes possible to write portions of a larger Android app with custom Processing-based views, and to integrate them with Android native views and UI.

We will learn how use each one of these integration approaches in the next sections.

Exporting a Sketch as a Gradle Project

Android mode has an option in the File menu called "Export Android Project" (Figure A-2). After we select this option, the mode will create a complete Gradle project, including assets and resources, from our sketch, ready to compile from the command line. The project is placed in the android folder inside the sketch folder.

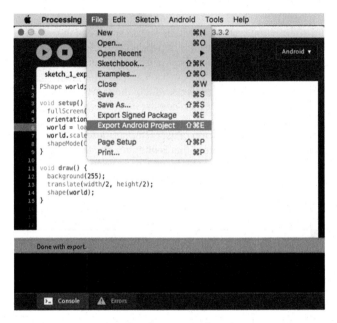

Figure A-2. *Export Android Project in the PDE*

Listing A-1 shows a simple sketch to test the export functionality in Android mode.

Listing A-1. Sketch to Export as Android Project

```
PShape world;

void setup() {
  fullScreen(P2D);
  orientation(LANDSCAPE);
  world = loadShape("World-map.svg");
  world.scale(height/world.getHeight());
  shapeMode(CENTER);
}

void draw() {
  background(255);
  translate(width/2, height/2);
  shape(world);
}
```

After exporting it, the resulting Gradle project should have the folder structure shown in Figure A-3. The original sketch includes an SVG file in its data folder, which will be placed inside src/main/assets in the exported project.

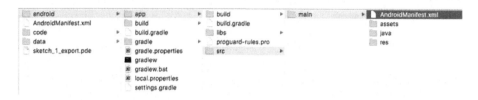

Figure A-3. *File structure of an exported Android project*

Gradle projects are organized in a hierarchical structure, with a main build.gradle file in the top-level folder containing the master options, and another build.gradle file inside the app sub-folder with the specific options to build the project, such as the dependencies and target SDK level. The Java source code generated from the sketch's code is inside app/src/main/java, and all files in the data folder are copied to the assets folder. The processing core library is placed as a jar file inside the libs folder.

Once we have generated this exported project, we can compile it using the gradlew command-line program included in the android folder. In order to do so, we need to open a terminal, change to the project folder, and run the command: `./gradlew build`.

The results of a successful build are the debug and release (unsigned) packages, which we will find in app/build/outputs/apk as app-debug.apk and app-release-unsigned.apk. The package name will be the one we set in the manifest file, or the Processing default if we did not edit the manifest that Processing generates automatically for us. This manifest file will also be copied into the exported project so we can further customize it.

Importing into Android Studio

Once we have exported our Processing sketch as Gradle project, we can easily import it into Android Studio, since an Android Studio project is essentially a Gradle project with some additional files.

From inside Android Studio, we go to the File Menu and select "New|Import Project…". We can also select "Import Project (Eclipse ADT, Gradle, etc.)" from the Welcome screen, as seen in Figure A-4.

Figure A-4. *Importing a Gradle project from the File menu (top) or the Welcome screen (bottom)*

The import functionality will prompt us to browse for the folder containing the Gradle project (Figure A-5).

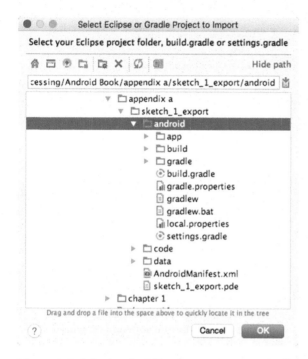

Figure A-5. *Selecting the folder that contains our Gradle project exported from Processing*

The exported Gradle project from Processing is linked to the SDK we use in Processing's Android mode. If it is different from Android Studio's SDK, then we will be prompted to choose to use one or the other in the imported Android Studio project. In general, it is recommended to use Processing's SDK, because it will be certain to work with the project, but a newer SDK in Android Studio should be compatible as well.

After importing the project, we can use all the functionality in Android Studio to edit and debug the code (Figure A-6). We also have access to any function from Processing's API since the core library is included as a dependency in the project.

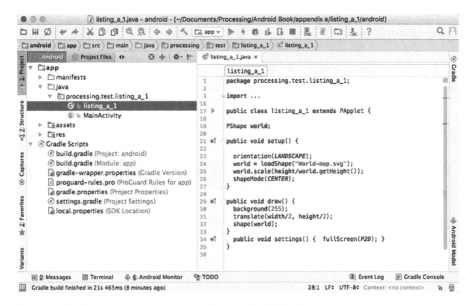

Figure A-6. *Processing sketch imported into Android Studio*

The code from our original Processing sketch is converted into two separate classes, the first for the main activity, and the second containing the sketch itself, which is a sub-class of PApplet, the core class that holds most of the functions and variables in the Processing API. See Listing A-2.

Listing A-2. Exported Sketch Code in Android Studio

```
package processing.test.listing_a_1;

import processing.core.*;

public class listing_a_1 extends PApplet {
  PShape world;
  public void setup() {
    orientation(LANDSCAPE);
    world = loadShape("World-map.svg");
    world.scale(height/world.getHeight());
    shapeMode(CENTER);
  }
  public void draw() {
    background(255);
    translate(width/2, height/2);
    shape(world);
  }
  public void settings() {  fullScreen(P2D); }
}
```

Notice an important change with respect to our original sketch code: fullScreen() is now inside a new function called settings(), which is needed to properly initialize our sketch when running it outside the PDE, and which always gets called before setup(). If we were using size() instead, it would also go inside settings().

Listing A-3 shows the main activity where the Processing sketch object is initialized and attached to a containing fragment inside the activity. This code is automatically generated by Processing when we export the Android project.

Listing A-3. Main Activity for an Exported Processing Sketch

```
package processing.test.listing_a_1;
import android.os.Bundle;
import android.content.Intent;
import android.view.ViewGroup;
import android.widget.FrameLayout;
import android.support.v7.app.AppCompatActivity;

import processing.android.PFragment;
import processing.android.CompatUtils;
import processing.core.PApplet;

public class MainActivity extends AppCompatActivity {
  private PApplet sketch;

  @Override
  protected void onCreate(Bundle savedInstanceState) {
    super.onCreate(savedInstanceState);
    FrameLayout frame = new FrameLayout(this);
    frame.setId(CompatUtils.getUniqueViewId());
    setContentView(frame, new ViewGroup.LayoutParams(
                    ViewGroup.LayoutParams.MATCH_PARENT,
                    ViewGroup.LayoutParams.MATCH_PARENT));

    sketch = new listing_a_1();
    PFragment fragment = new PFragment(sketch);
    fragment.setView(frame, this);
  }

  @Override
  public void onRequestPermissionsResult(int requestCode,
                                         String permissions[],
                                         int[] grantResults) {
    if (sketch != null) {
      sketch.onRequestPermissionsResult(
      requestCode, permissions, grantResults);
    }
  }
```

```
@Override
public void onNewIntent(Intent intent) {
  if (sketch != null) {
    sketch.onNewIntent(intent);
  }
}
}
```

It is important to keep the onRequestPermissionResult() event handler
so that our sketch can respond to the result of a dangerous permission request,
as well as onNewIntent(), which is needed to handle any new intent sent to the
activity (https://developer.android.com/reference/android/app/Activity.
html#onNewIntent(android.content.Intent)).

Let's take a closer look at the code relevant to creating our sketch object and adding
it to an existing view (Listing A-4), which we used in the onCreate() method in the
previous listing.

Listing A-4. Adding a Sketch Object to a Fragment View

```
sketch = new MySketch();
PFragment fragment = new PFragment(sketch);
fragment.setView(frame, this);
```

Here, MySketch is the class encapsulating our Processing code, like listing_a_1
before. PFragment is a system class from the Processing core library that handles
integration with Android fragments. All we need to do after creating it is to set the
view with the containing layout (in this case a FrameLayout) and the main activity as
arguments. These steps can be used in more complex projects with multiple views.
However, in such cases we would need to add a reference to the actual view object we
want to use, which we will discuss in more detail next.

Adding a Processing Sketch to a Layout

Advanced users might want to work with Android Studio directly, using Processing as a
library in their projects. To do so, we need to consider two important aspects:

1. How to include the Processing core library as a dependency in
the project

2. Attaching a Processing sketch to a layout in the UI of the
project

The Processing core library for Android mode is included in the mode folder (e.g.,
<sketchbook folder>/modes/AndroidMode), with the name processing-core.zip. All
we need to do is copy this file to the libs sub-folder (shown in Figure A-7) and change
its extension to .jar. At the time of this writing, Android's processing-core is not available
as an artifact in Maven Central Repository, but this feature is planned for inclusion in a
near future.

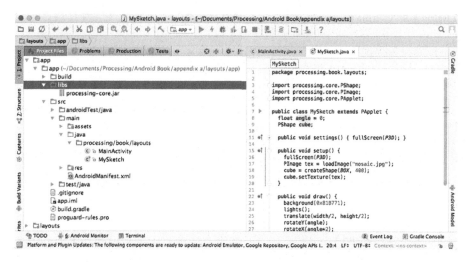

Figure A-7. *Location of the libs folder in the project files*

Once `processing-core.jar` is copied to the `libs` folder, we can add it into the project by opening the module settings for the app module (by right-clicking it in the Android view), going to the Dependencies tab, where we can add a jar dependency, and then selecting the file, the steps for which are shown in Figure A-8.

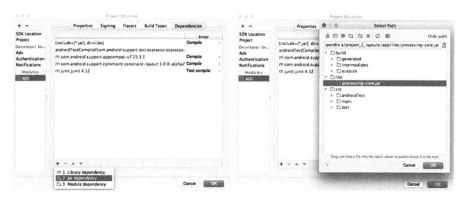

Figure A-8. *Adding processing-core.jar as a dependency to a new project in Android Studio*

Once we have added `processing-core` as a dependency, we can write the class containing the sketch, an example of which is presented in Listing A-5.

Listing A-5. Writing Processing Code in Android Studio

```
package processing.book.layouts;

import processing.core.PShape;
import processing.core.PImage;
import processing.core.PApplet;

public class MySketch extends PApplet {
  float angle = 0;
  PShape cube;

  public void settings() {
    fullScreen(P3D);
  }

  public void setup() {
    fullScreen(P3D);
    PImage tex = loadImage("mosaic.jpg");
    cube = createShape(BOX, 400);
    cube.setTexture(tex);
  }

  public void draw() {
    background(0x81B771);
    lights();
    translate(width/2, height/2);
    rotateY(angle);
    rotateX(angle*2);
    shape(cube);
    angle += 0.01;
  }
}
```

As we saw earlier, the screen size must be initialized in settings() instead of in setup() when working outside of the PDE.

Now, we will integrate the sketch into an existing layout. UI elements in Android are declared in layouts (https://developer.android.com/guide/topics/ui/declaring-layout.html), which in turn are described by XML files that are "inflated" as objects during runtime. If we create a new Basic Activity Project in Android Studio, we will end up with a layout for the main activity and a content layout. If we want to add the sketch to the content layout, then we would need to retrieve the reference to the content layout and its ID from the resources object, as is done in Listing A-6.

Listing A-6. Adding a Sketch Object to a Fragment View

```
sketch = new MySketch();
PFragment fragment = new PFragment(sketch);
fragment.setLayout(R.layout.content_main, R.id.content_main, this);
```

If the content layout does not have an ID, we can add it by editing the corresponding XML file and adding an android:id attribute, as seen in Figure A-9.

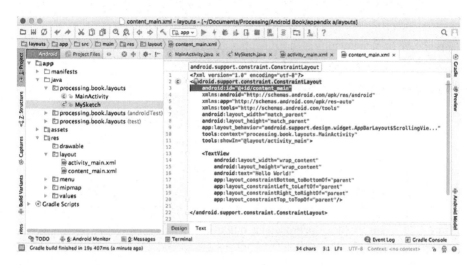

Figure A-9. *Setting a name for the content layout to add to our sketch*

With all of this in place, we can implement the onCreate() method in the main activity to look something like Listing A-7, where we set the layout of the fragment holding the sketch.

Listing A-7. Creating the Activity That Contains the Processing Fragment

```
@Override
protected void onCreate(Bundle savedInstanceState) {
  super.onCreate(savedInstanceState);
  setContentView(R.layout.activity_main);
  Toolbar toolbar = (Toolbar) findViewById(R.id.toolbar);
  setSupportActionBar(toolbar);
  FloatingActionButton fab = (FloatingActionButton) findViewById(R.id.fab);
  fab.setOnClickListener(new View.OnClickListener() {
    @Override
    public void onClick(View view) {
      Snackbar.make(view, "Replace with your own action",
              Snackbar.LENGTH_LONG)
            .setAction("Action", null).show();
    }
  });
  sketch = new MySketch();
  PFragment fragment = new PFragment(sketch);
  fragment.setLayout(R.layout.content_main, R.id.content_main, this);
}
```

If we use the requestPermission() function in our sketch to request critical permissions, then we would also need to add the onRequestPermissionsResult() handler, as seen in Listing A-8. We did not need to do this when exporting the sketch as an Android project from the PDE, since in that case Processing adds this handler automatically.

Listing A-8. Implementation of the onRequestPermissionsResult() handler

```
@Override
public void onRequestPermissionsResult(int requestCode,
                                       String permissions[],
                                       int[] grantResults) {
  if (sketch != null) {
    sketch.onRequestPermissionsResult(requestCode, permissions,
                                      grantResults);
  }
}
```

We can now run our project, and we should see a screen similar that shown in Figure A-10, where we have the Processing output inside the layout containing the sketch fragment.

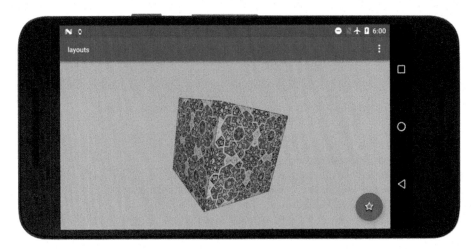

Figure A-10. *Running app with the Processing fragment embedded inside a content layout*

Processing Libraries

In this appendix, we will review the contributed libraries that can be used in Android mode and how we can create our own.

Extending Processing with Libraries

Two fundamentals of Processing have contributed to its adoption as a teaching and prototyping tool: first, a minimal core API that is easy to learn, and, second, a library architecture that extends the Processing core with new functionality and hardware support. Some libraries offering important features (such as video or networking) were developed by the Processing Foundation, but many more were contributed by the Processing community.

There are contributed libraries for a wide range of applications: 3D, computer vision, user interface, data handling, audio, and so forth. A few of these libraries are specific to Android, while others are only for PC or Mac platforms; many can be used across both Java and Android modes.

Installing a library is very simple to do through the Contribution Manager (although libraries can be installed manually as well). Search for the library using a keyword, by category, or simply by scrolling through the list, as shown in Figure B-1.

© Andrés Colubri 2017

A. Colubri, *Processing for Android*, https://doi.org/10.1007/978-1-4842-2719-0

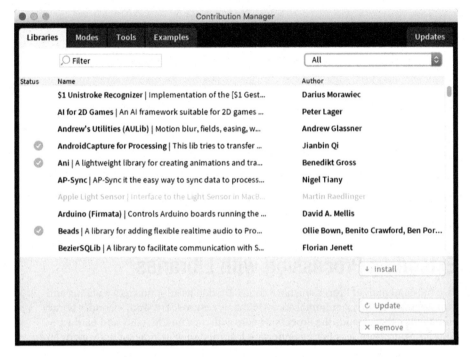

Figure B-1. *Contribution Manager showing the Libraries tab*

Once you find a library you would like to try out, all you need to do is to click the Install button. After you have installed it, you can update it if there is a new version available, or you can remove it.

Contributed libraries typically include examples that demonstrate their functionality. These examples can be found by opening the "Examples" option in the File menu and browsing to the Contributed Libraries category in the listing window (Figure B-2).

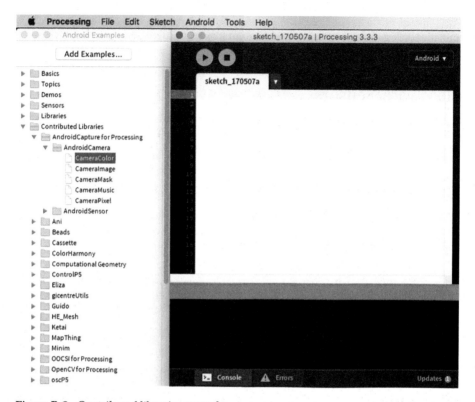

Figure B-2. *Contributed libraries examples*

In the next sections, we will look at several Processing libraries that are specific to Android mode or explicitly support it. However, this does not mean that these are the only libraries that could be used on Android, since many libraries that were originally written for Java mode are compatible with Android mode.

Data

The AndroidCapture for Processing library (https://github.com/onlylemi/ processing-android-capture) allows you to transfer Android camera and sensor data from the Android device to a Processing sketch running on the computer.

GUI

ControlP5 (http://www.sojamo.de/libraries/controlP5/) is a GUI library used to build custom user interfaces for desktop and Android modes. It has been around for a long time, so there are many examples of it in use, and it has a very characteristic look and feel. It is important to keep in mind that, when used on Android, ControlP5 does not rely on the native UI widgets or the standard UI creation techniques.

The SelectFile library (https://github.com/pif/android-select-file/tree/dlg) provides dialogs for selecting input and output files and folders, since the core API does not provide that functionality on Android (it does on PC/Mac).

Hardware/Sensors

Ketai (http://ketai.org/) is an Android library that provides comprehensive support for sensors, cameras, multi-touch, networking, Bluetooth, Wi-Fi Direct, near-field communication, and SQLite. We covered Ketai in chapters 7 and 8 of the book.

Geometry/Utilities

The Proscene (https://github.com/remixlab/proscene) library makes it easier to create interactive scenes in 2D and 3D by handling all the complexity of camera movement, coordinate systems, and input events (Figure B-3).

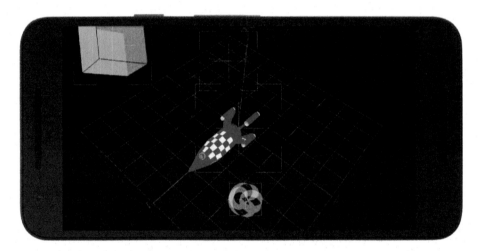

Figure B-3. *Example from Proscene library running on Android*

Sound and Video

In this category, we have Cassette (https://github.com/shlomihod/cassette), which provides sound playback functionality, and Processing Video for Android (https://github.com/omerjerk/processing-video-android), which exposes an API for video playback and capture similar to that available in the Processing video library for desktop.

Writing New Libraries

A common situation is when we find ourselves using some code in our sketches over and over again. It would be easier to include the code in future projects if we were able to package it as a library. Also, if this code implements some general functionality that other people might find useful, we could consider sharing it with the rest of the Processing community. As we saw in the previous section, there is very little restriction on what a library can do, and even though writing a Processing library involves some technical steps, it is not that hard to do.

The first step in the creation of a library is to modularize the functionality we want in a separate class that takes our sketch object as a parameter. Processing puts all of our sketch code inside a class called PApplet, and this class also holds most of the Processing API we have seen throughout the book. For example, let's imagine we wrote a number of functions to draw regular polyhedrons:

```
void setup() {
  fullScreen(P3D);
}

void draw() {
  background(255);
  drawTetrahedron();
  drawOctahedron();
  drawDodecahedron();
  drawIcosahedron();
}

void drawTetrahedron() {
  beginShape();
  ...
  endShape();
}

void drawDodecahedron() {
  beginShape();
  ...
  endShape();
}

...
```

If we move the drawing code inside a new class, we could do something like this:

```
Polyhedron poly;

void setup() {
  fullScreen(P3D);
  poly = new Polyhedron(this);
}

void draw() {
  background(255);
  poly.drawTetrahedron();
  poly.drawOctahedron();
  poly.drawDodecahedron();
  poly.drawIcosahedron();
}

class Polyhedron {
  PApplet parent;

  Polyhedron(PApplet parent) {
    this.parent = parent;
  }

  void drawTetrahedron() {
    parent.beginShape();
    ...
    parent.endShape();
  }
}
```

Note how we create an instance of the Polyhedron class with the this keyword, which is a reference to the current sketch. This reference is stored in the parent field in the Polyhedron class, which we can use to perform any Processing call.

Once we have organized the code in this way, although it does not bring much immediate benefit to the sketch, it is easy to move the class encapsulating the special functionality into a separate library. The Processing Foundation provides a Processing Android library template with all the required files to create an Eclipse project to build our library. In that template, we can incorporate our custom code, such as the one we discussed here. The library template is available at https://github.com/processing/processing-android-library-template and includes a detailed step-by-step guide on how to import the template into Eclipse and use it as the basis for a library project.

Index

A

Acceleration, 157
    audio playing, 165
    audio-visual mapping, 160
    control animation, 164
    onStepDetectorEvent()
        event, 163
    random colored dots, 161
    shake detection, 158
    step counter, 159
Accelerometer, 143
Ambient light, 294
Android devices
    Android library, 8
    emulator, 14
    installation, 9
    interface of, 10
    mobile apps, 8
    processing, 8
    sketch code, 12
Android Virtual Device
    (AVD), 14, 218

B

beginContour() and endContour()
    functions, 73
beginShape() and endShape()
    function, 61
Body sensors
    heart rate, 244
    step counter, 243

C

Contribution Manager (CM), 7
curveVertex() function, 64

D

Directional light, 295
3D Processing, 275
    lights and textures, 293
        light sources and material
            properties, 294
        map() function, 301
        material properties, 297
        setTextureUV() function, 302
        texture mapping, 298
        textureMode() function, 300
    P3D (*see* P3D renderer)
    shapes
        2D and 3D primitives, 284
        getShapeCenter() function, 292
        loadStrings() function, 289
        OBJ file format, 291
        PShape objects, 288
        QUADS, 286
        setVertex() function, 289
    3D transformations
        rotation, 281
        scaling, 282
        transformation composition, 283
        translations, 281
Drawing app (VR)
    3D drawing, 339
        background() function, 340
        current forward vectors, 340
        drawing tab, 342
        Geo tab, 346
        main tab, 341
        previous forward vectors, 340
        tab structure, 340
        UI tab, 344
        updateStrokes() function, 342, 344
        working drawing app, 346

© Andrés Colubri 2017
A. Colubri, *Processing for Android*, https://doi.org/10.1007/978-1-4842-2719-0

Drawing app (VR) (*cont.*)
  experience, 331
    class activities, 332
    Google Tilt Brush, 332
    sketches, 333
  fly-by through, 347
    drawing tab, 351
    mouseReleased() function, 349
    tab modifications, 347
    transition, 352
    UI tab modification, 349
  icons and package export, 354
  intro text, 353
  UI (*see* User interface (UI))

■ E

Extending processing, 7

■ F

fromAngle() method, 66

■ G, H

Geolocation sensors
  location data, 181
  processing sketch, 182
    event threads and
      concurrency, 186
    Ketai, 190
    location data, 192
    onLocationChanged()
      function, 186
    path-tracking sketch, 190
    permissions, 183
  Street View images, 194
    Google API, 195
    offscreen drawing surface, 202
    Pgraphics Object, 203
    Street View Collage, 204
    updatePositions() function, 209
    Voronoi tessellations, 197
    wallpaperPreview() function, 209
getChildren() function, 79
getTessellation() function, 101
Global positioning system
  (GPS), 181
Gradle projects, 357
  build automation system, 359
  export Android project, 359

file structure, 361
import project, 361
interface, 357–358
layout option
  content layout, 369
  fragment view, 368
  libs folder, 367
  onCreate() method, 369
  processing-core.jar, 367
  requestPermission() function, 370
  sketch fragment, 370
  steps, 366
processing sketch object, 364
Graphics processing unit (GPU), 59
growTree() function, 263–264
Gyroscope, 144, 174
  controlling navigation, 177
  control rotation, 175
  2D rotation, 176
  recentering data, 176
  rotational angles, 174

■ I, J

Image-flow wallpaper, 128
  hue() and saturation() functions, 136
  loading, resizing and cropping
    images, 128
  loadImage() and image() function, 80
  loadRandomImage() function, 135
  texturing shapes, 81
  threads, 134
  tint() and noTint() function, 80
  touch-based particle system, 130
  wrapping up, 138

■ K

Ketai library, 150, 157
  accelerometer, 151
  event handlers, 153
  gyroscope, 152
  installation, 150
  mousePressed()/touchMoved()
    functions, 151
Keyboard input and touchscreen
    input, 32
  ellipses, 33
  free-hand drawing, 34
  fullScreen() function, 33, 34
  size() function, 33

■ L

Libraries, 7, 371
    contribution manager, 371–372
    creation, 375
    data, 373
    file menu and
        browsing, 372
    geometry/utilities, 374
    GUI, 373
    hardware/sensors, 374
    sound and video, 374
    teaching and prototyping
        tool, 371
Live wallpapers, 111
    fullScreen() function, 112
    handling permissions, 116
    image (*see* Image-flow wallpaper)
    multiple home screens
        full-screen mode, 113
        image() function, 113
        image ratio, 114
        image-scroll interaction, 114
        offset function, 115
    particle systems, 120
        autonomous agents, 121
        code-based projects, 120
        draw() function, 125
        image flow field, 126
        pen and paper
          sketches, 121
        update() method, 125
    writing and installation, 111
loadFont() and textFont() functions, 83
loadImage() function, 130
loadPixels() function, 126
loadShape() function, 78
loadTable() function, 255

■ M, N

Magnetic sensor/magnetometer
    compass app, 170
    compass sketch, 170
    getOrientation() function, 172, 173
    getRotationMatrix() methods, 172
    magnetic field, 169
Magnetometer, 144
Monoscopic rendering, 308
mousePressed()/touchMoved()
    function, 105

■ O

onAccuracyChanged() method, 146
onGyroscopeEvent method, 152
onSensorChanged() function, 146, 263

■ P, Q

P3D renderer, 275
    camera, 277
    createShape() function, 280
    3D Hello World, 275
    immediate *vs.* retained rendering, 279
    orthographic projection, 278
    perspective() and ortho()
        functions, 278
Point light, 294
Processing development environment
    (PDE), 4
Processing project, 3
    Android (*see* Android devices)
    code sketchbook, 5
    extending processing, 7
    language, 3
    Mac, 6
    PDE process, 4
    software sketchbook, 3
PShape class, 74
    createShape() function, 75
    creation, 75
    SVG, 78
pushMatrix() and popMatrix()
    function, 31
pushStyle() and popStyle() function, 72

■ R

Renderers, 59
    full-screen output, 60
    size() and fullScreen() functions, 59
requestImage() function, 196

■ S

Sensor data, 157
    accelerometer, 143
    data in accelerometer, 147
    gyroscope, 144
    Ketai (*see* Ketai library)
    listener, 146
    location, 144

Sensor data (*cont.*)
  magnetometer, 144
  manager, 145
  mobile devices, 143
  reading data (gyroscope), 149
Shapes, 60
  attributes, 70
  contours, 73
  curve shapes, 62
  styles, 72
  types, 60
Sketchbook
  artists and designers, 17
  code-based drawing
    line() function, 20
  setup/draw structure, 17
    animation line, 18
    color, 27
    draw() function, 18–19
    form, 23
    geometric transformations, 30
    noLoop() and loop() functions, 19
    screen coordinates, 21
    setup() function, 17, 19
    static sketch, 20
    style attributes, 20
  user input, 32
  vine-drawing app, 34
Sketching and debugging, 4
  checkpoints, 44
  definition, 41
  integrated debugger, 44
  logcat, 43
  processing console, 42
  public release
    config.ini file, 50
    device DPI, 45
    display density, 46
    emulator, 48
    export signed package, 52
    fullScreen() method, 46
    icons and package name, 51
    package name and version, 51
    vine-drawing app, 51, 55
  reporting processing bugs, 45
  terminal session, 43
Software Development Kit (SDK), 9
Spotlight, 295
surfaceTouchEvent() function, 105

▓ **T**

Text drawing, 82
  attributes, 85
  font loading and
    creation, 83
  scaling text, 86
Texture mapping, 298
Time visualization
  sundials
    concentric circles, 230
    control motion, 228
    digital representations, 228
    smartwatches, 227
    square *vs.* round watch
      faces, 231
    technical and cultural
      background, 227
  watch face concept, 235
    crescent moon, 235
    elapsed/remaining time, 235
    interaction, 237
    load/display images, 239
Touchscreen interaction
  clear button, 95
  draw() function, 95
  interface actions, 96
  keyboard, 108
  line drawing, 93
  mouse events, 91
  mousedDragged() function, 91
  mousePressed() function, 91
  mouseReleased()
    function, 91, 95
  mouse variables, 90
  multi-touch events
    accessing properties, 96
    mouseDragged() function, 97
    multiple brushes, 99
    startTouch() function, 97
    touchEnded() and touchMoved()
      function, 98
  positions of mouse, 93
  scrolling bar, 102
  setVelocity() method, 94
  shape selection, 101
  swipe and pinch, 105
  track touch position, 90
  virtual/software keyboards, 89

▨ U

updateSteps() functions, 263
User interface (UI)
    base shape and dummy
        object, 336
    createBase() functions, 336
    createButtons() function, 338
    drawBase() function, 336
    drawBox() function, 336
    drawing app, 334
    screenX() and screenY() function, 338

▨ V

vertex() function, 62
    and bezierVertex() functions, 66
Vine-drawing app
    flower/leaf sketch, 36
    output of, 40
    randomized spirals, 38
    Sketches, 35
    spiral parametric equation, 36–37
Virtual reality (VR)
    drawingapp (see Drawing app, VR)
    Google, 303
        cardboard and
            daydream, 303
        hardware requirements, 304
        Vive/Oculus, 303
    interaction, 309
        box selection, 318
        eye and world coordinates, 310
        getObjectMatrix() function, 318
        intersectsLine() function, 322
        line of sight, 312
        screen coordinates, 315, 317
    movement, 322
        automatic movement, 324
        calculate() function, 326
        free-range movement, 326
        prepare() function, 323
        stationary reference
        object, 323

processing
    Android menu, 304
    fullScreen() function, 304
    monoscopic rendering, 308
    output window, 305
    sketch, 304
    stereo rendering, 306
Visualization
    bodysensors (see Body sensors)
    real-time, 245
        arc() function, 249
        BODY_SENSORS permission, 248
        heart-rate data, 250
        heart-rate sensor, 246
        permission request, 248
        sensor debugging, 253
        step-count data, 249
        step-counter sensor, 245
    tree generation, 257
        algorithms, 257
        particle system, 258
        step-count sensor, 260
        tree blooming, 264
        watch face, 263
Voronoi tessellations, 197

▨ W, X, Y, Z

wallpaperHomeCount() function, 114
wallpaperOffset() function, 114
Wearable devices
    smartwatches, 213
        Android watches, 214
        design concepts, 222
        screen shape and insets, 223
        trackers, 213
        watch face preview icons, 225
    watch face sketches
        ambient mode, 218
        emulator, 218
        step counter, 221
        time displays, 220
        watch, 215
        Wi-Fi debugging, 216

Get the eBook for only $5!

Why limit yourself?

With most of our titles available in both PDF and ePUB format, you can access your content wherever and however you wish—on your PC, phone, tablet, or reader.

Since you've purchased this print book, we are happy to offer you the eBook for just $5.

To learn more, go to http://www.apress.com/companion or contact support@apress.com.

Apress®

Printed by Printforce, United Kingdom